Learning Vue

Core Concepts and Practical Patterns
for Reusable, Composable, and
Scalable User Interfaces

Maya Shavin

Beijing · Boston · Farnham · Sebastopol · Tokyo

Learning Vue

by Maya Shavin

Published by O'Reilly Media, Inc., 1005 Gravenstein Highway North, Sebastopol, CA 95472.

O'Reilly books may be purchased for educational, business, or sales promotional use. Online editions are also available for most titles (*http://oreilly.com*). For more information, contact our corporate/institutional sales department: 800-998-9938 or *corporate@oreilly.com*.

Acquisitions Editor: Amanda Quinn	**Indexer:** Potomac Indexing, LLC
Development Editor: Michele Cronin	**Interior Designer:** David Futato
Production Editor: Ashley Stussy	**Cover Designer:** Karen Montgomery
Copyeditor: Piper Editorial Consulting, LLC	**Illustrator:** Kate Dullea
Proofreader: Liz Wheeler	

December 2023:   First Edition

Revision History for the First Edition

2023-12-01:   First Release

See *http://oreilly.com/catalog/errata.csp?isbn=9781492098829* for release details.

978-1-492-09882-9

[LSI]

Table of Contents

Preface

The JavaScript framework plays a significant role in modern web frontend development. When developing web projects, companies choose a framework for various reasons, including the quality of the final product, the cost of development, coding standard, and ease of development. Hence, learning to work with a JavaScript framework, such as Vue, is essential for any modern web developer (or frontend developer or full stack developer).

This book is for programmers who want to learn and develop Web applications using Vue library, in JavaScript and TypeScript, from end to end. It focuses solely on how Vue and its ecosystem can help you build scalable and interactive web applications in the most straightforward and comfortable direction. While covering the basics, we will also get into Vue Router and Pinia for state management, testing, animation, deployment, and server-side rendering, making sure you are ready to move on and start developing complex Vue projects right away.

It's OK if you are not familiar with Vue or the concept of Virtual DOM. This book doesn't assume any prior knowledge of Vue or any similar framework. I will introduce and guide you through all Vue's basics from scratch. I will also walk you through the Virtual DOM concept and reactivity system in Vue in Chapter 2, as the foundation for the rest of the book.

This book doesn't require you to know TypeScript, though you will be better prepared if you are familiar with TypeScript basics. You will also be better prepared for the contents of the book if you have prior basic knowledge of HTML, CSS, and JavaScript. A solid foundation of these three is always crucial before diving to any web (or frontend) Javascript framework.

Conventions Used in This Book

The following typographical conventions are used in this book:

Italic

Indicates new terms, URLs, email addresses, filenames, and file extensions.

`Constant width`

Used for program listings, as well as within paragraphs to refer to program elements such as variable or function names, databases, data types, environment variables, statements, and keywords.

`Constant width bold`

Shows commands or other text that should be typed literally by the user.

`Constant width italic`

Shows text that should be replaced with user-supplied values or by values determined by context.

 This element signifies a tip or suggestion.

 This element signifies a general note.

 This element indicates a warning or caution.

Using Code Examples

Supplemental material (code examples, exercises, etc.) is available for download at *https://github.com/mayashavin/learning-vue-app*.

If you have a technical question or a problem using the code examples, please send email to *bookquestions@oreilly.com*.

This book is here to help you get your job done. In general, if example code is offered with this book, you may use it in your programs and documentation. You do not need to contact us for permission unless you're reproducing a significant portion of the code. For example, writing a program that uses several chunks of code from this book does not require permission. Selling or distributing examples from O'Reilly books does require permission. Answering a question by citing this book and quoting example code does not require permission. Incorporating a significant amount of example code from this book into your product's documentation does require permission.

We appreciate, but generally do not require, attribution. An attribution usually includes the title, author, publisher, and ISBN. For example: "*Learning Vue* by Maya Shavin (O'Reilly). Copyright 2024 Maya Shavin, 978-1-492-09882-9."

If you feel your use of code examples falls outside fair use or the permission given above, feel free to contact us at *permissions@oreilly.com*.

O'Reilly Online Learning

O'REILLY® For more than 40 years, *O'Reilly Media* has provided technology and business training, knowledge, and insight to help companies succeed.

Our unique network of experts and innovators share their knowledge and expertise through books, articles, and our online learning platform. O'Reilly's online learning platform gives you on-demand access to live training courses, in-depth learning paths, interactive coding environments, and a vast collection of text and video from O'Reilly and 200+ other publishers. For more information, visit *http://oreilly.com*.

How to Contact Us

Please address comments and questions concerning this book to the publisher:

> O'Reilly Media, Inc.
> 1005 Gravenstein Highway North
> Sebastopol, CA 95472
> 800-889-8969 (in the United States or Canada)
> 707-829-7019 (international or local)
> 707-829-0104 (fax)
> *support@oreilly.com*
> *https://www.oreilly.com/about/contact.html*

We have a web page for this book, where we list errata, examples, and any additional information. You can access this page at *https://oreil.ly/learning-vue-1e*.

For news and information about our books and courses, visit *https://oreilly.com*.

Find us on LinkedIn: *https://linkedin.com/company/oreilly-media*

Follow us on Twitter: *https://twitter.com/oreillymedia*

Watch us on YouTube: *https://youtube.com/oreillymedia*

Acknowledgments

As I embarked on the journey of writing this book, my family was navigating a tumultuous period, full of highs and lows. Despite enjoying every moment, writing this book required a lot of time, effort, and dedication, and I wouldn't be able to commit to it without the support from my family, particularly my husband, Natan. His encouragement, belief in my programming skills, humor about frontend development, parenting our children during my work travels, lending an ear to my daily grievances, and helping me balance work with personal life have been invaluable. Without Natan, I would not be where I am today.

Just as quality code demands thorough review, this book's excellence owes much to critical technical insights and encouragement from Jakub Andrzejewski, Chris Fritz, Lipi Patnaik, Edward Wong, and Vishwesh Ravi Shrimali. Your valuable feedback has been pivotal in sharpening my focus and elevating the quality of this work.

My heartfelt appreciation goes to my O'Reilly team: Zan McQuade and Amanda Quinn, for guiding me through the acquisition process of *Learning Vue,* and to my exceptional editor, Michele Cronin. Michele, your insightful feedback, professionalism, and empathy, particularly during the challenging final stages of the book, were extraordinary. The production editing skills of Ashley Stussy and the copyediting expertise of Beth Richards were crucial in elevating my manuscript to production quality. This book wouldn't have materialized as envisioned without your collective efforts.

I extend a special thank you to the Vue core team for developing such a great framework and ecosystem, and to the Vue community members and friends for their support and inspiration. The knowledge and insights I gained from you are immeasurable and continue to enrich me daily.

Finally, my profound gratitude to you, the readers. Choosing this book from the plethora of resources available, including countless videos and tutorials, demonstrates a trust in my work that I deeply appreciate. I hope *Learning Vue* serves as a valuable tool in your journey, whether you aspire to be a web, frontend, or full-stack developer.

Thank you, from the bottom of my heart. And remember, in the world of web development, always "react with a Vue."

CHAPTER 1

Welcome to the Vue.js World!

Initially released in 2014, Vue.js has experienced rapid adoption, especially in 2018. Vue is a popular framework within the developer community, thanks to its ease of use and flexibility. If you are looking for a great tool to build and ship excellent performant web applications to end users, Vue.js is the answer.

This chapter highlights the core concepts of Vue.js and walks you through the tools you need for your Vue.js development environment. It also explores helpful tools that make your Vue.js development process more manageable. By the end of the chapter, you will have a working environment with a simple Vue.js application ready to start your journey in learning Vue.js.

What Is Vue.js?

Vue.js, or Vue, means view in French; it is a JavaScript engine for building progressive, composable, and reactive *user interfaces* (UI) in frontend applications.

 We will use the term Vue to indicate Vue.js from this point on.

Vue is written on top of JavaScript and offers an organized mechanism to structure and build a web application. It also acts as the trans-compiler (*transpiler*) that compiles and translates Vue code (as a Single File Component, which we will discuss further in "Vue Single File Component Structure" on page 57) into equivalent HTML, CSS, and JavaScript code in build time before deploying. In a standalone mode (with a generated script file), the Vue engine performs the code translation at run-time instead.

Vue follows the MVVM (*Model–View–ViewModel*) pattern. Unlike MVC (*Model–View–Controller*) (*https://oreil.ly/GHu2u*),[1] the ViewModel is the binder that binds data between the View and Model. Allowing direct communication for the view and model progressively enables the component's reactivity.

In short, Vue was created to focus only on the View layer but is incrementally adaptable to integrate with other external libraries for more complex usage.

Since Vue focuses solely on the View layer, it empowers the development of single-page applications (*https://oreil.ly/FWJ2p*) (SPAs). SPAs can move quickly and fluidly while communicating data continuously with the backend.

The official website for Vue (*https://oreil.ly/03RbI*) includes API documentation, installation, and primary use cases for reference.

The Benefits of Vue in Modern Web Development

A significant advantage of Vue is its well-written, easy-to-understand documentation. In addition, the ecosystem and supporting community built around Vue, such as Vue Router, Vuex, and Pinia, helps developers set up and run their projects with minimum effort.

Vue APIs are straightforward and familiar to anyone who has worked with AngularJS or jQuery before. Its powerful template syntax minimizes the learning effort required and makes it easier to work with data or listen to Document Object Model (DOM) events in your application.

Another significant benefit Vue offers is its size. The size of a framework is a substantial aspect of the application's performance, especially the initial loading time on delivery. At the time of writing, Vue stands as the fastest and most lightweight framework (~10kB in size). This advantage results in less time-consuming downloading and better run-time performance from a browser perspective.

With the release of Vue 3, the built-in support for TypeScript now offers developers the benefit of typing in types and making their codebase more readable, organized, and maintainable in the long term.

---

1 The MVC pattern helps implement an application by separating its structure into the UI (View), the data (Model), and the controlling logic (Controller). While the View and the Controller can be two-way binding, only the Controller manipulates the Model.

Installing Node.js

Working with Vue requires setting up the development ecosystem and prior coding knowledge to keep up with the learning process. Node.js and NPM (or Yarn) are necessary development tools to install before you start working on any application.

Node.js (or Node) is an open source JavaScript server environment built on Chrome's V8 JavaScript run-time engine. Node allows developers to code and run JavaScript applications locally or in a hosted server, outside a browser.

> Chromium-based browsers like Chrome and Edge also use the V8 engine to interpret JavaScript code into efficient low-level computer code and execute it.

Node is cross-platform supported and easy to install. If you are not sure you installed Node, open your terminal (or command prompt in Windows) and run the following command:

```
node -v
```

The output should be a Node version or "Command not found" if Node is not installed.

If you haven't installed Node, or your Node version is *lower* than 12.2.0, please visit the Node project website (*https://oreil.ly/E6xr-*) and download the installer for the latest version based on your operation system (Figure 1-1).

Once the download finishes, click on the installer and follow the instructions to set it up.

When installing Node, besides the node command, you also have the npm command added to the command-line tool. If you type the node -v command, you should see the installed version number displayed.

Figure 1-1. Latest version for download in Node's official website

NPM

The Node Package Manager (NPM) is the default package manager for Node. It will be installed together with Node.js by default. It lets developers download and install other remote Node packages with ease. Vue and other frontend frameworks are examples of helpful Node packages.

NPM is a powerful tool for developing complex JavaScript applications, with the ability to create and run task scripts (to start a local development server, for instance) and automatically download project package dependencies.

Similar to the Node version check, you can perform an NPM version check through the npm command:

```
npm -v
```

To update your NPM version, use the following command:

```
npm install npm@latest -g
```

With parameter @latest, your current NPM tool automatically updates its version to the latest version. You can run npm -v again to ensure it is updated correctly. You can also replace the latest word to target any specific NPM version (in the format xx.x.x). Additionally, you need to indicate the installation at the global scope with the -g flag for the npm command to be available everywhere on your local machine. For example, if you run the command npm install npm@6.13.4 -g, the tool will target the NPM package version 6.13.4 for installing and updating.

NPM Version for This Book

I recommend installing NPM version 7.x to be able to follow all the NPM code examples in this book.

A Node project depends on a collection of Node packages[2] (or dependencies) to be up and running. In the *package.json* file within the project directory, you can find these installed packages. This *package.json* file also describes the project, including the name, author(s), and other scripting commands applied to the project exclusively.

When you run the command npm install (or npm i) within the project folder, NPM will refer to this file and install all the listed packages into a folder called *node_modules*, ready for the project to use. Also, it will add a *package-lock.json* file to keep track of the package installed version and compatibility between common dependencies.

To start a project from scratch with dependencies, use the following command within the project directory:

```
npm init
```

This command walks you through some questions related to the project and initializes an empty project with a `package.json` file containing your answers.

You can search for any public open source packages at the NPM official website (*https://oreil.ly/LD4W8*).

Yarn

If NPM is the standard package manager tool, then Yarn is an alternative and popular package manager developed by Facebook.[3] Yarn is faster, more secure, and more reliable due to its parallel downloading and caching mechanism. It is compatible with all NPM packages; thus it can be used as a drop-in replacement for NPM.

---

2 These are commonly known as NPM packages.

3 Facebook has been known as Meta since 2021.

You can install the latest version of Yarn based on your operating system by visiting the Yarn official website (*https://oreil.ly/TX-qT*).

If you are working on a macOS computer and have Homebrew installed, you can install Yarn directly using the command:

```
brew install yarn
```

This command installs Yarn and Node.js (if not available) globally.

You can also install Yarn globally using the NPM package management tool with the following command:

```
npm i -g yarn
```

You should now have Yarn installed on your machine and ready to use.

To check if Yarn is installed and to verify its version, use the following command:

```
yarn -v
```

To add a new package, use the following command:

```
yarn add <node package name>
```

To install the dependencies for a project, instead of `npm install`, you only need to run the `yarn` command within the project directory. Once this finishes, similar to NPM, Yarn will also add a *yarn.lock* file in your project directory.

> We will use Yarn as our package manager tool for the code presented in this book.

At this point, you have set up your essential coding environment for Vue development. In the next section, we'll look at the Vue Developer Tools and what they offer us in working with Vue.

Vue Developer Tools

Vue Developer Tools (or Vue Devtools) are the official tools to help you work with your Vue projects locally. These tools include extensions for Chrome and Firefox, and an Electron desktop application for other browsers. You should install one of these tools during the development process.

Chrome users can head to the extension link in the Chrome Web Store (*https://oreil.ly/XvXLO*) and install the extension, as shown in Figure 1-2.

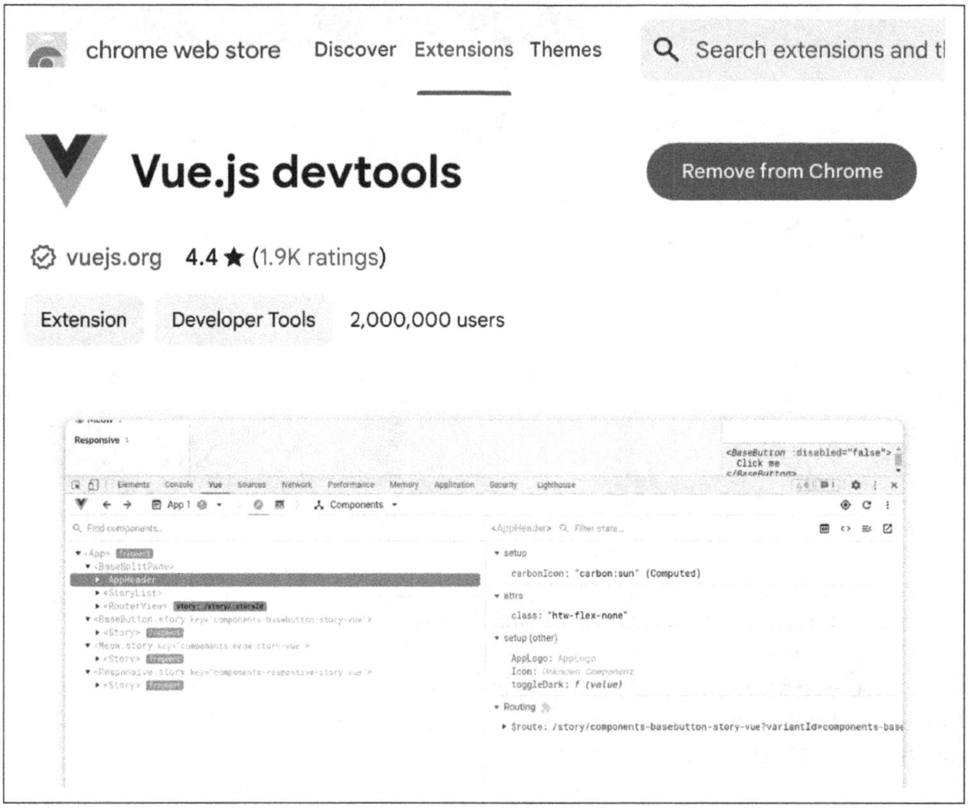

Figure 1-2. Vue Devtools extension page for Chrome

For Firefox, you can use the extension link from the Firefox Add-on page (*https://oreil.ly/oWT_C*), shown in Figure 1-3.

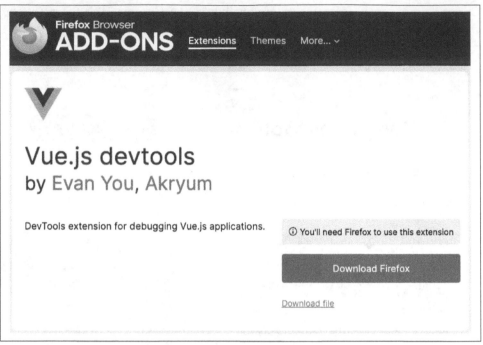

Figure 1-3. Vue Devtools extension page for Firefox

Once your extension is installed and enabled, you can detect if any site currently uses Vue in production. When a site is built with Vue, the Vue icon on the browser toolbar highlights as shown in Figure 1-4.

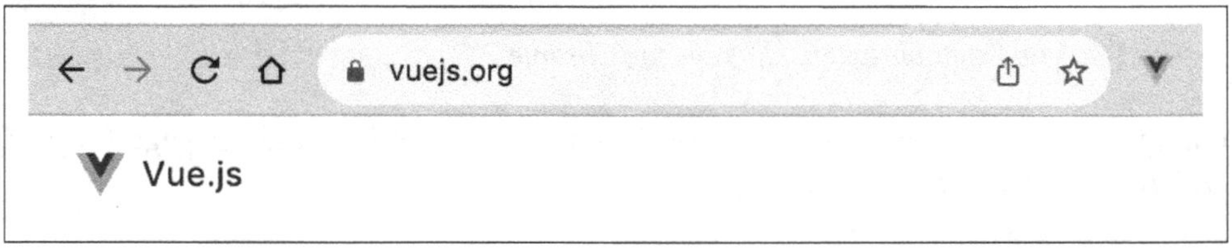

Figure 1-4. Icon confirms the Vue official site is built with Vue

The Vue Devtools enable you to inspect the Vue component tree, component props and data, events, and routing information within the browser's developer console. Vue Devtools divide the information into various tabs, providing helpful insights for debugging and inspecting behaviors of any Vue component within the project.

Vite.js as a Builder Management Tool

Introduced in 2020, Vite.js (or Vite) is a JavaScript development server that uses the native ES module[4] import during development instead of bundling your code into chunks of JavaScript files like Webpack, Rollup, etc.

 We will use the term Vite to indicate Vite.js from this point on.

This approach allows Vite to perform a hot reload[5] during development at an insane speed, making the development experience seamless. It also offers many out-of-the-box features such as TypeScript support and on-demand compilation, which is quickly gaining popularity and adaption among the developer community.

The Vue community has replaced the Vue CLI tool[6] (which uses Webpack under the hood) with Vite to be the default builder tool for creating and managing Vue projects.

Create a New Vue Application

With Vite, there are various ways to create a new Vue application project. The most straightforward way is to use the following command syntax in your command prompt or terminal:

```
npm init vue@latest
```

This command will first install **create-vue**, an official scaffolding tool, and then present you with a list of essentials questions to configure your Vue application.

As shown in Figure 1-5, the configurations used for the Vue application in this book include:

The Vue project name, all in lower-case format
   Vite uses this value to create a new project directory nested in your current directory.

TypeScript
   A typed programming language built on top of JavaScript.

---

4 ES modules stands for ECMAScript modules, a popular standard for working with modules since the ES6 release, first for Node.js and recently in browsers.

5 Hot reload automatically applies the new code changes to a running application without restarting the application or refreshing the page.

6 Vue command-line interface.

JSX[7]

In Chapter 2, we will discuss how Vue supports writing code in JSX standard (writing HTML syntax directly in JavaScript code block).

Vue Router

In Chapter 8, we will implement routing in our application using Vue Router.

Pinia

In Chapter 9, we will discuss using Pinia to manage and share data across the application.

Vitest

This is the official unit testing tool for any Vite project, which we will explore further in Chapter 11.

ESLint

This tool checks your code according to a set of ESLint rules, helping to maintain your coding standard, make it more readable, and avoid hidden coding errors.

Prettier

This tool formats your code styles automatically to keep your code clean, beautiful, and following a coding standard.

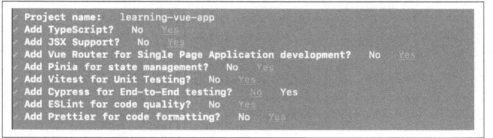

Figure 1-5. Configurations for a new Vue application project

Upon receiving the desired configurations, `create-vue` scaffolds for the project accordingly. Once done, it will present a set of in-order commands for you to execute and get your project up and running locally (see Figure 1-6).

---

7 JavaScript XML, commonly used in React

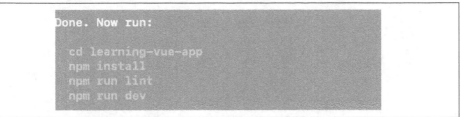

```
Done. Now run:

  cd learning-vue-app
  npm install
  npm run lint
  npm run dev
```

Figure 1-6. In-order commands to execute for the newly created project

Next, we will explore the file structure of our newly created project.

File Repository Structure

A new Vue project contains the following initial structure within the src directory:

assets
: Folder where you can put project images, graphics, and CSS files.

components
: Folder where you create and write Vue components following the Single File Component (SFC) concept.

router
: Folder where all the routing configurations reside.

stores
: Folder where you create and manage project global data by store using Pinia.

views
: Folder where all the Vue components that bind to defined routes reside.

App.vue
: The main Vue application component, acts as the root to host all other Vue components within the application.

main.ts
: Contains the TypeScript code responsible for mounting the root component (App.vue) into an HTML element on the DOM page. This file is also where you set up plugins and third-party libraries in the application, such as Vue Router, Pinia, etc.

Figure 1-7 shows the structure of our Vue project.

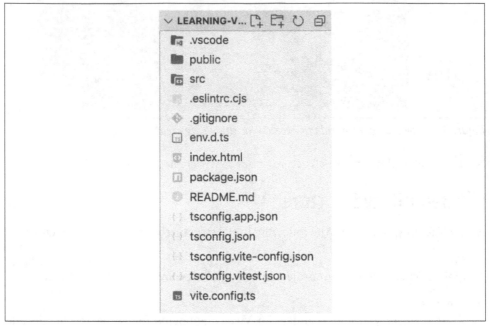

Figure 1-7. File structure of our created learning-vue-app project

In the project's root directory is an `index.html` file, which is the entry point for loading your application in the browser. It imports the `main.ts` file using the `<script>` tag and provides the target element for the Vue engine to load the Vue application by executing the code in `main.ts`. This file will likely stay unchanged during the development process.

You can find all the example code in the dedicated Github repository (*https://github.com/mayashavin/learning-vue*). We organize these code files by chapter.

Summary

In this chapter, we learned about the benefits of Vue and how to install the essential tools for our Vue development environment. We also discussed the Vue Developer Tools and other tools for effectively building a Vue project, such as Vite. Now that we have created our first Vue project, we are ready to learn Vue, starting with the basics: the Vue instance, the built-in directives, and how Vue handles reactivity.

CHAPTER 2

How Vue Works: The Basics

In the previous chapter, you learned the essential tools for building a Vue application and also created your first Vue application, preparing you for the next step: learning how Vue works by writing Vue code.

This chapter introduces you to the concepts of Virtual Document Object Model (Virtual DOM) and the fundamentals of writing a Vue component with Vue Options API. It also explores further Vue directives and the Vue reactivity mechanism. By the end of the chapter, you will understand how Vue works and be able to write and register a Vue component for use in your application.

Virtual DOM Under the Hood

Vue doesn't work directly with the Document Object Model (DOM). Instead, it implements its Virtual DOM to optimize the application's performance on run-time.

To build a solid understanding of how Virtual DOM works, we start with the concept of the DOM.

The DOM represents the HTML (or XML) document content on the web, in the form of an in-memory tree-like data structure (as shown in Figure 2-1). It acts as a programming interface that connects the web page and the actual programming code (such as JavaScript). Tags, such as <div> or <section>, in the HTML document are represented as programmatic nodes and objects.

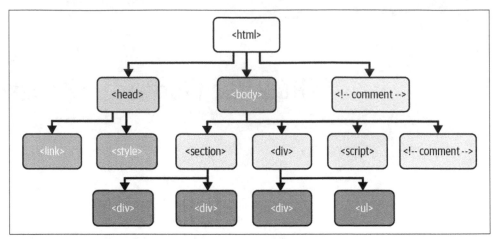

Figure 2-1. Example of a DOM tree

After the browser parses the HTML document, the DOM will be available for interaction immediately. Upon any layout changes, the browser then paints and repaints the DOM constantly in the background. We call the process parsing, and painting the DOM screen rasterization or the *pixel-to-screen* pipeline. Figure 2-2 demonstrates how rasterization works:

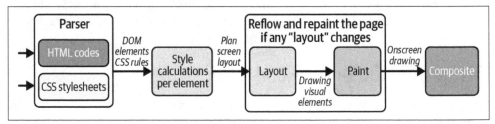

Figure 2-2. Browser rasterization process

The Layout Update Problem

Each paint is costly to the browser's performance. Since the DOM may consist of many nodes, querying and updating single or multiple nodes can be extremely expensive.

Here is a simple example of a list of li elements in the DOM:

```
<ul class="list" id="todo-list">
  <li class="list-item">To do item 1</li>
  <li class="list-item">To do item 2</li>
  <!--so on…-->
</ul>
```

Adding/removing a li element or modifying its content requires querying the DOM for that item using document.getElementById (or document.getElementsByClass Name). Then you need to perform the desired updates using the appropriate DOM APIs.

For instance, if you want to add a new item to the previous example, you need to do the following steps:

1. Query the containing list element by its id attribute's value—"todo-list"
2. Add the new li element using document.createElement()
3. Set the textContent and the relevant attributes to match other element's standard using setAttribute().
4. Append that element to the list element found in step 1 as its child using append Child():

```
const list = document.getElementById('todo-list');

const newItem = document.createElement('li');
newItem.setAttribute('class', 'list-item');
newItem.textContent = 'To do item 3';
list.appendChild(newItem);
```

Similarly, suppose you want to change the text content of the 2nd li item to "buy groceries". In that case, you perform step 1 to get the containing list element, then query the target element using getElementsByClassName(), and finally change its textContent to the new content:

```
const secondItem = list.getElementsByClassName('list-item')[1];
secondItem.textContent = 'Buy groceries'
```

Querying and updating the DOM on a small scale usually do not enormously impact performance. However, these actions can slow the page if performed more repetitively (within a few seconds) and on a more complex web page. The performance impact is significant when there are consecutive minor updates. Many frameworks, such as Angular 1.x, fail to acknowledge and address this performance issue as the codebase grows. The Virtual DOM is designed to solve the layout update problem.

What Is Virtual DOM?

Virtual DOM is the *in-memory virtual copy version* of the actual DOM in the browser, but it is lighter weight and has extra functionalities. It mimics the real DOM structure, with a different data structure (usually Object) (see Figure 2-3).

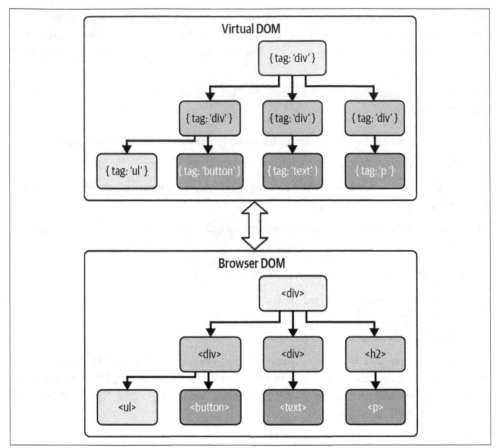

Figure 2-3. The browser DOM vs. the Virtual DOM

Behind the scenes, the Virtual DOM still uses the DOM API to construct and render updated elements in the browser. Thus, it still causes the browser's repainting process, but more efficiently.

In short, Virtual DOM is an abstract pattern aiming to free the DOM from all the actions that can lead to performance inefficiencies, such as manipulating attributes, handling events, and manually updating DOM elements.

How Virtual DOM Works in Vue

The Virtual DOM sits between the real DOM and the Vue application code. The following is an example of what a node in the Virtual DOM looks like:

```
const node = {
  tag: 'div',
  attributes: [{ id: 'list-container', class: 'list-container' }],
  children: [ /* an array of nodes */]
}
```

Let's call this node VNode. VNode is a *virtual node* that resides within the Virtual DOM and represents the actual DOM element in the real DOM.

Through UI interactions, the user tells Vue what state they wish the element to be in; Vue then triggers the Virtual DOM to update that element's represented object (node) to the desired shape while keeping track of those changes. Finally, it communicates with the actual DOM and performs accurate updates on the changed nodes accordingly.

Since the Virtual DOM is a tree of custom JavaScript objects, updating a component equals updating a custom JavaScript object. This process doesn't take long. Because we don't call any DOM API, this update action doesn't cause a DOM repainting.

Once the Virtual DOM finishes updating itself, it syncs in batch with the actual DOM, leading the changes to be reflected on the browser.

Figure 2-4 illustrates how updates from the Virtual DOM to the actual DOM work when adding a new list item and changing the list item's text.

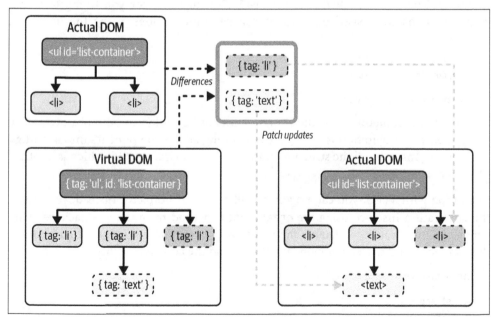

Figure 2-4. Updating from Virtual DOM to actual DOM adding a new element and updating the text of an existing element in the list

Since the Virtual DOM is a tree of objects, we can easily track the specific updates that need to be synced with the actual DOM when modifying the Virtual DOM. Instead of querying and updating directly on the actual DOM, we can now schedule and call the updated APIs with a single render function in one update cycle to maintain performance efficiency.

Now that we understand how Virtual DOM works, we will explore the Vue instance and the Vue Options API.

The Vue App Instance and Options API

Every Vue application starts with a single Vue component instance as the application root. Any other Vue component created in the same application needs to be nested inside this root component.

You can find the initialization code example in `main.ts` of our Vue project. Vite automatically generates the code as part of its scaffolding process.

You will also find the example code of this chapter within this file.

In Vue 2, Vue exposes a `Vue` class (or JavaScript function) for you to create a Vue component instance based on a set of configuration options, using the following syntax:

```
const App = {
  //component's options
}
const app = new Vue(App)
```

`Vue` receives a component, or the component's configuration to be more precise. A component's configuration is an `Object` containing all the component's initial configuration options. We call the structure of this argument *Options API*, which is another of Vue's core APIs.

Beginning with Vue 3, you can no longer call `new Vue()` directly. Instead, you create the application instance using the `createApp()` method from the `vue` package. This change in functionality enhances the isolation of each Vue instance created both on dependencies and shared components (if any) and the code readability:

```
import { createApp } from 'vue'

const App = {
  //component's options
}

const app = createApp(App)
```

`createApp()` also accepts an `Object` of the component's configurations. Based on these configurations, Vue creates a Vue component instance as its application root `app`. Then you need to mount the root component `app` to the desired HTML element using the `app.mount()` method, as follows:

```
app.mount('#app')
```

`#app` is the unique id selector for the application's root element. The Vue engine queries for the element using this id, mounts the app instance to it, then renders the application in the browser.

The next step is to provide the configurations for Vue to build a component instance according to Options API.

 From this point on, we write code according to Vue 3 API standards.

Exploring the Options API

Options API is Vue's core API for initializing a Vue component. It contains the component's configurations structured in an Object format.

We divide its essential properties into four main categories:

State handling
> Including `data()`, which returns the local data state for the component, `computed`, `methods`, and `watch` for enabling observation on specific local data, and `props` for the incoming data.

Rendering
> `template` for the HTML view template and `render()` as the rendering logic for the component.

Lifecycle hooks
> Such as `beforeCreate()`, `created()`, `mounted()`, etc., for handling different stages of a component's lifecycle.

Others
> Such as `provide()`, `inject()` for handling different customization and communication between components. And `components`, a collection of nested component templates to use within the component.

The following is an example structure of our root `App` component based on Options API:

```
import { createApp } from 'vue'

const App = {
  template: "This is the app's entrance",
}

const app = createApp(App)
app.mount('#app')
```

In the previous code, an HTML template displays regular text. We can also define a local `data` state using `data()` function, which we will discuss further in "Creating Local State with Data Properties" on page 22.

You can also rewrite the previous code to use the `render()` function:

```
import { createApp } from 'vue'

const App = {
  render() {
    return "This is the app's entrance"
  }
}

const app = createApp(App)
app.mount('#app')
```

Both codes will generate the same result (Figure 2-5).

This is the app's entrance

Figure 2-5. Sample output of writing a root component using Options API

If you open the Elements tab in the browser's Developer Tools, you will see the actual DOM now contains a div with `id="app"` and a text content *This is the app's entrance* (Figure 2-6).

```
▼<body>
    <div id="app" data-v-app>This is the app's entrance</div>
    <script type="module" src="/src/main.ts?t=1653374850644"></script>
  </body>
```

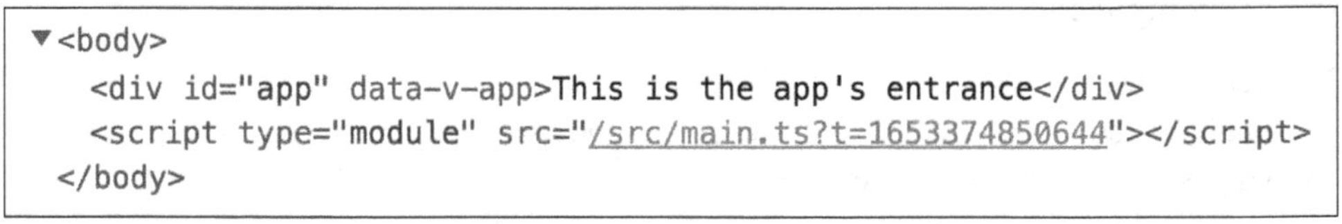

Figure 2-6. The DOM tree in the browser has a div containing the app's text content

You can also create a new component, `Description`, which renders a static text and passes it to `components` of the `App`. Then you can use it as a nested component in the `template`, like in Example 2-1.

Example 2-1. Declare an internal component template to use in the App

```
import { createApp } from 'vue'

const Description = {
 template: "This is the app's entrance"
};

const App = {
 components: { Description },
 template: '<Description />'
}

const app = createApp(App)
app.mount('#app')
```

The output stays the same as in Figure 2-6.

Note here you must declare either `template` or `render()` function (see "The Render Function and JSX" on page 173) for the component. However, you don't need these properties in case you are writing the component in Single File Component (SFC) standard. We will discuss this component standard in Chapter 3.

Next, let's look at the `template` property syntax.

The Template Syntax

In Options API, `template` accepts a single string that contains valid HTML-based code and represents the component's UI layout. The Vue engine parses this value and compiles it into optimized JavaScript code, then accordingly renders the relevant DOM elements.

The following code demonstrates our root component App, whose layout is a single `div` displaying text—`This is the app's entrance`:

```
import { createApp } from 'vue'

const App = {
 template: "<div>This is the app's entrance</div>",
}

const app = createApp(App)
app.mount('#app')
```

For multi-level HTML template code, we can use backtick characters (JavaScript template literals), denoted by ` symbol, and maintain the readability. We can rewrite App's template in the previous example to include other `h1` and `h2` elements, as in the following:

```
import { createApp } from 'vue'

const App = {
 template: `
 <h1>This is the app's entrance</h1>
 <h2>We are exploring template syntax</h2>
 `,
}

const app = createApp(App)
app.mount('#app')
```

The Vue engine will render to the DOM with two headings (Figure 2-7).

This is the app's entrance
We are exploring template syntax

Figure 2-7. Output of a multi-level template for a component

The `template` property syntax is essential for creating the binding between a specific DOM element and the component's local data using directives and a dedicated syntax. We will explore how to define the data we want to display in the UI next.

Creating Local State with Data Properties

Most components keep their local state (or local data) or receive data from an external source. In Vue, we store the component's local state using the Options API `data()` function property.

`data()` is an anonymous function that returns an object representing the local data state of a component. We call that returned object the *data object*. When initializing the component instance, the Vue engine will add each property of this data object to its reactivity system for tracking its changes and triggering the re-rendering of the UI template accordingly.

In short, the data object is the reactive state of a component.

To inject the data property in the template, we use the *mustache* syntax, denoted by double curly braces {{}}. Within the HTML template, we wrap the data property with the curly braces where we need to inject its value, as seen in Example 2-2.

Example 2-2. Inject title to display in the HTML template

```
import { createApp } from 'vue'

type Data = {
  title: string;
```

```
}
const App = {
 template: `
  <div>{{ title }}</div>
 `,
 data(): Data {
  return {
   title: 'My first Vue component'
  }
 }
}

const app = createApp(App)
app.mount('#app')
```

In the previous code, we declare the local data property `title` and inject its value in the template of `App` by using the `{{ title }}` expression. The output in the DOM equals the following code:

```
<div>My first Vue component</div>
```

You can also combine an inline static text with double curly braces within the same element tag:

```
const App = {
 template: `
  <div>Title: {{ title }}</div>
 `,
 /**... */
}
```

Vue automatically preserves the static text and replaces only the expression with the correct value. The result equals the following:

```
<div>Title: My first Vue component</div>
```

All data object properties are available for access directly and internally through the component instance `this`. And `this` is accessible in any component's local methods, computed properties, and lifecycle hooks. For example, we can print out `title` to the console after creating a component with the hook `created()`:

```
import { createApp, type ComponentOptions } from 'vue'

const App = {
 /**... */
 created() {
  console.log((this as ComponentOptions<Data>).title)
 }
}

const app = createApp(App)
app.mount('#app')
```

We cast this as a ComponentOptions<Data> type. We will enable full TypeScript support for the Vue component in Vue 3 using defineComponent, which we will discuss further in "Using define-Component() for TypeScript Support" on page 60.

You can debug the reactivity of a data property by using the Vue Devtools. On the main page of our application, open the browser's Developer Tools, head to the Vue tab, and select the Root component displayed in the Inspector panel. Once this is selected, a right-side panel will appear, showing the component data object's properties. When you hover on the title property, a pen icon will appear, allowing you to edit the property value (Figure 2-8).

Figure 2-8. How to debug and edit a data property using Vue Devtools

Click on that edit icon button, modify the title value, and hit Enter; the application UI instantly reflects the new value.

You have learned how to use data() and double curly braces {{}} to inject the local data to the UI template. This is a type of one-way data binding.

Before we explore the two-way binding and other directives in Vue, let's look at reactivity in Vue.

How Reactivity in Vue Works

To understand how reactivity works, let's take a quick look at how the Virtual DOM processes all the received information, creates, and keeps track of created VNodes before yielding to the actual DOM (Figure 2-9).

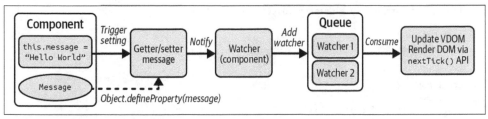

Figure 2-9. The flow of Virtual DOM's rendering process

We can describe the previous process diagram as follows:

1. Once you define the local data, in Vue.js 2.0, the internal Vue engine uses JavaScript's built-in `Object.defineProperty()` to establish the *getters and setters* for each related piece of data and enables relevant data reactivity. In Vue.js 3.0, however, the Vue engine uses the ES5 Proxy-based mechanism[1] for performance enhancement, doubling run-time performance and reducing the memory needed by half. We will explain more about this reactivity mechanism in Chapter 3.

2. After setting up the reactivity mechanism, the Vue engine uses *watcher* objects to keep track of any data update triggered by the setters. Watchers help the Vue engine detect changes and update the Virtual DOM and the actual DOM through a *Queue* system.

3. Vue uses the Queue system to avoid inefficient multiple updates of the DOM within a short time. A watcher adds itself to the Queue upon a related component's data change. The Vue engine sorts it by a specific order for consumption. Until the Vue engine finishes consuming and flushing that watcher from the Queue, only one watcher of the same component exists within the Queue, regardless of the number of data changes. This consumption process is done by `nextTick()` API, which is a Vue function.

4. Finally, after the Vue engine consumes and flushes all the watchers, it triggers the `run()` function of each watcher to update the component's real DOM and Virtual DOM automatically, and the application renders.

Let's perform another example. This time we use `data()` and the help of `created()` to demonstrate reactivity in the application. `created()` is the lifecycle hook that the Vue engine triggers after creating the component instance and before mounting it to the DOM element. At this point, we won't discuss this hook further but use this hook to perform a timer update on a data property `counter` with `setInterval`:

---

1 Visit the JavaScript Proxy documentation (*https://oreil.ly/SRqbn*).

```
import { createApp, type ComponentOptions } from 'vue'

type Data = {
  counter: number;
}

const App = {
 template: `
  <div>Counter: {{ counter }}</div>
  `,
 data(): Data {
  return {
   counter: 0
  }
 },
 created() {
  const interval = setInterval(() => {
   (this as ComponentOptions<Data>).counter++
  }, 1000);

  setTimeout(() => {
   clearInterval(interval)
  }, 5000)
 }
}

const app = createApp(App)
app.mount('#app')
```

This code increments the counter every one second.[2] We also use setTimeout() to clear the interval after 5 seconds. On the browser, you can see the displayed value changing from 0 to 5 every second. The final output will equal the string:

```
Counter: 5
```

After understanding the concept of reactivity and rendering in Vue, we are ready to explore how to perform two-way data binding.

Two-Way Binding with v-model

Two-way binding refers to how we sync data between a component's logic and its view template. When a component's data field changes programmatically, the new value reflects on its UI view. And vice versa, when a user makes changes to the data field on the UI view, the component automatically gets and saves the updated value, keeping both the internal logic and the UI synchronized. A good example of two-way binding is the form input field.

---

2 1 second = 1000 milliseconds

Two-way data binding is a complex yet beneficial use case for application development. One common scenario for two-way binding is form input synchronization. Proper implementation saves developing time and reduces complexity to maintain data consistency between the actual DOM and component data. But implementing two-way binding is a challenge.

Fortunately, Vue makes two-way binding much simpler with the v-model directive. Binding the v-model directive to a component's data model will automatically trigger updating the template when the data model changes, and vice versa.

The syntax is straightforward; the value passing to v-model is the name alias declared in the data return object.

Assume we have a NameInput component that receives text input from the user, with the following template code:

```
const NameInput = {
 template: `
 <label for="name">
  <input placeholder="Enter your name" id="name">
 </label>`
}
```

We want to sync the the input value received with a local data model, naming name. To do so, we add v-model="name" to the input element and declare the data model in data() accordingly:

```
const NameInput = {
 template: `
 <label for="name">
  Write your name:
  <input
   v-model="name"
   placeholder="Enter your name"
   id="name"
  >
 </label>`,
 data() {
  return {
   name: '',
  }
 }
}
```

The value of name will change whenever the user changes the input field on run-time.

To have this component render in the browser, we add `NameInput` as one of the components for the application:

```
import { createApp } from 'vue'

const NameInput = {
  /**... */
}

const app = createApp({
  components: { NameInput },
  template: `<NameInput />`,
})

app.mount('#app')
```

You can track this data change by opening the Vue tab in the browser's Developer Tools. Within the Inspector tab, find and select the `NameInput` element under the Root element, and you will see the component's data displayed on the right panel of the Vue tab (Figure 2-10).

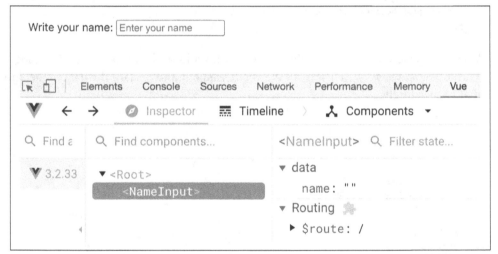

Figure 2-10. Debug the input component using the Vue tab in Developer Tools

When you change the input field, the `name` property under `data` displayed on the right side of the Vue tab also will get the updated value (Figure 2-11).

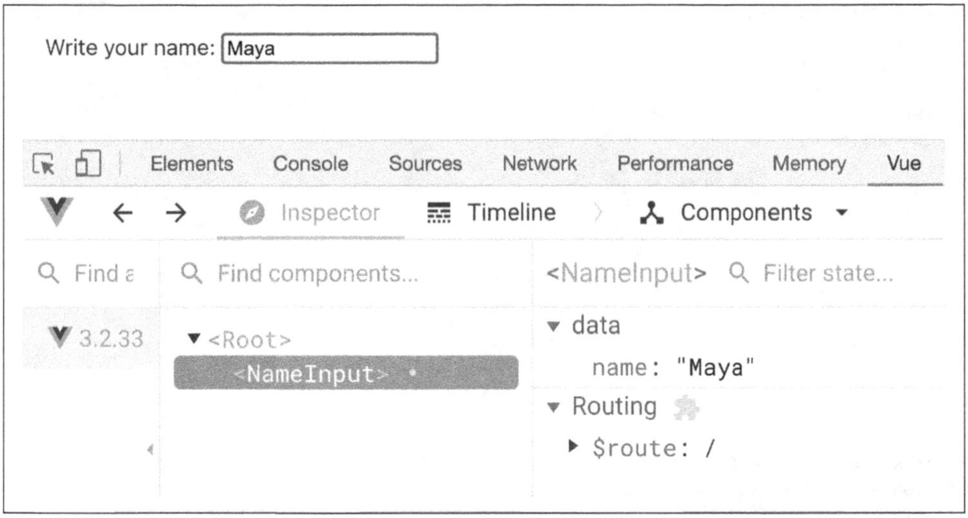

Figure 2-11. Input value changes sync with the relevant component's data model

You can use the same approach for building a checklist with multiple options. In this scenario, you need to declare the data model as an `Array` and add the `v-model` binding on each checkbox input field. Example 2-3 demonstrates how it looks for a `CourseChecklist`.

Example 2-3. Create a course checklist using `v-model` and checkbox input

```
import { createApp } from 'vue'

const CourseChecklist = {
 template: `
<div>The course checklist: {{list.join(', ')}}</div>
<div>
<label for="chapter1">
 <input
  v-model="list"
  type="checkbox"
  value="chapter01"
  id="chapter1"
 >
 Chapter 1
</label>
<label for="chapter2">
 <input
  v-model="list"
  type="checkbox"
  value="chapter02"
  id="chapter2"
 >
 Chapter 2
</label>
```

```
<label for="chapter3">
 <input
  v-model="list"
  type="checkbox"
  value="chapter03"
  id="chapter3"
 >
 Chapter 3
</label>
</div>
`,
data() {
 return {
  list: [],
 }
}
}

const app = createApp({
 components: { CourseChecklist },
 template: `<CourseChecklist />`,
})

app.mount('#app')
```

Vue automatically adds or removes an input value to the list array according to the user's interaction (Figure 2-12).

The course checklist: chapter01, chapter02

☑ Chapter 1 ☑ Chapter 2 ☐ Chapter 3

Figure 2-12. Screenshot of the list value after the user makes a selection

Using v-model.lazy Modifier

Updating a data value on every user keystroke can be too much, especially when displaying that input value in other places. Remember Vue re-renders the template UI according to the data changes. By enabling two-way syncing on every input key received, you expose your application to potential unnecessary re-rendering. To reduce this overhead, you can use the v-model.lazy modifier instead of the regular v-model to bind with the data model:

```
const NameInput = {
 template: `
 <label for="name">
  Write your name:
  <input
   v-model.lazy="name"
   placeholder="Enter your name"
   id="name"
  >
```

```
    </label>`,
  data() {
   return {
    name: '',
   }
  }
 }
```

This modifier ensures the v-model will only track changes triggered by the onChange event of that input element.

Using v-model.number and v-model.trim Modifiers

If the data model you are binding to v-model should be a number type, you can use the modifier v-model.number to convert the input value to a number.

Similarly, if you want to ensure the string data model free from trailing whitespaces, you can use v-model.trim instead.

That's all for two-way binding. Next we'll examine the more common directive v-bind for one-way binding.

Binding Reactive Data and Passing Props Data with v-bind

Previously we learned to use v-model for two-way binding and double curly braces {{}} for one-way data injection. But to perform one-way binding of data to another element as an attribute's values or other Vue components as props, we use v-bind.

v-bind, denoted by :, is the most used Vue directive in any application. We can bind an element's attribute (or component's props) or more to JavaScript expressions, following this syntax:

```
v-bind:<attribute>="<expression>"
```

Or, for short, with : syntax:

```
:<attribute>="<expression>"
```

For example, we have imageSrc data, an image URL. To display the image using <img> tag, we perform the following binding to its src attribute:

Example 2-4. Binding a source to an image

```
import { createVue } from 'vue'

const App = {
 template: `
  <img :src="imageSrc" />
  `,
```

```
  data() {
    return {
     imageSrc: "https://res.cloudinary.com/mayashavin/image/upload/TheCute%20Cat"
    }
  }
}

const app = createApp(App)

app.mount('#app')
```

Vue takes the value of `imageSrc` and binds it to the `src` attribute, resulting in the following code on the DOM:

```
<img src="https://res.cloudinary.com/mayashavin/image/upload/TheCute%20Cat" >
```

Vue updates the `src` whenever `imageSrc`'s value changes.

Also, you can add `v-bind` on an element as a standalone attribute. `v-bind` accepts an object containing all the attributes to bind as properties and the expressions as their values. Example 2-5 rewrites Example 2-4 to demonstrate this use case:

Example 2-5. Binding source and alt text to an image using an object

```
import { createVue } from 'vue'

const App = {
 template: `
  <img v-bind="image" />
 `,
 data() {
   return {
    image: {
     src: "https://res.cloudinary.com/mayashavin/image/upload/TheCute%20Cat",
     alt: "A random cute cate image"
    }
   }
  }
}

const app = createApp(App)

app.mount('#app')
```

In Example 2-5, we bind an object `image` with two properties, `src` for the image URL and `alt` for its alt text to the element `<img>`. The Vue engine will automatically parse `image` into relevant attributes by its properties' names, and then generate the following HTML code in the DOM:

```
<img
  src="https://res.cloudinary.com/mayashavin/image/upload/TheCute%20Cat"
  alt="A random cute cate image"
  >
```

Binding to Class and Style Attributes

When binding to `class` or `style` attributes, you can pass expressions in array or object type. The Vue engine knows how to parse and unite them into the proper styling or class name string.

For example, let's add some classes to our `img` in Example 2-5:

```
import { createVue } from 'vue'

const App = {
 template: `
  <img v-bind="image" />
  `,
 data() {
  return {
   image: {
    src: "https://res.cloudinary.com/mayashavin/image/upload/TheCute%20Cat",
    alt: "A random cute cate image",
    class: ["cat", "image"]
   }
  }
 }
}

const app = createApp(App)

app.mount('#app')
```

This code generates an `<img>` element with the class as a single string `"cat image"`, as in the following:

```
<img
 src="https://res.cloudinary.com/mayashavin/image/upload/TheCute%20Cat"
 alt="A random cute cate image"
 class="cat image"
>
```

You can also perform dynamic class names by binding the `class` attribute to an object whose properties' values are according to the Boolean `isVisible` data value:

```
import { createVue } from 'vue'

const isVisible = true;

const App = {
 template: `
  <img v-bind="image" />
  `,
 data() {
  return {
   image: {
    src: "https://res.cloudinary.com/mayashavin/image/upload/TheCute%20Cat",
    alt: "A random cute cate image",
    class: {
     cat: isVisible,
```

```
        image: !isVisible
      }
    }
  }
 }
}

const app = createApp(App)

app.mount('#app')
```

Here we define the img element to have cat class when isVisible is true, and image otherwise. The generated DOM element for when isVisible is true now becomes:

```
<img
 src="https://res.cloudinary.com/mayashavin/image/upload/TheCute%20Cat"
 alt="A random cute cate image"
 class="cat" >
```

Output is similar when isVisible is false, with image instead of cat for the class name.

You can use the same approach with the style attribute or pass an object containing CSS rules in CamelCase format. For example, let's add some margins to our image in Example 2-5:

```
import { createVue } from 'vue'

const App = {
 template: `
  <img v-bind="image" />
 `,
 data() {
  return {
   image: {
    src: "https://res.cloudinary.com/mayashavin/image/upload/TheCute%20Cat",
    alt: "A random cute cate image",
    style: {
     marginBlock: '10px',
     marginInline: '15px'
    }
   }
  }
 }
}

const app = createApp(App)

app.mount('#app')
```

This code generates inline stylings for the img element with margin-block: 10px and margin-inline: 15px applied.

You can also combine several style objects into a single style array. Vue knows how to unite them into a single style rule string, as follows:

```
import { createVue } from 'vue'

const App = {
 template: `
  <img v-bind="image" />
 `,
 data() {
  return {
   image: {
    src: "https://res.cloudinary.com/mayashavin/image/upload/TheCute%20Cat",
    alt: "A random cute cate image",
    style: [{
     marginBlock: "10px",
     marginInline: "15px"
    }, {
     padding: "10px"
    }]
   }
  }
 }
}

const app = createApp(App)

app.mount('#app')
```

The output DOM element will be:

```
<img
 src="https://res.cloudinary.com/mayashavin/image/upload/TheCute%20Cat"
 alt="A random cute cate image"
 style="margin-block: 10px; margin-inline: 15px; padding: 10px" >
```

Using v-bind for Style

In general, inline style is not a good practice. Hence I don't recommend using v-bind for organizing component stylings. We will discuss the proper way of working with styling in Vue in Chapter 3.

Next, let's iterate over a data collection in a Vue component.

Iterating over Data Collection Using v-for

Dynamic list rendering is essential to reduce repetitive code, increase code reusability,
and maintain the format consistency between a group of similar element types. Some
examples are a list of articles, active users, and TikTok accounts you follow. The data
is dynamic in these examples, while the type of content and the UI layout remain
similar.

Vue provides a v-for directive to accomplish the goal of iterating through an iterative
data collection, such as an array or object. We use this directive directly on an element, following this syntax:

```
v-for = "elem in list"
```

elem is just an alias for each element in the data source list.

For example, if we want to iterate through an array of numbers [1, 2, 3, 4, 5] and print out the element value, we use the following code:

```
import { createApp } from 'vue'

const List = {
 template: `
  <ul>
   <li v-for="number in numbers" :key="number">{{number}}</li>
  </ul>
  `,
 data() {
  return {
   numbers: [1, 2, 3, 4, 5]
  };
 }
};

const app = createApp({
 components: { List },
 template: `<List />`
})

app.mount('#app')
```

This code equals writing the following native HTML code:

```
<ul>
 <li>1</li>
 <li>2</li>
 <li>3</li>
 <li>4</li>
 <li>5</li>
</ul>
```

One significant advantage of using v-for is to keep the template consistent and map the data content dynamically to the relevant element, regardless of how the data source may change over time.

Each block generated by the v-for iteration has access to other components' data and the specific list item. Take Example 2-6, for instance.

Example 2-6. Writing a task list component using v-for

```
import { createApp } from 'vue'

const List = {
 template: `
 <ul>
  <li v-for="task in tasks" :key="task.id">
   {{title}}: {{task.description}}
```

```
    </li>
  </ul>
  `,
  data() {
   return {
    tasks: [{
     id: 'task01',
     description: 'Buy groceries',
    }, {
     id: 'task02',
     description: 'Do laundry',
    }, {
     id: 'task03',
     description: 'Watch Moonknight',
    }],
    title: 'Task'
   }
  }
}

const app = createApp({
 components: { List },
 template: `<List />`
})

app.mount('#app')
```

Figure 2-13 displays the output:

- Task: Buy groceries
- Task: Do laundry
- Task: Watch Moonknight

Figure 2-13. Output of tasks list with the default title for each row

Keeping the Uniqueness with the Key Attribute

Here we *must* define a unique key attribute for each iterated element. Vue uses this attribute to keep track of each element rendered for a later update. See "Make the Element Binding Unique with Key Attribute" on page 39 for discussion on its importance.

Also, v-for supports an optional second argument, index, the current element's appearance index in the iterating collection. We can rewrite Example 2-6 as follows:

```
import { createApp } from 'vue'

const List = {
 template: `
 <ul>
  <li v-for="(task, index) in tasks" :key="task.id">
   {{title}} {{index}}: {{task.description}}
```

```
    </li>
  </ul>
  `,
  //...
}

//...
```

This code block generates the following output (Figure 2-14):

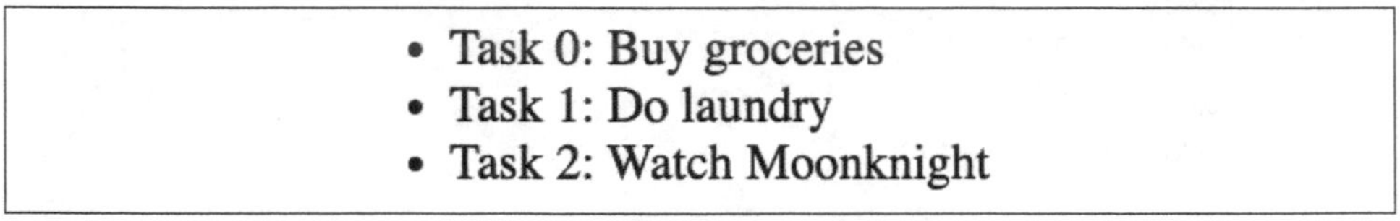

- Task 0: Buy groceries
- Task 1: Do laundry
- Task 2: Watch Moonknight

Figure 2-14. Output of the task list with each task's index

So far, we have covered iteration with array collection. Let's look at how we iterate through the properties of an object.

Iterating Through Object Properties

In JavaScript, an `Object` is a type of *key-value map table*, with each object's property being the *unique key* of the table. To iterate through the properties of an object, we use similar syntax with array iteration:

```
v-for = "(value, name) in collection"
```

Here `value` stands for the value of a property and `name` for that property's key.

The following shows how we iterate through properties of an object collection and print out each property's `name` and `value` according to the format `<name>: <value>`:

```
import { createApp } from 'vue'

const Collection = {
 data() {
  return {
   collection: { ❶
    title: 'Watch Moonknight',
    description: 'Log in to Disney+ and watch all the chapters',
    priority: '5'
   }
  }
 },
 template: `
<ul>
 <li v-for="(value, name) in collection" :key="name"> ❷
  {{name}}: {{value}}
 </li>
</ul>
 `,
}
```

```
const app = createApp({
 components: { Collection },
 template: `<Collection />`
})

app.mount('#app')
```

❶ Define a collection object with three properties: `title`, `description`, and `priority`

❷ Iterate through the properties of `collection`

Figure 2-15 shows the output.

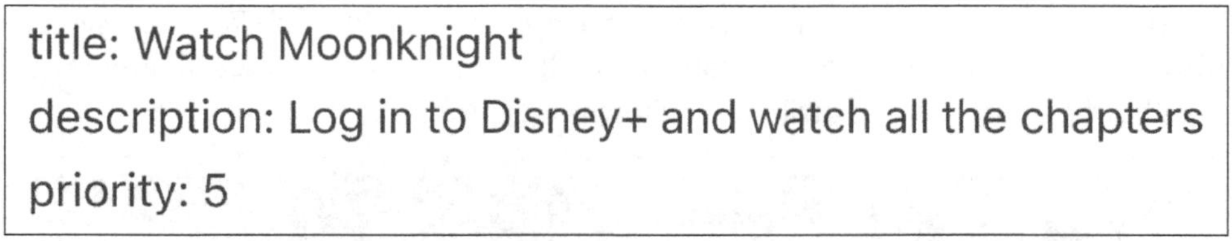

title: Watch Moonknight

description: Log in to Disney+ and watch all the chapters

priority: 5

Figure 2-15. Output of collection object with default title

We still have access to the index appearance of the present pair as the third argument, as in the following syntax:

```
v-for = "(value, name, index) in collection"
```

As noted earlier, we always have to define a key attribute value for each iterating element. This attribute is significant in making the element update binding unique. We will explore the key attribute next.

Make the Element Binding Unique with Key Attribute

The Vue engine tracks and updates the elements rendered with `v-for` by a simple in-place patch strategy. However, in various scenarios, we need to take complete control over list reordering or prevent unwanted behavior when the list element relies on its child component's state.

Vue provides an additional attribute: a key, as a *unique identity for each node element*, binds to a specific iterated list item. The Vue engine uses it as a hint to track, reuse, and reorder the rendered nodes and their nested elements instead of in-place patching.

The syntax usage of a key attribute is straightforward. We use v-bind:key (:key for short) and bind a *unique* value to that list element:

```
<div v-for="(value, name, index) in collection" :key="index">
```

Keeping the Key's Uniqueness

The key should be the item's *distinct identifier* (id) or its *appearance index* in the list.

As a good practice, you must always provide the key attribute when using v-for.

Nevertheless, Vue will throw a warning on the browser console if no key is presented. Also, if you enable ESLint in your application, it throws an error and instantly warns you about the missing key attribute, as shown in Figure 2-16.

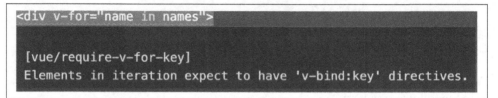

```
<div v-for="name in names">

[vue/require-v-for-key]
Elements in iteration expect to have 'v-bind:key' directives.
```

Figure 2-16. ESLint warning when no key is presented

Valid Values for the Key Attribute

A key should be a string or numeric value. An object or array is *not* a valid key to use.

The key attribute is helpful, even beyond the scope of v-for. Without a key attribute, applying the built-in list transition and animation effect is impossible. We'll discuss more about the benefits of key in Chapter 8.

Adding Event Listener to Elements with v-on

To bind a DOM event to a listener, Vue exposes the built-in directive v-on (for short @) for element tags. The v-on directive accepts the following value types:

- Some inline JavaScript statements in the form of a string
- Name of the component method declared in the component options under methods property

We use v-on with the following format:

```
v-on:<event>= "<inline JavaScript code / name of method>"
```

Or with the shorter version using @:

```
@<event>="<inline JavaScript code / name of method>"
```

 From this point on, we will use @ to denote v-on.

Then add this directive directly on any element as an attribute:

```
<button @click= "printMsg='Button is clicked!'">
Click me
</button>
```

For code readability, especially in a complex codebase, I recommend keeping the JavaScript expression inside a component's method and exposing the use through its name on the directive, as in Example 2-7.

Example 2-7. Change printMsg's value on button click using v-on directive

```
import { createApp, type ComponentOptions } from 'vue'

type Data = {
  printMsg: string;
}

const App = {
 template: `
  <button @click="printMessage">Click me</button>
  <div>{{ printMsg }}</div>
 `,
 methods: {
  printMessage() {
   (this as ComponentOptions<Data>).printMsg = "Button is clicked!"
  }
 },
 data(): Data {
  return {
   printMsg: "Nothing to print yet!",
  }
 }
}

const app = createApp(App)

app.mount("#app");
```

If the user hasn't clicked the button, the display message below the button will be "Nothing to print yet" (Figure 2-17).

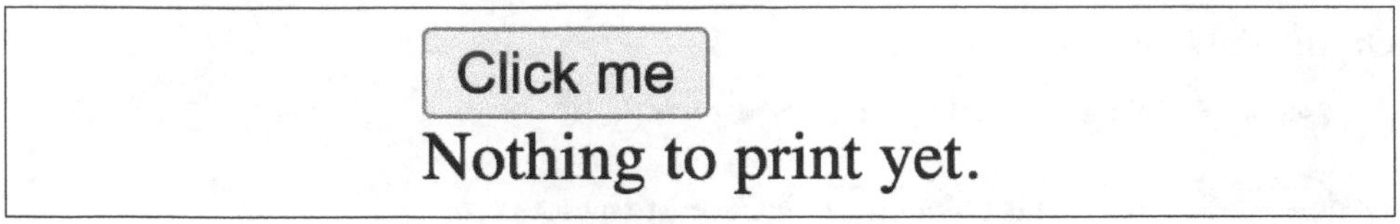

Figure 2-17. "Nothing to print yet" message appears as default

Otherwise, the message will change to "Button is clicked!" (Figure 2-18).

Figure 2-18. "Button is clicked!" message appears after user clicks the button

Handling Events with v-on Event Modifiers

Before the browser dispatches an event on a target element, it constructs that event's propagation path list using the current DOM tree structure. The last node in this path is the target itself, and the other preceding nodes are its ancestors, respectively, in order. Once dispatched, the event travels through one or all three main event phases (Figure 2-19):

Capturing (or capture phase)
> The event travels (or propagates) from the top ancestor down to the target element.

Target
> The event is at the target element.

Bubbling
> The event travels (or bubbles) from the target element up to its ancestor.

We usually interfere with this event propagation flow programmatically within the listener logic. With v-on's modifiers, we can interfere directly on the directive level.

Use v-on modifiers following this format:

```
v-on:<event>.<modifier>
```

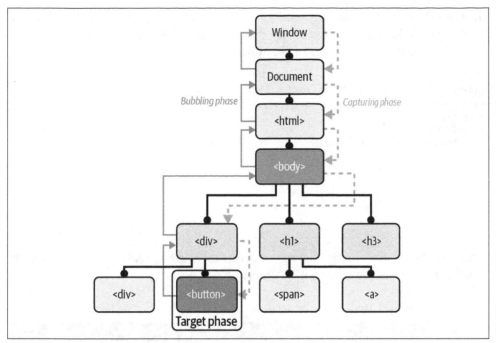

Figure 2-19. Flow of propagation for a click event

One advantage of modifiers is that they keep the listener as generic and reusable as possible. We do not need to worry internally about event-specific details, such as `preventDefault` or `stopPropagation`.

Take Example 2-8, for instance.

Example 2-8. Manually stop the propagation using `stopPropagation()`

```
const App = {
 template: `
  <button @click="printMessage">Click me</button>
 `,
 methods: {
  printMessage(e: Event) {
   if (e) {
    e.stopPropagation()
   }

   console.log("Button is clicked!")
  }
 },
}
```

Here we have to stop the propagation ourselves with `e.stopPropagation`, adding another validation layer to make sure e exists. Example 2-9 shows how we can rewrite Example 2-8 using the `@click.stop` modifier.

Example 2-9. Stop propagation using `@click.stop` modifier

```
const App = {
 template: `
  <button @click.stop="printMessage">Click me</button>
 `,
 methods: {
  printMessage() {
   console.log("Button is clicked!")
  }
 },
}
```

Table 2-1 shows the complete list of event modifiers available, briefly explaining the equivalent event functionalities or behavior.

Table 2-1. Event modifiers for `v-on` directive

Modifier	Description
`.stop`	Instead of calling `event.stopPropagation()`
`.prevent`	Instead of calling `event.preventDefault()`
`.self`	Trigger the event listener *only if* the event's target is the element where we attach the listener.
`.once`	Trigger the event listener *at most once*
`.capture`	Instead of passing `{ capture: true }` as the third parameter for `addEventListener()`, or `capture="true"` in the element. This modifier triggers the listener in the *capturing phase* order, instead of regular bubbling phase order.
`.passive`	Mainly to opt-in for *better scroll performance* and prevent triggering `event.preventDefault()`. We use it instead of passing `{ passive: true }` as the third parameter for `addEventListener()` or adding `passive="true"` to the element.

Chaining Modifiers

Event modifiers support chaining. This means you can write expressions such as `@click.stop.prevent=" printMessage">` on the element tag. This expression equals calling both `event.stopPropagation()` and `event.preventDefault()` inside the event handler, in the order in which they appear.

Detecting Keyboard Events with Key Code Modifiers

While event modifiers are for interfering with the event propagation flow, *key modifiers* help detect special keys of keyboard events such as keyup, keydown, and key press.

Usually, to detect a specific key, we need to perform two steps:

1. Identify the key code, key, or the code represented by that key. For instance, the keyCode for Enter is 13, its key is "Enter", and its code is "Enter."
2. When firing the event handler, within the handler, we need to check manually that event.keyCode (or event.code or event.key) matches the target key code.

This approach is not efficient for maintaining reusable and clean code in a large codebase. v-on comes with built-in key modifiers as a better alternative. If we want to detect if the user types the *Enter* key, we add the modifier .enter to the related key down event, following the same syntax when using event modifiers.

Let's assume we have an input element, and we log a message to the console whenever a user presses *Enter*, as seen in Example 2-10.

*Example 2-10. Manual check if **keyCode** is 13 stands for Enter key*

```
const App = {
 template: `<input @keydown="onEnter" >`,
 methods: {
  onEnter(e: KeyboardEvent) {
   if (e.keyCode === '13') {
    console.log('User pressed Enter!')
   }

   /*...*/
  }
 }
}
```

We now can rewrite it using @keydown.enter.

*Example 2-11. Checking for Enter key pressed by **@keydown.enter** modifier*

```
const App = {
 template: `<input @keydown.enter="onEnter" >`,
 methods: {
  onEnter(e: KeyboardEvent) {
    console.log('User pressed Enter!')
   /*...*/
  }
 }
}
```

The app behaves the same in both cases.

A few other commonly used key modifiers are `.tab`, `.delete`, `.esc`, and `.space`.

Another popular use case is to capture a special keys combination, such as *Ctrl & Enter* (*CMD & Enter* for MacOS) or *Shift + S*. In these scenarios, we chain the *system key modifiers* (`.shift`, `.ctrl`, `.alt` and `.meta` for *CMD* key in MacOS) with *key code modifiers*, as in the following example:

```
<!-- Ctrl + Enter -->
<input @keyup.ctrl.13="onCtrlEnter">
```

Or chaining the shift modifier and key code modifier for S key (keyCode is 83):

```
<!-- Shift + S -->
<input @keyup.shift.83="onSave">
```

Chaining System Modifiers and Key Code Modifiers

You *must* use key code modifiers instead of standard key modifiers, meaning `.13` in place of `.enter` for this type of chaining.

Also, to capture the exact key combinations for triggering an event, we use the `.exact` modifier:

```
<button @click.shift.exact="onShiftEnter" />
```

Combining `.shift` and `.exact` makes sure the click event fires when the user presses *only* the Shift key while clicking the button.

Conditional Rendering Elements with v-if, v-else, and v-else-if

We also can generate or remove an element from the DOM, a scenario called *conditional rendering*.

Assume we have a Boolean data property `isVisible`, which decides if Vue should render a text element into the DOM and make it visible to the user. Binding directive `v-if` to `isVisible` by placing `v-if="isVisible"` on the text element enables reactively rendering the element only when `isVisible` is `true` (Example 2-12).

Example 2-12. Example usage for `v-if`

```
import { createVue } from 'vue'

const App = {
 template: `
  <div>
```

```
  <div v-if="isVisible">I'm the text in toggle</div>
  <div>Visibility: {{isVisible}}</div>
 </div>
 `,
 data() {
  return {
   isVisible: false
  }
 }
}

const app = createApp(App)

app.mount('#app')
```

When setting `isVisible` to `false`, the generated DOM elements will look like this:

```
<div>
 <!--v-if-->
 <div>Visibility: false</div>
</div>
```

Otherwise, the text element will be visible in the DOM:

```
<div>
 <div>I'm the text in toggle</div>
 <div>Visibility: true</div>
</div>
```

If we want to render a different component for the opposite condition (`isVisible` is `false`), `v-else` is the right choice. Unlike `v-if`, you use `v-else` without binding to any data property. It takes the correct condition value based on the immediate preceding `v-if` usage in the same context level.

Using v-else

`v-else` works only when `v-if` exists, and it must always present last in a chaining conditional rendering.

For example, as Example 2-13 shows, we can create a component with the following code block with both `v-if` and `v-else`.

Example 2-13. Conditional display of different texts using `v-if` and `v-else`

```
import { createVue } from 'vue'

const App = {
 template: `
  <div>
   <div v-if="isVisible">I'm the visible text</div>
   <div v-else>I'm the replacement text</div>
  </div>
```

```
  `,
  data() {
    return {
     isVisible: false
    }
   }
}

const app = createApp(App)

app.mount('#app')
```

In short, you can translate the previous conditions into similar logical expressions as:

```
<!--if isVisible is true, then render -->
<div>I'm the visible text</div>
<!-- else render -->
<div>I'm the replacement text</div>
```

As in any if…else logic expression, we can always extend the condition check with an else if condition block. This condition block equals a v-else-if directive and also requires a JavaScript condition statement. Example 2-14 shows how to display a text, I'm the subtitle text, when isVisible is false and showSubtitle is true.

Example 2-14. Condition chaining with v-if, v-else-if, and v-else

```
import { createVue } from 'vue'

const App = {
 template: `
  <div v-if="isVisible">I'm the visible text</div>
  <div v-else-if="showSubtitle">I'm the subtitle text</div>
  <div v-else>I'm the replacement text</div>
  `,
 data() {
   return {
    isVisible: false,
    showSubtitle: false,
   }
  }
}

const app = createApp(App)

app.mount('#app')
```

Order of v-else-if

If we use v-else-if, we *must* present it on elements appearing after the element with assigned v-if attribute.

While using `v-if` means to render an element conditionally, there are situations where it won't be efficient to mount/unmount an element from the DOM so frequently.

In such cases, it's better to use `v-show`.

Conditional Displaying Elements with v-show

Unlike `v-if`, `v-show` only toggles the visibility of the target element. Vue still renders the target element regardless of the status of the condition check. Once rendered, Vue controls the visibility using the CSS `display` rule to hide/show the element conditionally.

Let's take Example 2-12 and change the directive from `v-if` to `v-show`, as in Example 2-15.

Example 2-15. Hide/show the element using `v-show`

```
import { createVue } from 'vue'

const App = {
 template: `
  <div>
   <div v-show="isVisible">I'm the text in toggle</div>
   <div>Visibility: {{isVisible}}</div>
  </div>
 `,
 data() {
  return {
   isVisible: false
  }
 }
}

const app = createApp(App)

app.mount('#app')
```

The UI output is the same as when we use `v-if`. However, in the browser DOM (*you can debug in the Elements tab of the Developer Tools*), the text element exists in the DOM but is not visible to the user:

```
<div>
 <div style="display: none;">I'm the text in toggle</div>
 <div>Visibility: false</div>
</div>
```

The target element has an inline `style` with `display:none` applied. When toggling `isVisible` to `true`, Vue will remove this inline style.

v-show is more efficient if the toggling frequency is high at run-time, while v-if is an ultimate choice if the condition is not likely to change.

Dynamically Displaying HTML Code with v-html

We use v-html to inject plain HTML code into the DOM dynamically, in the form of a string, as in Example 2-16.

Example 2-16. Using v-html to render inner HTML content

```
import { createVue } from 'vue'

const App = {
 template: `
  <div v-html="innerContent" />
 `,
 data() {
  return {
   innerContent: `
    <div>Hello</div>
   `
  }
 }
}

const app = createApp(App)

app.mount('#app')
```

The Vue engine will parse the directive value as *static HTML code* and place it into the innerHTML property of the div element. The result should look like:

```
<div>
 <div>Hello</div>
</div>
```

 Security Concern with v-html

You should use v-html to render only trusted content or perform server-side rendering.

Also, a valid HTML string can contain a script tag and the browser will trigger the code within this script tag, leading to a potential security threat. Thus, using this directive on client-side rendering is not recommended.

Displaying Text Content with v-text

v-text is an alternative way of injecting data as the element's content besides the double curly braces {{}}. However, unlike {{}}, Vue won't update the text rendered if there are any changes.

This directive is beneficial when you need to predefine a placeholder text, then override the text only once after a component finishes loading:

```
import { createVue } from 'vue'

const App = {
 template: `
  <div v-text="text">Placeholder text</div>
 `,
 data() {
  return {
   text: `Hello World`
  }
 }
}

const app = createApp(App)

app.mount('#app')
```

Here Vue will render the application displaying *placeholder text* and will eventually replace it with "Hello World" received from text.

Optimizing Renders with v-once and v-memo

v-once helps render static content and preserves performance from the re-rendering static element. Vue renders elements with this directive presented *only once* and will not update it regardless of any re-rendering.

To use v-once, place the directive as is on the element tag:

```
import { createVue } from 'vue'

const App = {
 template: `
  <div>
   <input v-model="name" placeholder="Enter your name" >
  </div>
  <div v-once>{{name}}</div>
 `,
 data() {
  return {
   name: 'Maya'
  }
 }
}
```

```
const app = createApp(App)

app.mount('#app')
```

In the previous example, Vue renders `name` once for the `div` tag, and regardless of what value `name` receives from the user through `input` field and by `v-model`, the content of this `div` won't be updated (Figure 2-20).

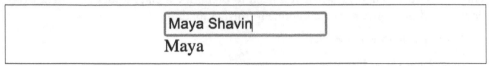

Figure 2-20. Text remains the same though the input value has changed

While `v-once` is excellent for defining a block of elements as static content, we use `v-memo` to memorize a block of parts (or components) within a template conditionally.

`v-memo` accepts an array of JavaScript expressions as its value. We place it on the top element where we want to control its and its children's re-rendering. Vue then validates these JavaScript conditional expressions and only triggers the re-rendering on the target block of elements when fulfilling those condition(s).

Take rendering a gallery of image cards, for instance. Assume we have an array of images. Each image is an object with a `title`, `url`, and `id`. Users can select an image card by clicking on the card, and the selected card will have a blue border.

First, let's define the `images` data array and `selected` image card id in the component data object:

```
const App = {
  data() {
    return {
    selected: null,
    images: [{
      id: 1,
      title: 'Cute cat',
      url:
'https://res.cloudinary.com/mayashavin/image/upload/w_100,h_100,c_thumb/TheCute%20Cat',
    }, {
      id: 2,
      title: 'Cute cat no 2',
      url:
'https://res.cloudinary.com/mayashavin/image/upload/w_100,h_100,c_thumb/cute_cat',
    }, {
      id: 3,
      title: 'Cute cat no 3',
      url:
'https://res.cloudinary.com/mayashavin/image/upload/w_100,h_100,c_thumb/cat_me',
    }, {
      id: 4,
      title: 'Just a cat',
```

```
      url:
'https://res.cloudinary.com/mayashavin/image/upload/w_100,h_100,c_thumb/cat_1',
      }]
    }
  }
}
```

Then we define the layout for the list rendering to the `template`, adding a conditional memorization `v-memo` for the list item to re-render only if the image item is no longer selected, or vice versa:

```
const App = {
 template: `
 <ul>
  <li
   v-for="image in images"
   :key="image.id"
   :style=" selected === image.id ? { border: '1px solid blue' } : {}"
   @click="selected = image.id"
   v-memo="[selected === image.id]" ❶
  >
   <img :src="image.url">
   <div>{{image.title}}</h2>
  </li>
 </ul>
 `,
 data() {
  /*..*/
 }
}
```

❶ We set the re-rendering to only if the condition check `selected === image.id` results differently from the previous check.

The output will look like Figure 2-21.

Figure 2-21. Images gallery output

Every time you select an image by clicking on the image card, Vue will only re-render two items: the previously selected item and the currently selected one. For optimizing large list rendering, this directive can be very powerful.

v-memo Availability

v-memo is available only in Vue 3.2 and above.

We have learned how to write a component using the `template` syntax and some common Vue directives, except `v-slot`. We will resume discussing the power of `v-slot` in Chapter 3.

Next, we will learn how to register a component globally, making it available for use in other components of the same application without explicitly importing them.

Registering a Component Globally

Using the `components` property of Options API to register a component only enables its availability explicitly within the current component. Any of the present component's nested elements won't have access to use the registered one.

Vue exposes the instance method `Vue.component()`, which receives two input parameters as arguments:

- A string stands for the component's registered name (alias).
- A component instance, either an SFC imported as a module or an object containing the component's configurations, following Options API.

To register a component globally, we trigger `component()` on the created `app` instance, as seen in Example 2-17.

Example 2-17. Register MyComponent as global component and use it in the App template

```
/* main.ts */
import { createApp } from 'vue'

//1. Create the app instance
const app = createApp({
 template: '<MyComponent />'
});

//2. Define the component
const MyComponent = {
 template: 'This is my global component'
}

//3. Register a component globally
app.component('MyComponent', MyComponent)

app.mount('#app')
```

If you have a `MyComponent` as an SFC file (see Chapter 3), you can rewrite Example 2-17 to the following:

```
/* main.ts */
import { createApp } from 'vue'
import App from './App.vue'
import MyComponent from './components/MyComponent.vue'

//1. Create the app instance
const app = createApp(App);

//2. Register a component globally
app.component('MyComponent', MyComponent);
```

And `MyComponent` will always be available for reuse in any component nested within the `app` instance.

Importing the same component again in every component file can be repetitive and inconvenient. In reality, sometimes you need to reuse a component multiple times across an application. In this scenario, registering components as global components is an excellent practice.

Summary

This chapter explored Virtual DOM and how Vue uses it to achieve its performance goal. We learned how to control the component rendering with JSX and functional components, handle built-in Vue directives, and use them to process the component's local data for displaying on the UI template reactively. We also learned about the reactivity fundamentals and how to create and register the Vue component using Options API with the template syntax. These are the basics for going further into the Vue component mechanism in the next chapter.

CHAPTER 3

Composing Components

In the previous chapter, you learned the fundamentals of Vue and how to write a Vue component with common directives using Options API. You are now ready to deep dive into the next level: composing more complex Vue components with reactivity and hooks.

This chapter introduces the Vue Single File Component (SFC) standard, component lifecycle hooks, and other advanced reactive features such as computed properties, watchers, methods, and refs. You will also learn to use slots to dynamically render different parts of the component while maintaining the component's structure with styles. By the end of this chapter, you will be able to write complex Vue components in your application.

Vue Single File Component Structure

Vue introduces a new file format standard, Vue SFC, denoted by the `.vue` extension. With SFC, you can write the HTML template code, the JavaScript logic, and the CSS stylings for a component in the same file, each in its dedicated code section. A Vue SFC contains three essential code sections:

Template
> This HTML code block renders the UI view of the component. It should only appear *once* per component at the highest level element.

Script
> This JavaScript code block contains the component's main logic and only appears *a maximum of once* per component file.

Style

This CSS code block contains the stylings for the component. It is optional and can appear as *many times* as required per component file.

Example 3-1 is an example of an SFC file structure for a Vue component named `MyFirstComponent`.

Example 3-1. SFC structure of `MyFirstComponent` component

```
<template>
 <h2 class="heading">I am a a Vue component</h2>
</template>
<script lang="ts">
export default {
 name: 'MyFistComponent',
};
</script>
<style>
.heading {
  font-size: 16px;
}
</style>
```

We can also refactor a non-SFC component code into SFC, as shown in Figure 3-1.

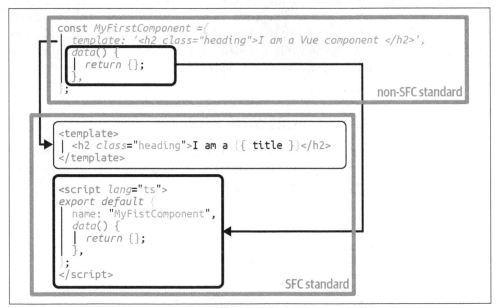

Figure 3-1. Refactoring the component from non-SFC format to SFC format

As Figure 3-1 shows, we perform the following refactoring:

- Move the HTML code presented as the string value of the `template` field into the `<template>` section of the Single File Component.

- Move the rest of `MyFirstComponent` logic into the `<script>` section of the Single File Component, as part of the `export default {}` object.

Tip for Using TypeScript

You should add the attribute `lang="ts"` for TypeScript to the `<script>` syntax, as `<script lang="ts">` , so the Vue engine knows to handle the code format accordingly.

Since the `.vue` file format is a unique extension standard, you need to use a special build tool (compiler/transpiler) such as Webpack, Rollup, etc., to pre-compile the relevant files into proper JavaScript and CSS for serving on the browser side. When creating a new project with Vite, Vite already sets up these tools as part of the scaffolding process. You then can import the component as an ES module and declare it as internal `components` to use in other component files.

Following is an example of importing `MyFirstComponent` located in the `components` directory to use in the `App.vue` component:

```
<script lang="ts">
import MyFirstComponent from './components/MyFirstComponent.vue';

export default {
 components: {
  MyFirstComponent,
 }
}
</script>
```

As Example 3-2 shows, you can use the imported component by referring to its name, either by CamelCase or snake case, in the `template` section:

Example 3-2. How to use the imported component

```
<template>
 <my-first-component />
 <MyFirstComponent />
</template>
```

This code generates the MyFirstComponent component's content twice, as shown in Figure 3-2.

I am a a Vue component
I am a a Vue component

Figure 3-2. MyFirstComponent output

> A component's `template` in Example 3-2 contains two root elements. This fragmentation capability is available only in Vue 3.x onward.

We learned how to create and use a Vue component using the SFC format. As you have noticed, we define `lang="ts"` in the `script` tag to inform the Vue engine about our usage of TypeScript. And thus, the Vue engine will apply stricter type validation on any code or expressions presented in the `script` and `template` sections of the component.

However, to fully enjoy TypeScript's benefits in Vue, we need to use the `defineCompo nent()` method when defining a component, which we will learn in the next section.

Using defineComponent() for TypeScript Support

The `defineComponent()` method is a wrapper function that accepts an object of configurations and returns the same thing with type inference for defining a component.

> The `defineComponent()` method is available only in Vue 3.x onward and relevant only when TypeScript is required.

Example 3-3 illustrates using `defineComponent()` to define a component.

Example 3-3. Defining a component with defineComponent()

```
<template>
  <h2 class="heading">{{ message }}</h2>
</template>
<script lang="ts">
import { defineComponent } from 'vue';

export default defineComponent({
  name: 'MyMessageComponent',
  data() {
```

```
    return {
      message: 'Welcome to Vue 3!'
    }
  }
});
</script>
```

If you use VSCode as your IDE, and have Volar extension (*https://oreil.ly/lmnvd*) installed, you will see the type of `message` as `string` when hovering on `message` in the template section, as shown in Figure 3-3.

```
components >  ▼ MyFirstComponent.vue > {} script > [●] default
  <template>                    (property) message: string
    <h2 class="heading">{{ message }}</h2>
  </template>
```

Figure 3-3. Generated type for `message` property of `MyMessageComponent` displayed on hover

You should use `defineComponent()` for TypeScript support only in complex components such as accessing a component's properties through `this` instance. Otherwise, you can use the standard method for defining an SFC component.

> In this book, you will see a combination of the traditional component definition approach and `defineComponent()` when suitable. You are free to decide which method works best for you.

Next, we will explore the lifecycle of a component and its hooks.

Component Lifecycle Hooks

The lifecycle of a Vue component starts when Vue instantiates the component and ends when destroying the component instance (or unmounting).

Vue divides the component's lifecycle into the phases (Figure 3-4).

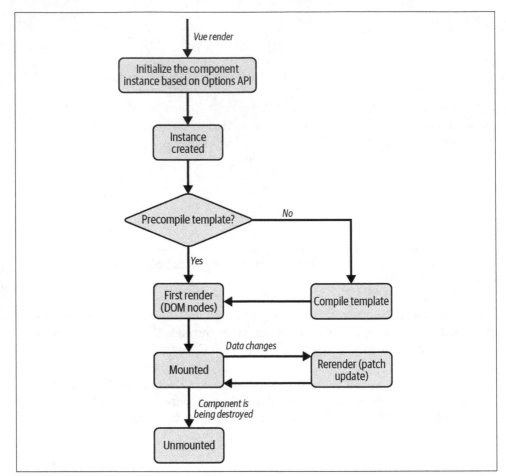

Figure 3-4. Flow graph of a Vue component lifecycle

Initialize phase

The Vue renderer loads the component's option configurations and prepares for the component instance creation.

Creating phase

The Vue renderer creates the component instance. If the template requires compiling, there will be an additional step to compile it before moving forward to the next phase.

First render phase

The Vue renderer creates and inserts the DOM nodes for the component in its DOM tree.

Mounting phase

The component's nested elements are already mounted and attached to the component's DOM tree, as seen in Figure 3-5. The Vue renderer then attaches the component to its parent container. From this phase onward, you have access to the component's $el property, representing its DOM node.

Updating phase

Only relevant if the component's reactive data changes. Here the Vue renderer re-renders the DOM nodes for the component with the new data and performs a patch update. Similar to the mounting phase, the update process finishes with the child elements first and then the component itself.

Unmounting phase

The Vue renderer detaches the component from the DOM and destroys the instance and all its reactive data effects. This phase is the last phase of the lifecycle, happening when the component is no longer in use in the application. Similar to the updating and mounting stages, a component can only unmount itself after all its children are unmounted.

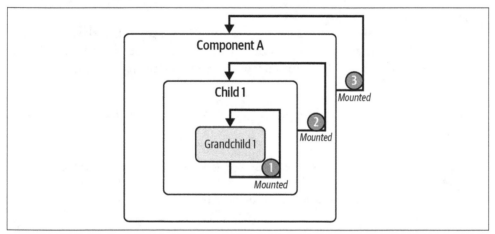

Figure 3-5. Mounting order for a component and its children

Vue allows you to attach some events to specific transitions between these lifecycle phases for better component flow control. We call these events lifecycle hooks. The lifecycle hooks available in Vue are described in the following sections.

setup

setup is the first event hook before the component's lifecycle starts. This hook runs *once* before Vue instantiates the component. At this phase, no component instance exists; hence *there is no access* to this:

```
export default {
  setup() {
    console.log('setup hook')
    console.log(this) // undefined
  }
}
```

An alternative to the setup hook is adding the setup attribute to the script tag section of the component (<script setup>).

The setup hook is mainly for use with the Composition API (we will learn more in Chapter 5). Its syntax is:

```
setup(props, context) {
  // ...
}
```

setup() takes two arguments:

props

> An object that contains all the props passed to the component, declared using the props field of the component's options object. Each of props's properties is reactive data. You don't need to return props as part of the setup() return object.

context

> A non-reactive object that contains the component's context, such as attrs, slots, emit, and expose.

If you use <script setup>, you need to use defineProps() to define and access these props. See "Declaring Props Using define-Props() and withDefaults()" on page 116.

setup() returns an object that contains all the references to the component's internal reactive state and methods and any static data. Suppose you use <script setup>; you don't need to return anything. In that case, Vue will automatically translate all the variables and functions declared within this syntax into the appropriate setup() return object during compilation. You then can access them in the template or other parts of the component's options object using the this keyword.

Example 3-4 shows using setup() hook to define a component that prints out a static message.

Example 3-4. Defining a component with the setup() hook

```
import { defineComponent } from 'vue';

export default defineComponent({
  setup() {
    const message = 'Welcome to Vue 3!'
    return {
      message
    }
  }
})
```

Note here that `message` is not reactive data. To make it reactive, you must wrap it with the `ref()` function from the Composition API. We will learn more about this in "Handling Data with ref() and reactive()" on page 138. Also, we no longer need to define `message` as part of the `data()` object, reducing the amount of undesired reactive data in a component.

Alternatively, as Example 3-5 shows, you can write the previous component using the <script setup> syntax.

Example 3-5. Defining a component with <script setup> syntax

```
<script setup lang='ts'>
const message = 'Welcome to Vue 3!'
</script>
```

One great thing about using <script setup> instead of `setup()` is that it has built-in TypeScript support. As a result, there is no need for `defineComponent()`, and writing components takes less code.

When using `setup()` hook, you can also combine with the h() render function to return a renderer for the component based on the `props` and `context` arguments, as Example 3-6 shows.

Example 3-6. Defining a component with the setup() hook and h() render function

```
import { defineComponent, h } from 'vue';

export default defineComponent({
  setup(props, context) {
    const message = 'Welcome to Vue 3!'
    return () => h('div', message)
  }
})
```

It is helpful to use `setup()` with `h()` when you want to create a component that renders a different static DOM structure based on the props passed to it or a stateless functional component (Figure 3-6 shows the output of Example 3-6 in the Vue tab of Chrome Devtools).

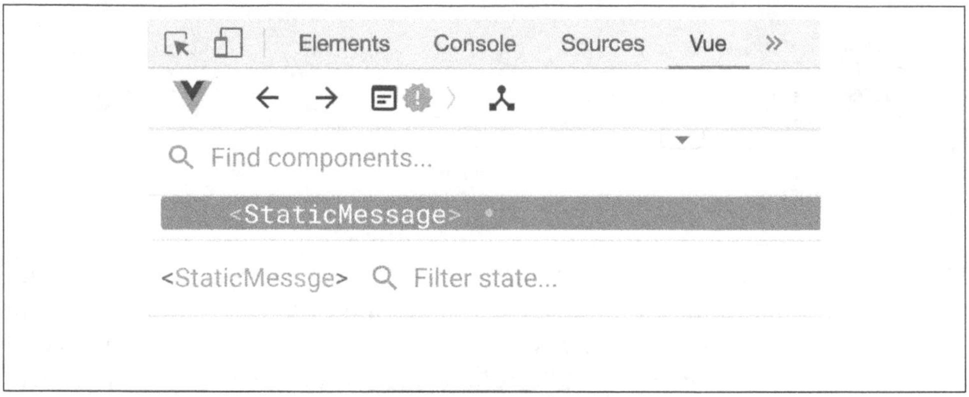

Figure 3-6. How the stateless component using the h() render function looks in Vue Devtools

> From this point on, we will use `<script setup>` syntax to demonstrate use cases component's `setup()` hook due to its simplicity, whenever applicable.

beforeCreate

`beforeCreate` runs *before* the Vue renderer creates the component instance. Here the Vue engine has initialized the component but hasn't yet triggered the `data()` function or calculated any `computed` properties. Thus, there is no reactive data available.

created

This hook runs *after* the Vue engine creates the component instance. At this stage, the component instance exists with reactive data, watchers, computed properties, and defined methods. However, the Vue engine hasn't yet mounted it to the DOM.

The `created` hook runs *before the first render* of the component. It helps perform any task that requires `this` to be available, such as loading data from an external resource into the component.

beforeMount

This hook runs after `created`. Here the Vue render has created the component instance and compiled its template for rendering before the first render of the component.

mounted

This hook runs after the first render of the component. At this phase, the component's rendered DOM node is available for you to access through the ++ property. You can use this hook to perform additional side-effect calculations with the component's DOM node.

beforeUpdate

The Vue renderer updates the component's DOM tree when the local data state changes. This hook runs *after* the update process starts, and you can still use it to modify the component's state internally.

updated

This hook runs after the Vue renderer updates the component's DOM tree.

> updated, beforeUpdate, beforeMount and mounted hooks are not available in server-side rendering (SSR).

Use this hook with caution *since it runs after any DOM update occurs to the component.*

> **Update local state inside updated hook**
>
> You *must not* mutate the component's local data state in this hook.

beforeUnmount

This hook runs before the Vue renderer starts unmounting the component. At this point, the component's DOM node $el is still available.

unmounted

This hook runs after the unmounting process completes successfully and the component instance is no longer available. This hook can clean up additional observers or effects, such as DOM event listeners.

In Vue 2.x, you should use `beforeDestroy` and `destroyed` in place of `beforeUnmount` and `mounted`, respectively.

`beforeUnmounted` and `unmounted` hooks are not available in server-side rendering (SSR).

In summary, we can redraw our component's lifecycle diagram with the lifecycle hooks, as in Figure 3-7.

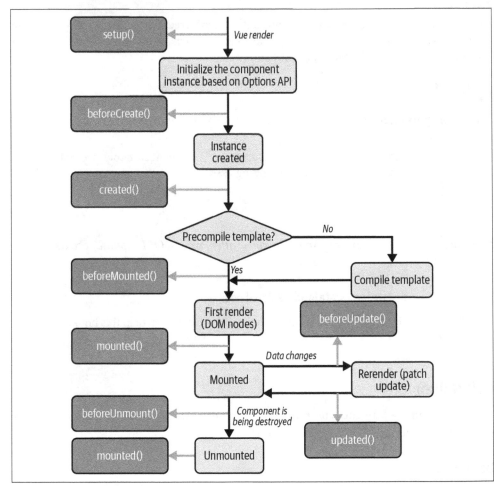

Figure 3-7. Flowchart of a Vue component lifecycle with hooks

We can experiment with the execution order for each lifecycle hook with the component in Example 3-7.

Example 3-7. Console log of lifecycle hooks

```
<template>
    <h2 class="heading">I am {{message}}</h2>
    <input v-model="message" type="text" placeholder="Enter your name" />
</template>
<script lang="ts">
  import { defineComponent } from 'vue'

  export default defineComponent({
    name: 'MyFistComponent',
    data() {
      return {
        message: ''
      }
    },
    setup() {
      console.log('setup hook triggered!')
      return {}
    },
    beforeCreate() {
      console.log('beforeCreate hook triggered!')
    },
    created() {
      console.log('created hook triggered!')
    },
    beforeMount() {
      console.log('beforeMount hook triggered!')
    },
    mounted() {
      console.log('mounted hook triggered!')
    },
    beforeUpdate() {
      console.log('beforeUpdate hook triggered!')
    },
    updated() {
      console.log('updated hook triggered!')
    },
    beforeUnmount() {
      console.log('beforeUnmount hook triggered!')
    },
  });
</script>
```

When we run this code in the browser's Inspector console, we will see the output shown in Figure 3-8.

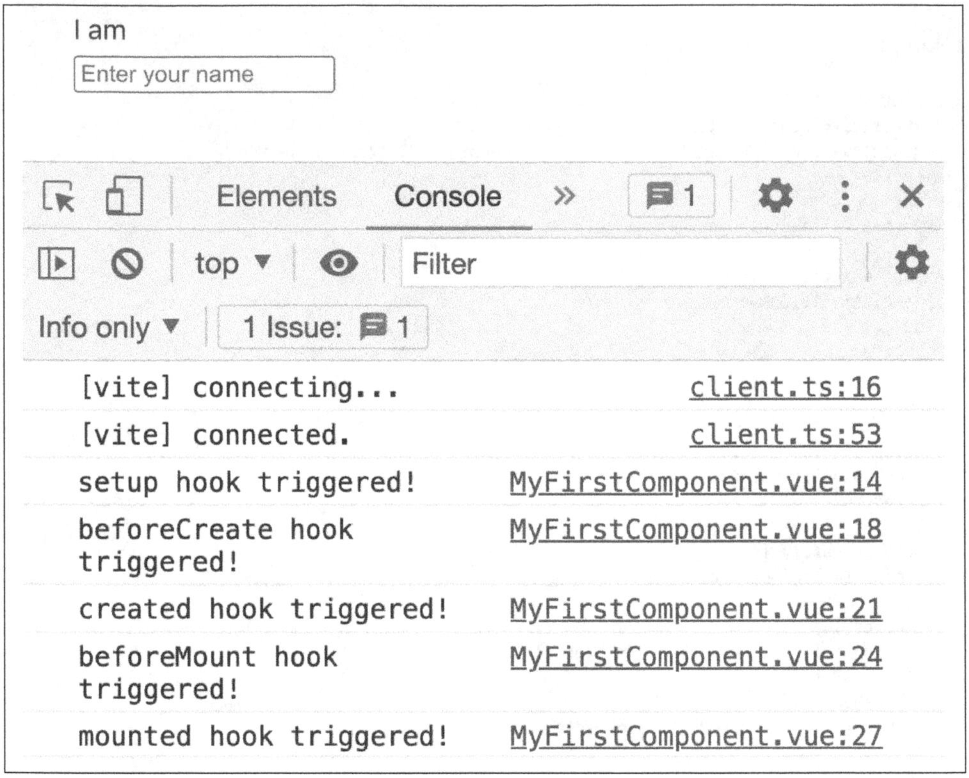

I am

Enter your name

| | | Elements | Console | » | 1 | ⚙ | ⋮ | ✕ |

top ▾ | ⊘ | ◉ | Filter | ⚙

Info only ▾ | 1 Issue: 1

[vite] connecting...		client.ts:16
[vite] connected.		client.ts:53
setup hook triggered!	MyFirstComponent.vue:14
beforeCreate hook triggered!	MyFirstComponent.vue:18
created hook triggered!	MyFirstComponent.vue:21
beforeMount hook triggered!	MyFirstComponent.vue:24
mounted hook triggered!	MyFirstComponent.vue:27

Figure 3-8. Console log output hook order for `MyFirstComponent` in the first render

When we change the value of the `message` property, the component re-renders, and the console outputs as shown in Figure 3-9.

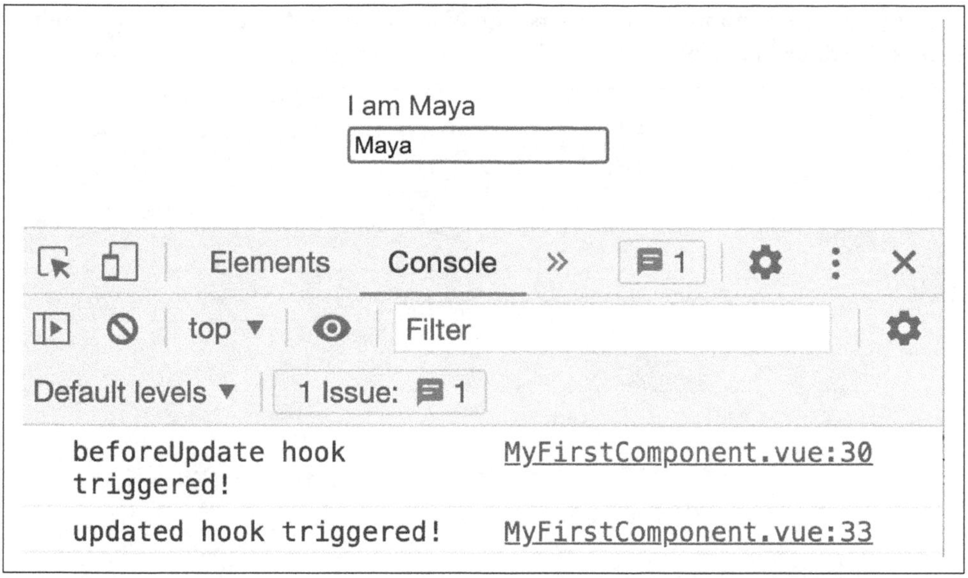

Figure 3-9. Only *beforeUpdate* and *updated* hooks are triggered on the second render

We can also review this lifecycle order in the Timeline tab—Performance section of Vue Devtools, as in Figure 3-10 for the first render.

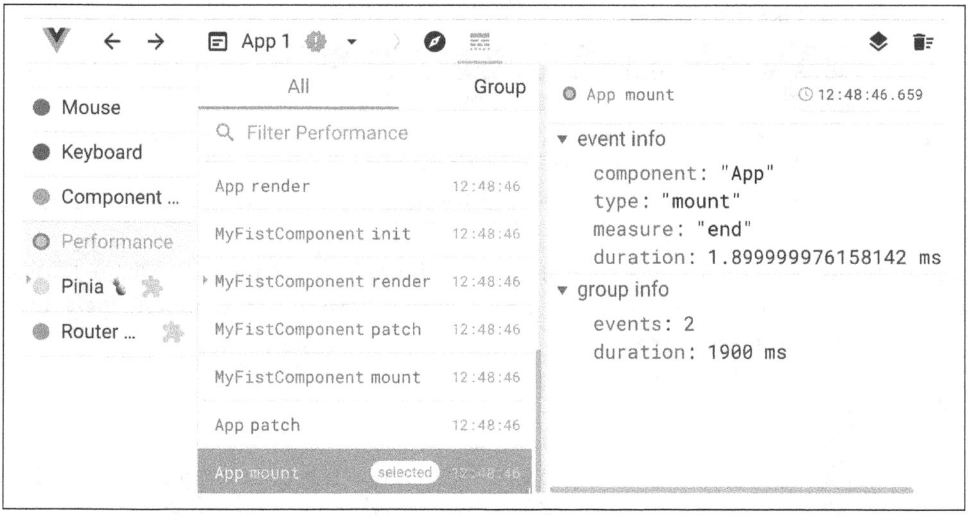

Figure 3-10. Timeline for *MyFirstComponent* in the first render

And when the component re-renders, the Vue Devtools tab displays the timeline event records as in Figure 3-11.

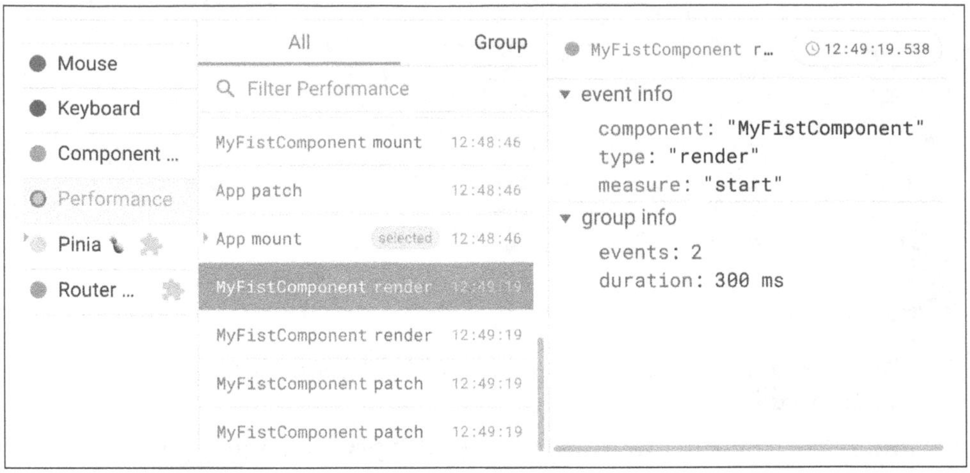

Figure 3-11. Timeline for *MyFirstComponent* in the second render

Each of the previous lifecycle hooks can be beneficial. In Table 3-1, you will find the most common use cases per hook.

Table 3-1. Using the right hook for the right purpose

Lifecycle hook	Use case
beforeCreate	When you need to load external logic *without* modifying the component's data.
created	When you need to load external data into the component. This hook is preferable to the mounted one for reading or writing data from external resources.
mounted	When you need to perform any DOM manipulation or access the component's DOM node this.$el.

To this point, we have learned the component's lifecycle order and its available hooks. Next, we will look at how to create and organize common component logic into methods with the method property.

Methods

Methods are logic that does not depend on the component's data, even though we can access the component's local state using a this instance within a method. Components' methods are functions defined within the methods property. As Example 3-8 shows, we can define a method to reverse the message property.

Example 3-8. Defining a method to reverse the `message` property

```ts
<script lang="ts">
import { defineComponent } from 'vue'

export default defineComponent({
  name: 'ReversedMessage',
  data() {
    return {
      message: '',
    };
  },
  methods: {
    reverseMessage():string {
      return this.message.split('').reverse().join('')
    },
  },
});
</script>
```

Example 3-9 shows how we can use the `reverseMessage` method in the component's template.

Example 3-9. Output the reversed message on the template

```
<template>
  <h2 class="heading">I am {{reverseMessage()}}</h2>
  <input v-model="message" type="text" placeholder="Enter your message" />
</template>
```

When a user inputs a message's value in the browser, we see the output in Figure 3-12.

Figure 3-12. Reversed message based on the value of `message`

You can also modify the `reverseMessage` method to accept a string argument, making it more reusable and less dependent on `this.message`, as in Example 3-10.

Example 3-10. Defining a method to reverse a string

```ts
<script lang="ts">
import { defineComponent } from 'vue'

export default defineComponent({
  name: 'MyFistComponent',
  data() {
    return {
      message: '',
    };
  },
  methods: {
    reverseMessage(message: string):string {
      return message.split('').reverse().join('')
    },
  },
});
</script>
```

And in the `template` section, we refactor Example 3-9 and pass `message` as input parameter for the `reverseMessage` method:

```
<template>
  <h2 class="heading">I am {{reverseMessage(message)}}</h2>
  <input v-model="message" type="text" placeholder="Enter your message" />
</template>
```

The output stays the same as in Figure 3-12.

Also, we can trigger a component's method within its other properties or lifecycle hooks using the `this` instance. For example, we can split `reverseMessage` into two smaller methods, `reverse()` and `arrToString()`, as in the following code:

```
/**... */
  methods: {
    reverse(message: string):string[] {
      return message.split('').reverse()
    },
    arrToString(arr: string[]):string {
      return arr.join('')
    },
    reverseMessage(message: string):string {
      return this.arrToString(this.reverse(message))
    },
  },
```

Methods are beneficial in keeping your component's logic organized. Vue triggers a method only when it is relevant (such as being called in the template as in Example 3-9), allowing us to compute a new data value from local data dynamically. However, for methods, Vue does not cache the result of every trigger, and it will always rerun the method whenever a re-render occurs. Thus, in scenarios where you need to calculate new data, it is better to use computed properties, which we will explore next.

Computed Properties

Computed properties are Vue's unique features that allow you to calculate new reactive data properties from any reactive data of a component. Each computed property is a function that returns a value and resides within the `computed` property field.

Example 3-11 shows how we define a newly computed property, `reversedMessage`, which returns the component's local data `message` in reversed order.

Example 3-11. A computed property that returns the component's local message in reversed order

```
import { defineComponent } from 'vue'

export default defineComponent({
  name: 'ReversedMessage',
  data() {
    return {
      message: 'Hello Vue!'
    }
  },
  computed: {
    reversedMessage() {
      return this.message.split('').reverse().join('')
    }
  }
})
```

You can access `reversedMessage` computed with the same approach as any component's local data. Example 3-12 shows how we can output the calculated `reversedMessage` based on the input value of `message`.

Example 3-12. Computed property example

```
<template>
  <h2 class="heading">I am {{ reversedMessage }}</h2>
  <input v-model="message" type="text" placeholder="Enter your message" />
</template>
```

Example 3-12 has the same output as in Figure 3-12.

You can also track the computed property in the Components tab of the Vue Devtools (Figure 3-13).

Figure 3-13. Computed properties `reversedMessage` in the Components tab

Similarly, you can access a computed property's value in the component's logic through the `this` instance as its local data property. You can also calculate a new computed property based on the computed property's value. As Example 3-13 shows, we can add the length of the `reversedMessage` property value into a new property, `reversedMessageLength`.

Example 3-13. Adding `reversedMessageLength` computed property

```
import { defineComponent } from 'vue'

export default defineComponent({
  /**... */
  computed: {
    reversedMessage() {
      return this.message.split('').reverse().join('')
    },
    reversedMessageLength() {
      return this.reversedMessage.length
    }
  }
})
```

The Vue engine automatically caches the value of computed properties and re-computes the value only when related reactive data changes. As in Example 3-12, Vue will update the value of `reversedMessage` computed property only when `message` changes. If you want to display or reuse the `reversedMessage` value in another location within the component, Vue will not need to recalculate its value.

Using computed properties helps organize complex data modification into reusable data blocks. Thus, it reduces the amount of code required and keeps code clean while improving your component's performance. Using computed properties also allows you to quickly set up an automatic watcher for any reactive data property, by having them appear in the implementation logic of the computed property function.

However, in some scenarios, this automatic watcher mechanism can create overhead to keep the component's performance stable. In such cases, we can consider using watchers through the `watch` property field of the component.

Watchers

Watchers allow you to programmatically watch for changes in any reactive data property of a component and handle them. Each watcher is a function that receives two arguments: the new value (`newValue`) and the current value (`oldValue`) of the observed data. It then performs any logic based on these two input parameters. We define a watcher for reactive data by adding it to the `watch` property field of the component's options, following this syntax:

```
watch: {
  'reactiveDataPropertyName'(newValue, oldValue) {
    // do something
  }
}
```

You need to replace the `reactiveDataPropertyName` with the name of the target component's data that we want to observe.

Example 3-14 shows how we define a new watcher to observe for changes in the component's local data `message`.

Example 3-14. A watcher that observes for changes in the component's local message

```
export default {
  name: 'MyFirstComponent',
  data() {
    return {
      message: 'Hello Vue!'
    }
  },
  watch: {
    message(newValue: string, oldValue: string) {
      console.log(`new value: ${newValue}, old value: ${oldValue}`)
    }
  }
}
```

In this example, we have defined a `message` watcher that observes changes in the `message` property. The Vue engine triggers the watcher whenever the value of `message` changes. Figure 3-14 shows the console log output for this watcher.

Figure 3-14. Console log output when the message changes

We can implement the `reservedMessage` in Example 3-11 using a watcher on `message` and `data()` field instead of computed properties, as seen in Example 3-15.

Example 3-15. A watcher that observes for changes in the component's local message and updates the value of reversedMessage

```
import { defineComponent } from 'vue'

export default defineComponent({
  name: 'MyFirstComponent',
  data() {
    return {
      message: 'Hello Vue!',
      reversedMessage: 'Hello Vue!'.split('').reverse().join('')
    }
  },
  watch: {
    message(newValue: string, oldValue: string) {
      this.reversedMessage = newValue.split('').reverse().join('')
    }
  }
})
```

The output remains the same as in Figure 3-12. However, this approach is not recommended in this specific case, as it is less efficient than using computed properties.

Side effects are any additional logic triggered by the watcher or within the computed property. Side effects can impact the component's performance; you should handle them with caution.

You can assign the handler function directly to the watcher name. The Vue engine will automatically call the handler with a set of default configurations for watchers. However, you can also pass an object to the watcher's name to customize the watcher's behavior, using the fields in Table 3-2.

Table 3-2. The watcher object's fields

Watcher's field	Description	Accepted type	Default value	Required?
`handler`	The callback function to trigger when the target data's value changes.	function	N/A	Yes
`deep`	Indicates whether Vue should observe for changes in the nested properties of the target data (if any).	boolean	`false`	No
`immediate`	Indicates whether to trigger the handler immediately after mounting the component.	boolean	`false`	No
`flush`	Indicates the timing order of the handler's execution. By default, Vue triggers the handler before updating the Vue component.	pre, post	`pre`	No

Observing for Changes in Nested Properties

The `deep` option field allows you to observe changes in all nested properties. Take a `user` object data in a `UserWatcherComponent` component with two nested properties: `name` and `age`, for instance. We define a `user` watcher that observes for changes in the `user` object's nested properties using the `deep` option field, as in Example 3-16.

Example 3-16. A watcher that observes for changes in the user object's nested properties

```
import { defineComponent } from 'vue'

type User = {
  name: string
  age: number
}

export default defineComponent({
  name: 'UserWatcherComponent',
  data(): { user: User } {
    return {
      user: {
        name: 'John',
        age: 30
```

```
      }
    }
  },
  watch: {
    user: {
      handler(newValue: User, oldValue: User) {
        console.log({ newValue, oldValue })
      },
      deep: true
    }
  }
})
```

As Example 3-17 shows, in the template section of the UserWatcherComponent component, we receive the input for the user object's fields, name and age.

Example 3-17. Template section for the UserWatcherComponent

```
<template>
  <div>
    <div>
      <label for="name">Name:
        <input v-model="user.name" placeholder="Enter your name" id="name" />
      </label>
    </div>
    <div>
      <label for="age">Age:
        <input v-model="user.age" placeholder="Enter your age" id="age" />
      </label>
    </div>
  </div>
</template>
```

In this case, the Vue engine triggers the user watcher whenever the value of user.name or user.age changes. Figure 3-15 shows the console log output for this watcher when we change the value of user.name.

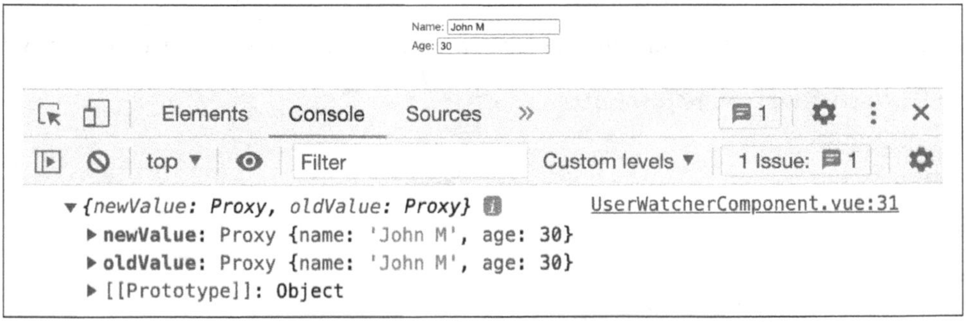

Figure 3-15. Console log output when the user object's nested properties change

Figure 3-15 shows the new and old value of `user` is identical. This happens because the `user` object is still the same instance and only its `name` field's value changed.

Also, once we turn on the `deep` flag, the Vue engine will traverse all the properties of the `user` object and their nested properties, then observe for changes in them. Thus, it may cause performance issues when the `user` object structure contains a more complex internal data structure. In this case, it's better to specify which nested properties you wish to monitor, as shown in Example 3-18.

Example 3-18. A watcher that observes for changes in the user's name

```
//...
export default defineComponent({
  //...
  watch: {
    'user.name': {
      handler(newValue: string, oldValue: string) {
        console.log({ newValue, oldValue })
      },
    },
  }
});
```

Here we observe changes only in `user.name` property. Figure 3-16 shows the console log output for this watcher.

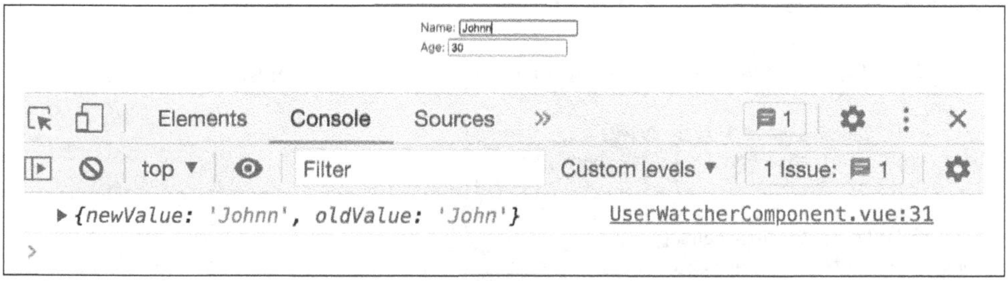

Figure 3-16. Console log outputs only when the user object's name changes

You can use the dot-delimited path approach to enable watching a specific child property, regardless of how deeply nested it is. For example, if the `user` has this:

```
type User = {
  name: string;
  age: number;
  address: {
    street: string;
    city: string;
    country: string;
    zip: string;
  };
}
```

Suppose you need to watch for changes in `user.address.city`; you can do so by using *"user.address.city"* as the watcher name, and so on. By taking this approach, you can avoid undesired performance issues on deep watching and narrow the scope of the watcher to only the properties you need.

Using the this.$watch() Method

In most cases, the `watch` option is enough to handle your watcher needs. However, there are scenarios where you don't want to enable certain watchers when not necessary. For instance, you may want to enable the `user.address.city` watcher only when the `user` object's `address` property is not `null`. In this case, you can use the `this.$watch()` method to create the watcher upon creating the component conditionally.

The `this.$watch()` method accepts the following parameters:

- Name of the target data to watch as a string
- The callback function as a watcher's handler to trigger when the target data's value changes

`this.$watch()` returns a function you can call to stop the watcher. The code in Example 3-19 shows how to use the `this.$watch()` method to create a watcher that observes for changes in `user.address.city`.

Example 3-19. A watcher that observes for changes in city field in the user's address

```
import { defineComponent } from "vue";
import type { WatchStopHandle } from "vue";

//...
export default defineComponent({
  name: "UserWatcherComponent",
  data(): { user: User; stopWatchingAddressCity?: WatchStopHandle } {
    return {
      user: {
        name: "John",
        age: 30,
        address: {
          street: "123 Main St",
          city: "New York",
          country: "USA",
          zip: "10001",
        },
      },
      stopWatchingAddressCity: undefined, ❶
    };
  },
  created() {
    if (this.user.address) { ❷
```

```
      this.stopWatchingAddressCity = this.$watch(
        "user.address.city",
        (newValue: string, oldValue: string) => {
          console.log({ newValue, oldValue });
        }
      );
    }
  },
  beforeUnmount() {
    if (this.stopWatchingAddressCity) { ❸
      this.stopWatchingAddressCity();
    }
  },
});
```

❶ Define a `stopWatchingAddressCity` property for storing the watcher's return function.

❷ Create a watcher for `user.address.city` only when the user object's `address` object property is available.

❸ Before unmounting the component, trigger the `stopWatchingAddressCity` function to stop the watcher if relevant.

Using this approach, we can limit the number of unnecessary watchers created, such as the watcher for `user.address.city` when `user.address` doesn't exist.

Next, we will look at another interesting feature of Vue, the `slot` component.

The Power of Slots

Building a component is about more than just its data and logic. We often want to maintain the current component's sense and existing design but still allow users to modify parts of the UI template. This flexibility is crucial when building a customizable component library in any framework. Fortunately, Vue offers the `<slot>` component to allow us to dynamically replace the default UI design for an element when needed.

For instance, let's build a layout component `ListLayout` to render a list of items, with each item having the following type:

```
interface Item {
  id: number
  name: string
  description: string
  thumbnail?: string
}
```

For each item in the list, by default, the layout component should render its name and description, as shown in Example 3-20.

Example 3-20. The first template implementation of the ListLayout component

```
<template>
  <ul class="list-layout">
    <li class="list-layout__item" v-for="item in items" :key="item.id">
      <div class="list-layout__item__name">{{ item.name }}</div>
      <div class="list-layout__item__description">{{ item.description }}</div>
    </li>
  </ul>
</template>
```

We also define a sample list of items to render for ListLayout in its script section (Example 3-21).

Example 3-21. The script section of the ListLayout component

```
import { defineComponent } from 'vue'

//...

export default defineComponent({
  name: 'ListLayout',
  data(): { items: Item[] } {
    return {
      items: [
        {
          id: 1,
          name: "Item 1",
          description: "This is item 1",
          thumbnail:
"https://res.cloudinary.com/mayashavin/image/upload/v1643005666/Demo/supreme_pizza",
        },
        {
          id: 2,
          name: "Item 2",
          description: "This is item 2",
          thumbnail:
"https://res.cloudinary.com/mayashavin/image/upload/v1643005666/Demo/hawaiian_pizza",
        },
        {
          id: 3,
          name: "Item 3",
          description: "This is item 3",
          thumbnail:
"https://res.cloudinary.com/mayashavin/image/upload/v1643005666/Demo/pina_colada_pizza",
        },
      ]
    }
  }
})
```

Figure 3-17 shows the default rendered UI of a single item using the previous template (Example 3-20) and data (Example 3-21).

- Item 1

  This is item 1

- Item 2

  This is item 2

- Item 3

  This is item 3

Figure 3-17. A sample UI layout of the item in the ListLayout component

Based on this default UI, we can then offer users an option to customize each item's UI. To do so, we wrap the code block within a li element with a slot element, as shown in Example 3-22.

Example 3-22. ListLayout component with slot

```
<template>
  <ul class="list-layout">
    <li class="list-layout__item" v-for="item in items" :key="item.id">
      <slot :item="item">
        <div class="list-layout__item__name">{{ item.name }}</div>
        <div class="list-layout__item__description">{{ item.description }}</div>
      </slot>
    </li>
  </ul>
</template>
```

Notice how we bind the item variable received for each v-for iteration to the same item prop attribute of the slot component using : syntax. By doing so, we ensure the slot provides access to the same item data to its descendants.

 The slot component doesn't share the same data context with its host component (such as ListLayout). If you want to access any data property of the host component, you need to pass it as a prop to slot using v-bind syntax. We will learn more about giving props to nested elements in "Nested Components and Data Flow in Vue" on page 107.

However, we need more than having `item` available for the custom template content to make it work. In the parent component of `ListLayout`, we add `v-slot` directive to `<ListLayout>` tag to get access to the `item` passed to its `slot` component, following the syntax below:

```
<ListLayout v-slot="{ item }">
  <!-- Custom template content -->
</ListLayout>
```

Here we use the object destructuring syntax { `item` } to create a scoped slot reference to the data property we want to access. Then we can use `item` directly on our custom template content, as in Example 3-23.

Example 3-23. Compose `ProductItemList` from `ListLayout`

```
<!-- ProductItemList.vue -->
<template>
  <div id="app">
    <ListLayout v-slot="{ item }">
      <img
        v-if="item.thumbnail"
        class="list-layout__item__thumbnail"
        :src="item.thumbnail"
        :alt="item.name"
        width="200"
      />
      <div class="list-layout__item__name">{{ item.name }}</div>
    </ListLayout>
  </div>
</template>
```

In Example 3-23, we change the UI to display a thumbnail image and the item's name only. You can see the result in Figure 3-21.

This example is the most straightforward use case for the `slot` component when we want to enable customization in a single slot in the element. But what about more complex scenarios like a product card component containing a thumbnail, the main description area, and an area of actions, each of which requires customization? For such a case, we still can take advantage of the power of `slot`, with naming capability.

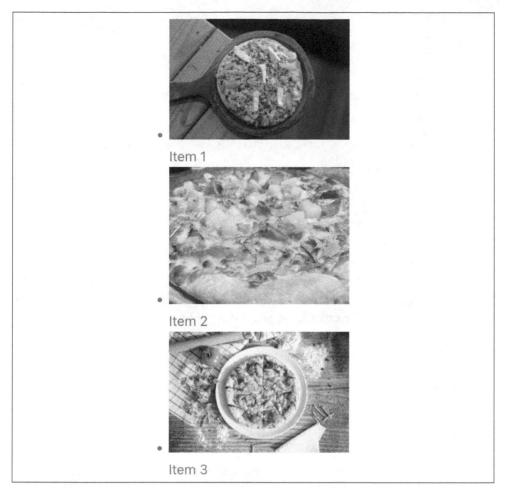

- Item 1

- Item 2

- Item 3

Figure 3-18. The UI layout of the `ProductItemList` component

Using Named Slots with Template Tag and v-slot Attribute

In Example 3-22, we only enable customization for the UI of the item's name and description as a single slot. To split the customization into several slot sections for a thumbnail, the main description area, and a footer of actions, we use `slot` with the attribute `name`, as in Example 3-24.

Example 3-24. `ListLayout` component with named slots

```
<template>
  <ul class="list-layout">
    <li class="list-layout__item" v-for="item in items" :key="item.id">
      <slot name="thumbnail" :item="item" />
      <slot name="main" :item="item">
        <div class="list-layout__item__name">{{ item.name }}</div>
        <div class="list-layout__item__description">{{ item.description }}</div>
      </slot>
      <slot name="actions" :item="item" />
    </li>
  </ul>
```

We assigned each slot with the names `thumbnail`, `main`, and `actions`, respectively. And for the `main` slot, we add a fallback content template to display the item's name and description.

When we want to pass the custom content to a specific slot, we wrap the content with a `template` tag. Then we pass the name declaring the desired slot (`slot-name` for example) to the `v-slot` directive of the `template`, following the syntax:

```
<template v-slot:slot-name>
  <!-- Custom content -->
</template>
```

We can also use the shorthand syntax # instead of `v-slot`:

```
<template #slot-name>
  <!-- Custom content -->
</template>
```

 From here on, we will use the syntax # to denote `v-slot` when using with the `template` tag.

Like using `v-slot` on the component tag, we can also give access to the slot's data:

```
<template #slot-name="mySlotProps">
  <!--<div> Slot data: {{ mySlotProps }}</div>-->
</template>
```

Using multiple slots

For multiple slots, you *must* use the v-slot directive for each relevant template tag, and *not* on the component tag. Otherwise, Vue will throw an error.

Let's go back to our ProductItemList component (Example 3-23) and refactor the component to render the following custom content sections for the product item:

- A thumbnail image
- An action button for adding the product to the cart

Example 3-25 shows how to implement that using template and v-slot.

Example 3-25. Compose ProductItemList with named slot

```
<!-- ProductItemList.vue -->
<template>
  <div id="app">
    <ListLayout>
      <template #thumbnail="{ item }">
        <img
          v-if="item.thumbnail"
          class="list-layout__item__thumbnail"
          :src="item.thumbnail"
          :alt="item.name"
          width="200"
        />
      </template>
      <template #actions>
        <div class="list-layout__item__footer">
          <button class="list-layout__item__footer__button">Add to cart</button>
        </div>
      </template>
    </ListLayout>
  </div>
</template>
```

The code results in the output shown in Figure 3-19.

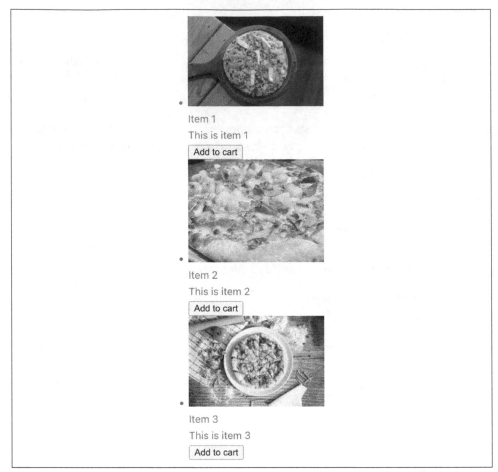

- Item 1
  This is item 1
  [Add to cart]

- Item 2
  This is item 2
  [Add to cart]

- Item 3
  This is item 3
  [Add to cart]

Figure 3-19. Output of `ProductItemList` with customized slot content

And that's it. You are ready to use slots to customize your UI components. With slots, you can now create some basic standard reusable layouts for your application, such as a page layout with a header and footer, a side panel layout, or a modal component that can be a dialog or notification. You will then find how handy slots are in keeping your code organized and reusable.

> Using `slot` also means the browser won't apply all relevant scoped styles defined in the component. To enable this functionality, see "Applying Scoped Styles to Slot Content" on page 101.

Next, we will learn how to access the mounted component instance or a DOM element using refs.

Understanding Refs

While Vue typically handles most of the DOM interactions for you, for some scenarios you may need to directly access a DOM element within a component for further manipulation. For instance, you may want to open a modal dialog when the user clicks a button or focus on a specific input field when mounting the component. In such cases, you can use the ref attribute to access the target DOM element instance.

The ref is a Vue built-in attribute that allows you to receive a direct reference to a DOM element or a mounted child instance. In the template section, you assign the value of the ref attribute to a string representing the reference name on the target element. Example 3-26 shows how to create a messageRef, which refers to the DOM element input.

Example 3-26. An input component with a ref attribute assigned to messageRef

```
<template>
  <div>
    <input type="text" ref="messageRef" placeholder="Enter a message" />
  </div>
</template>
```

You can then access the messageRef in the script section to manipulate the input element through a this.$refs.messageRef instance. The reference instance messageRef will have all the properties and methods of the input element. For instance, you can use this.$refs.messageRef.focus() to focus on the input element programmatically.

Accessing the ref attribute

The ref attribute is accessible only *after* mounting the component.

The reference instance contains all the properties and methods of a specific DOM element or the child component instance, depending on the target element type. In a scenario where you use the ref attribute on a looped element using v-for, the reference instance will be the array containing the looped elements without order.

Take a list of tasks, for instance. As Example 3-27 shows, you can use the ref attribute to access the list of tasks.

Example 3-27. A list of tasks with a ref attribute assigned to `taskListRef`

```ts
<template>
  <div>
    <ul>
      <li v-for="(task, index) in tasks" :key="task.id" ref="tasksRef">
        {{title}} {{index}}: {{task.description}}
      </li>
    </ul>
  </div>
</template>
<script lang="ts">
import { defineComponent } from "vue";

export default defineComponent({
  name: "TaskListComponent",
  data() {
    return {
      tasks: [{
        id: 'task01',
        description: 'Buy groceries',
      }, {
        id: 'task02',
        description: 'Do laundry',
      }, {
        id: 'task03',
        description: 'Watch Moonknight',
      }],
      title: 'Task',
    };
  }
});
</script>
```

Once Vue mounts the `TaskListComponent`, you can see the `tasksRef` contains three `li` DOM elements and nested in `refs` property of the component instance, as seen in the Vue Devtools screenshot in Figure 3-20.

You can now use `this.$refs.tasksRef` to access the list of the task elements and perform further modification when needed.

ref can also accept a function as its value, by adding a prefix, :, to it (:ref). The function accepts the reference instance as its input parameter.

We have learned about the `ref` attribute and how it can be helpful in many real-world challenges, such as building a reusable modal system (see "Implementing a Modal with Teleport and the <dialog> Element" on page 127). The following section will explore how to create and share standard configurations across components with mixins.

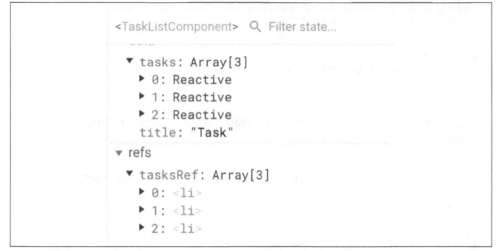

Figure 3-20. Vue Devtools showing the tasksRef reference instance

Sharing Component Configuration with Mixins

In reality, it is not uncommon for some components to share similar data and behaviors, such as a cafe and a dining restaurant component. Both elements share the logic of making reservations and accepting payments, but each has unique features. In such scenarios, you can use the `mixins` property to share the standard functionalities across these two components.

For instance, you can create a `restaurantMixin` object that contains the standard functionalities of the two components, `DiningComponent` and `CafeComponent`, as in Example 3-28.

Example 3-28. A restaurantMixin mixin object

```
/** mixins/restaurantMixin.ts */
import { defineComponent } from 'vue'

export const restaurantMixin = defineComponent({
  data() {
    return {
      menu: [],
      reservations: [],
      payments: [],
      title: 'Restaurant',
    };
  },
  methods: {
    makeReservation() {
      console.log("Reservation made");
    },
```

```
    acceptPayment() {
      console.log("Payment accepted");
    },
  },
  created() {
    console.log(`Welcome to ${this.title}`);
  }
});
```

You can then use the `restaurantMixin` object in the `mixins` property of Dining
Component, as seen in Example 3-29.

Example 3-29. Using the `restaurantMixin` mixins property of the `DiningComponent`

```
<template>
<!-- components/DiningComponent.vue -->
  <h1>{{title}}</h1>
  <button @click="getDressCode">getDressCode</button>
  <button @click="makeReservation">Make a reservation</button>
  <button @click="acceptPayment">Accept a payment</button>
</template>
<script lang='ts'>
import { defineComponent } from 'vue'
import { restaurantMixin } from '@/mixins/restaurantMixin'

export default defineComponent({
  name: 'DiningComponent',
  mixins: [restaurantMixin],
  data() {
    return {
      title: 'Dining',
      menu: [
        { id: 'menu01', name: 'Steak' },
        { id: 'menu02', name: 'Salad' },
        { id: 'menu03', name: 'Pizza' },
      ],
    };
  },
  methods: {
    getDressCode() {
      console.log("Dress code: Casual");
    },
  },
  created() {
    console.log('DiningComponent component created!');
  }
});
</script>
```

Example 3-30 shows the similar `CafeComponent`.

Example 3-30. Using the `restaurantMixin` mixins property of the CafeComponent

```
<template>
<!-- components/CafeComponent.vue -->
  <h1>{{title}}</h1>
  <p>Open time: 8am - 4pm</p>
  <ul>
    <li v-for="menuItem in menu" :key="menuItem.id">
      {{menuItem.name}}
    </li>
  </ul>
  <button @click="acceptPayment">Pay</button>
</template>
<script lang='ts'>
import { defineComponent } from 'vue'
import { restaurantMixin } from '@/mixins/restaurantMixin'

export default defineComponent({
  name: 'CafeComponent',
  mixins: [restaurantMixin],
  data() {
    return {
      title: 'Cafe',
      menu: [{
        id: 'menu01',
        name: 'Coffee',
        price: 5,
      }, {
        id: 'menu02',
        name: 'Tea',
        price: 3,
      }, {
        id: 'menu03',
        name: 'Cake',
        price: 7,
      }],
    };
  },
  created() {
    console.log('CafeComponent component created!');
  }
});
</script>
```

Upon creating the components, the Vue engine will merge the mixin logic into the component, with the component's data declaration taking precedence. In Examples 3-29 and 3-30, the DiningComponent and CafeComponent will have the same properties, menu, reservations, payments, and title, but with different values. Also, the methods and hooks declared in restaurantMixin will be available to both components. It is similar to the inheritance pattern, though the component doesn't override the mixin hooks' behavior. Instead, the Vue engine calls the mixin's hooks first, then the component's hooks.

When Vue mounts the `DiningComponent`, you will see the output in Figure 3-21 in the browser console.

```
Welcome to Dining                          restaurantMixin.ts:21
DiningComponent component created!         DiningComponent.vue:31
```

Figure 3-21. Output order of console log of the `DiningComponent`

Similarly, when Vue mounts the `CafeComponent`, you will see the output in Figure 3-22 in the browser console.

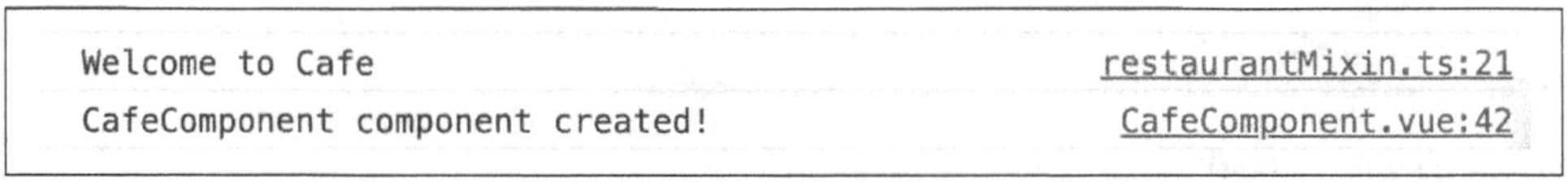

```
Welcome to Cafe                            restaurantMixin.ts:21
CafeComponent component created!           CafeComponent.vue:42
```

Figure 3-22. Output order of console log of the `CafeComponent`

Note that `title` value has changed between the two components, while Vue triggers the `created` hook of the `restaurantMixin` first, followed by the one declared on the element itself.

 The order of merging and triggering the hooks for multiple mixins is according to the order of the mixins array. Vue *always* calls the component's hooks last. Consider this order when putting multiple mixins together.

If you open the Vue Devtools, you will see the `restaurantMixin` is not visible, and the `DiningComponent` and `CafeComponent` are with their own data properties, as shown in Figures 3-23 and 3-24.

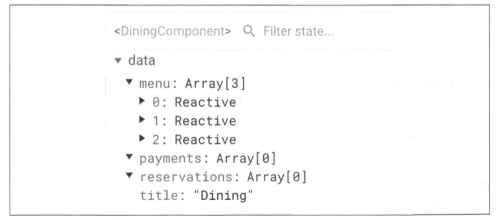

Figure 3-23. Vue Devtools showing the `DiningComponent`

```
<CafeComponent>   Q  Filte   [icon] <>  ≡  [icon]

 ▼ data
    ▼ menu: Array[3]
       ▶ 0: Reactive
       ▶ 1: Reactive
       ▶ 2: Reactive
    ▼ payments: Array[0]
    ▼ reservations: Array[0]
       title: "Cafe"
```

Figure 3-24. Vue Devtools showing the `CafeComponent`

Mixins are great for sharing common logic between components and keeping your code organized. However, too many mixins can confuse other developers in understanding and debugging, and in most cases, are considered bad practice. We recommend validating your use case before choosing mixins over alternatives, such as the Composition API (Chapter 5).

At this point, we have explored how to compose components' logic using advanced features in `template` and `script` sections. Next, let's learn how to make your component beautiful with Vue's built-in styling features in the `style` section.

Scoped Styling Components

Like a regular HTML page structure, we can define CSS stylings for an SFC component using the `<style>` tag:

```
<style>
h1 {
  color: red;
}
</style>
```

The `<style>` section usually comes last in the order of a Vue SFC component and can appear multiple times. Upon mounting the component to the DOM, the Vue engine will apply the CSS styles defined within the `<style>` tag to all the elements or matched DOM selectors within the application. In other words, all CSS rules that appeared in the `<style>` of a component apply globally once mounted. Take the HeadingComponent shown in Example 3-31, which renders a heading title with some stylings.

Example 3-31. Using the `<style>` tag in HeadingComponent

```
<template>
  <h1 class="heading">{{title}}</h1>
  <p class="description">{{description}}</p>
</template>
<script lang='ts'>
export default {
  name: 'HeadingComponent',
  data() {
    return {
      title: 'Welcome to Vue Restaurant',
      description: 'A Vue.js project to learn Vue.js',
    };
  },
};
</script>
<style>
.heading {
  color: #178c0e;
  font-size: 2em;
}

.description {
  color: #b76210;
  font-size: 1em;
}
</style>
```

In Example 3-31, we created two CSS class selectors: `heading` and `description` for `h1` and `p` elements of the component, respectively. When Vue mounts the component, the browser will paint these elements with the appropriate styles, as seen in Figure 3-25.

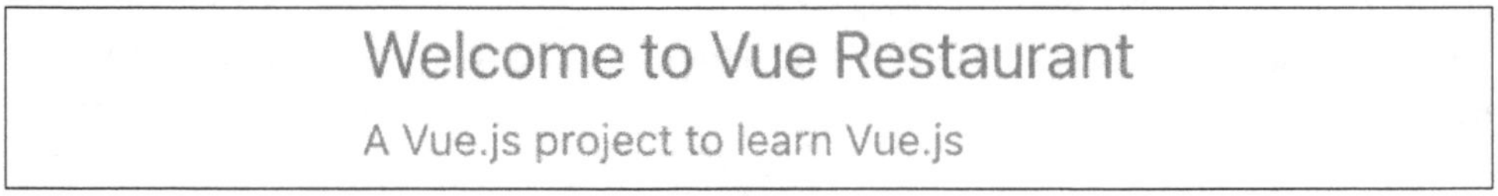

Figure 3-25. The `HeadingComponent` with styles applied

Example 3-32 shows adding a `span` element with the same `heading` class selector outside `HeadingComponent` in the parent component `App.vue`.

Example 3-32. Adding the same class selector to the parent component `App.vue`

```
<!-- App.vue -->
<template>
  <section class="wrapper">
    <HeadingComponent />
    <span class="heading">This is a span element in App.vue component</span>
  </section>
</template>
```

The browser then still applies the same styles to the span element, as shown in Figure 3-26.

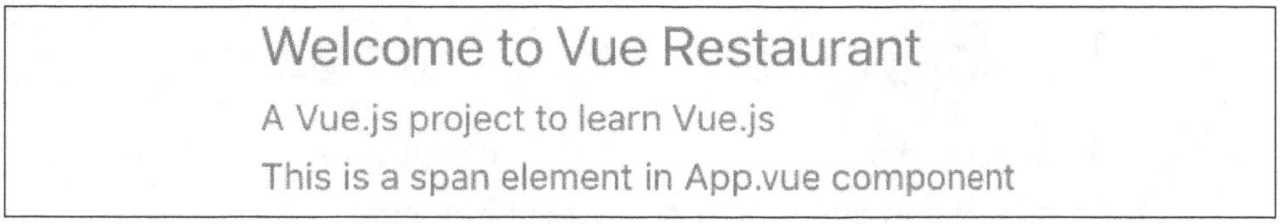

Welcome to Vue Restaurant

A Vue.js project to learn Vue.js

This is a span element in App.vue component

Figure 3-26. The span element in App.vue has the same CSS styles as the h1 element in the HeadingComponent

But if we don't use the HeadingComponent, or it does not yet exist in the application on run-time, the span element will not have the CSS rules of the heading class selector.

To avoid such a scenario and to have better control of style rules and selectors, Vue offers a unique feature, the scoped attribute. With the <style scoped> tag, Vue ensures the CSS rules will apply to relevant elements within the component and not leak them to the rest of the application. Vue achieved this mechanism by performing these steps:

1. Add a randomly generated data attribute on the target element tag with the prefix syntax data-v.

2. Transform the CSS selectors defined in the <style scoped> tag to include the generated data attribute.

Let's see how this works in practice. In Example 3-33, we add the scoped attribute to the <style> tag of the HeadingComponent.

Example 3-33. Adding the scoped attribute to the <style> tag of HeadingComponent

```
<!-- HeadingComponent.vue -->
<!--...-->
<style scoped>
.heading {
  color: #178c0e;
  font-size: 2em;
}

.description {
  color: #b76210;
  font-size: 1em;
}
</style>
```

The span element defined in App.vue (Example 3-32) will not have the same CSS styles as the h1 element in HeadingComponent, as shown in Figure 3-27.

Welcome to Vue Restaurant

A Vue.js project to learn Vue.js

This is a span element in App.vue component

Figure 3-27. The span element in App.vue now has default black color

When you open the Elements tab in the browser's Developer Tools, you can see the h1 and p elements now have the data-v-xxxx attribute, as shown in Figure 3-28.

```
▼ <section class="wrapper">
    <h1 data-v-6c9f22e5 class="heading">Welcome to Vue Restaurant</h1>
    <p data-v-6c9f22e5 class="description">A Vue.js project to learn Vue.js</p>
    <span class="heading">This is a span element in App.vue component</span>
  </section>
```

Figure 3-28. The h1 and p elements in HeadingComponent have the data-v-xxxx attribute

And if you select the h1 element and look at its styles on the right panel, you can see that the CSS selector .heading has become .heading[data-v-xxxx], as shown in Figure 3-29.

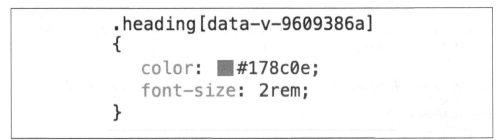

```
.heading[data-v-9609386a]
{
    color:  ■#178c0e;
    font-size: 2rem;
}
```

Figure 3-29. The CSS selector .heading is transformed to .heading[data-v-xxxx]

I strongly recommend you start working with the scoped attribute in your components as a good coding habit to avoid undesirable CSS bugs when your project grows.

> The browser follows the CSS specificity (*https://oreil.ly/x4iOg*) when deciding which order to apply the styles. Because Vue's scoped mechanism uses attribute selectors [data-v-xxxx], using the .heading selector solely is not enough to override the component's styles from the parent.

Applying CSS to a Child Component in Scoped Styles

Beginning with Vue 3.x, you can override or extend the styles of a child component from the parent with a scoped style by using the :deep() pseudo-class. For example, as Example 3-34 shows, we can override the scoped styles of paragraph element p in the HeadingComponent from its parent App.

Example 3-34. Overriding the scoped styles of paragraph element p in the Heading Component from its parent App

```
<!-- App.vue -->
<template>
  <section class="wrapper">
    <HeadingComponent />
    <span class="heading">This is a span element in App.vue component</span>
  </section>
</template>
<style scoped>
.wrapper :deep(p) {
  color: #000;
}
</style>
```

The p element in the HeadingComponent will have the color black instead of its scoped color, #b76210, as shown in Figure 3-30.

Figure 3-30. The p element in HeadingComponent has the color black

The browser will apply the newly defined CSS rules to any p elements nested in any child component of App and its children.

Applying Scoped Styles to Slot Content

By design, any styles defined in the `<style scoped>` tag is relevant only to the component's default `template` itself. Vue won't be able to transform any slotted content to include the `data-v-xxxx` attribute. To style any slotted content, you can use the `:slot([CSS selector])` pseudo-class or create a dedicated `style` section for them on the parent level and keep the code organized.

Accessing a Component's Data Value in Style Tag with v-bind() Pseudo-Class

We often need to access the component's data value and bind that value to a valid CSS property, such as changing dark or light mode or theme color for an application based on the user's preference. For such use cases, we use the pseudo-class v-bind().

v-bind() accepts the component's data property and JavaScript expressions as a string for its only argument. For example, we can change the color of the h1 element in the HeadingComponent based on the value of the titleColor data property, as shown in Example 3-35.

Example 3-35. Changing the color of the h1 element based on the value of the title Color

```
<!-- HeadingComponent.vue -->
<template>
  <h1 class="heading">{{title}}</h1>
  <p class="description">{{description}}</p>
</template>
<script lang='ts'>
export default {
  //...
  data() {
    return {
      //...
      titleColor: "#178c0e",
    };
  },
};
</script>
<style scoped>
.heading {
  color: v-bind(titleColor);
  font-size: 2em;
}
</style>
```

The v-bind() pseudo-class then transforms the value of the titleColor data property into an inline hashed CSS variable, as shown in Figure 3-31.

```
<h1 data-v-6c9f22e5 class="heading" style="--6c9f22e5-titleColor: #178c0e;">
Welcome to Vue Restaurant</h1>
<p data-v-6c9f22e5 class="description" style="--6c9f22e5-titleColor: #178c0e;
">A Vue.js project to learn Vue.js</p>
<span data-v-7a7a37b1 class="heading">This is a span element in App.vue
component</span>
```

Figure 3-31. The value of the titleColor data property is now a hashed CSS property in inline style

Let's open the Elements tab in the browser's Developer Tools and look at the element's styles. You can see the generated color property for the `.heading` selector remains static and has the same value as the developed hashed CSS property of `titleColor` (Figure 3-32).

Figure 3-32. The generated color property for the .heading selector has the same value as the generated hashed CSS property of `titleColor`

`v-bind()` helps retrieve a component's data value and then bind the desired CSS property to that dynamic value. However, this is only one-way binding. If you want to retrieve the defined CSS styles in the `template` for binding to the template's elements, you need to use CSS Modules, which we will cover in the next section.

Styling Components with CSS Modules

Another alternative for scoping your CSS styles per component is to use CSS Modules.[1] CSS Modules is an approach that allows you to write CSS styles regularly and then consume them as a JavaScript object (*module*) in our `template` and `script` sections.

To start using CSS Modules in a Vue SFC Component, you need to add the `module` attribute to the `style` tag, as shown in our `HeadingComponent` in Example 3-36.

Example 3-36. Using CSS Modules in `HeadingComponent`

```
<!-- HeadingComponent.vue -->
<style module>
.heading {
  color: #178c0e;
  font-size: 2em;
}
```

---

[1] CSS Modules (*https://oreil.ly/YQ6IJ*) started as an open source project for React.

```
.description {
  color: #b76210;
  font-size: 1em;
}
</style>
```

Now you will have access to these CSS selectors as fields of a $style property object of the component. We can remove the static class names heading and description assigned for h1 and p, respectively, in the template section. Instead, we will bind the classes of these elements to the relevant fields of the $style object (Example 3-37).

Example 3-37. Binding classes dynamically with $style object

```
<!-- HeadingComponent.vue -->
<template>
  <h1 :class="$style.heading">{{title}}</h1>
  <p :class="$style.description">{{description}}</p>
</template>
```

The output on the browser stays the same as Figure 3-27. However, when looking at the relevant elements on the Elements tab in the browser's Developer Tools, you will see Vue has hashed the generated class names to keep the styles scoped within the component, as in Figure 3-33.

```
<h1 class="_heading_e6bi0_2">Welcome to Vue Restaurant</h1>
<p class="_description_e6bi0_6">A Vue.js project to learn Vue.js
</p>
```

Figure 3-33. The generated class names heading and description are now hashed

Additionally, you can rename the CSS style object $style by assigning a name to the module attribute, as shown in Example 3-38.

Example 3-38. Renaming the CSS style object $style to headerClasses

```
<!-- HeadingComponent.vue -->
<style module="headerClasses">
.heading {
  color: #178c0e;
  font-size: 2em;
}

.description {
  color: #b76210;
  font-size: 1em;
}
</style>
```

And in the `template` section, you can bind the classes of the h1 and p elements to the `headerClasses` object instead (Example 3-39).

Example 3-39. Binding classes dynamically with headerClasses object

```
<!-- HeadingComponent.vue -->
<template>
  <h1 :class="headerClasses.heading">{{title}}</h1>
  <p :class="headerClasses.description">{{description}}</p>
</template>
```

> If you are using `<script setup>` or `setup()` function in your component (Chapter 5), you can use the `useCssModule()` hook to access the instance of the style object. This function accepts the name of the style object as its only argument.

The component now has a more isolated design than when using the `scoped` attribute in the `style` tag. The code looks more organized, and it is more challenging to override this component's styles from outside since Vue hashes the relevant CSS selectors randomly. Nevertheless, depending on your project's requirements, one approach may be better than the other, or it might be crucial to combine both `scoped` and `module` attributes to achieve the desired result.

Summary

In this chapter, we learned how to create a Vue component in the SFC standard and use `defineComponent()` to enable TypeScript support for the Vue application fully. We also learned to use `slots` to create a reusable component with isolated styles and shared mixin configurations in different contexts. We have explored further composing components using the component's lifecycle hooks, `computed`, `methods`, and `watch` properties in the Options API. Next, we will build on these foundations to create custom events and develop the interactions between components with the provide/inject patterns.

CHAPTER 4

Interactions Between Components

In Chapter 3, we deep-dived into composing a component with lifecycle hooks, computed properties, watchers, methods, and other features. We also learned about the power of slots and how to receive external data from other components using props.

Based on that foundation, this chapter guides you on how to build the interactions between components using custom events and provide/inject patterns. It also introduces Teleport API, which allows you to move elements around the DOM tree while keeping their order of appearance inside a Vue component.

Nested Components and Data Flow in Vue

Vue components can nest other Vue components inside them. This feature is handy in allowing users to organize their code into smaller, manageable, and reusable pieces in a complex UI project. We call nested elements child components and the component containing them their parent component.

Data flow in a Vue application is unidirectional by default, which means that the parent component can pass data to its child component but not the other way around. The parent can pass data to the child component using `props` (discussed briefly in "Exploring the Options API" on page 19), and the child component can emit events back to the parent component using custom events `emits`. Figure 4-1 demonstrates the data flow between components.

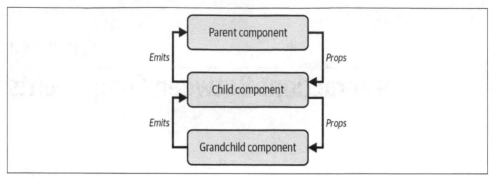

Figure 4-1. One-way data flow in Vue components

Passing Functions as Props

Unlike other frameworks, Vue does not allow you to pass a function as a prop to the child component. Instead, you can bind the function as a custom event emitter (see "Communication Between Components with Custom Events" on page 117).

Using Props to Pass Data to Child Components

In the form of an object or array, the props field of a Vue component contains all the available data properties that the component can receive from its parent. Each property of props is a prop of the target component. To start receiving data from the parent, you need to declare the props field in the component's options object, as shown in Example 4-1.

Example 4-1. Defining props in a component

```ts
export default {
  name: 'ChildComponent',
  props: {
    name: String
  }
}
```

In Example 4-1, the ChildComponent component accepts a name prop of type String. The parent component then can pass data to the child component using this name prop, as shown in Example 4-2.

Example 4-2. Passing static data as props to a child component

```
<template>
  <ChildComponent name="Red Sweater" />
</template>
<script lang="ts">
```

```
import ChildComponent from './ChildComponent.vue'
export default {
  name: 'ParentComponent',
  components: {
    ChildComponent
  },
}
</script>
```

The `ChildComponent` receives a static "Red Sweater" as a `name` value in the previous example. If you want to pass and bind a dynamic data variable to `name`, such as the first element in the `children` list, you can use the `v-bind` attribute, denoted by `:`, as shown in Example 4-3.

Example 4-3. Passing dynamic variables as props to a child component

```
<template>
  <ChildComponent :name="children[0]" />
</template>
<script lang="ts">
import ChildComponent from './ChildComponent.vue'
export default {
  //...
  data() {
    return {
      children: ['Red Sweater', 'Blue T-Shirt', 'Green Hat']
    }
  }
}
</script>
```

The output for the previous code is the same as passing a static string, `Red Sweater`, to the `name` prop.

> If the `name` prop is not of type `String`, you still need to use the `v-bind` attribute (or `:`) to pass static data to the child component, such as `:name="true"` for Boolean, or `:name="["hello", "world"]"` for `Array` type.

In Example 4-3, whenever the value of `children[0]` changes, Vue will also update the `name` prop in the `ChildComponent`, and the child component will re-render its content if needed.

If you have more than one prop in the child component, you can follow the same approach and pass each data to the relevant prop. For instance, to pass `name` and `price` of a product to the `ProductComp` component, you can perform this (Example 4-4).

Example 4-4. Passing multiple props to a child component

```
/** components/ProductList.vue */
<template>
  <ProductComp :name="product.name" :price="product.price" />
</template>
<script lang="ts">
import ProductComp from './ProductComp.vue'
export default {
  name: 'ProductList',
  components: {
    ProductComp
  },
  data() {
    return {
      product: {
        name: 'Red Sweater',
        price: 19.99
      }
    }
  }
}
</script>
```

And we can define the `ProductComp` component as in Example 4-5.

Example 4-5. Defining multiple props in `ProductComp`

```
<template>
  <div>
    <p>Product: {{ name }}</p>
    <p>Price: {{ price }}</p>
  </div>
</template>
<script lang="ts">
export default {
  name: 'ProductComp',
  props: {
    name: String,
    price: Number
  }
}
</script>
```

The output will be as follows:

```
Product: Red Sweater
Price: 19.99
```

Alternatively, you can use `v-bind` (*not* :) to pass the entire object `user` and have its properties bound to the relevant child component's props:

```
<template>
  <ProductComp v-bind="product" />
</template>
```

Note that only the child component will receive the relevant declared props. Hence, if you have another field, `product.description`, in the parent component, it will not be available for access in the child component.

 Another approach to declare your component's `props` is to use an array of strings, each representing the name of the prop it accepts, such as `props: ["name", "price"]`. This approach is practical when you want to prototype a component quickly. However, I strongly recommend you use the object form of `props` and declare all your props with types, as a good practice for code readability and bug prevention.

We have learned how to declare props with types, but how do we validate the data passed to the child's props when needed? How can we set a fallback value for a prop when no value is passed? Let's find out next.

Declaring Prop Types with Validation and Default Values

Back in Example 4-1, we declared the `name` prop as a `String` type. Vue will warn if the parent component passes a non-string value to the `name` prop during run-time. However, to be able to enjoy the benefit of Vue's type validation, we should use the full declaration syntax:

```
{
  type: String | Number | Boolean | Array | Object | Date | Function | Symbol,
  default?: any,
  required?: boolean,
  validator?: (value: any) => boolean
}
```

In which:

- `type` is the type of prop. It can be a constructor function (or custom class) or one of the built-in types.

- `default` is the prop's default value if no value is passed. For types `Object`, `Function`, and `Array`, the default value must be a function that returns the initial value.

- `required` is a boolean value indicating whether the prop is mandatory. If `required` is `true`, the parent component must pass a value to the prop. By default, all props are optional.

- `validator` is a function that validates the value passed to the prop, mainly for development debugging.

We can declare the `name` prop to be more specific, including a default value, as shown in Example 4-6.

Example 4-6. Defining prop as a string with a default value

```
export default {
  name: 'ChildComponent',
  props: {
    name: {
      type: String,
      default: 'Child component'
    }
  }
}
```

If the parent component does not pass a value, the child component will fall back to the default value *"Child component"* for the `name` prop.

We can also set `name` as a mandatory prop for the child component and add a validator for its received data, as shown in Example 4-7.

Example 4-7. Defining name as required with a prop validator

```
export default {
  name: 'ChildComponent',
  props: {
    name: {
      type: String,
      required: true,
      validator: value => value !== "Child component"
    }
  }
}
```

In this scenario, if the parent component does not pass a value to the `name` prop, or the given value matches *Child component*, Vue will throw a warning in development mode (Figure 4-2).

```
⚠ ▶ [Vue warn]: Invalid prop: custom     runtime-core.esm-bundler.js:40
    validator check failed for prop "name".
      at <ChildComponent name="Child component" >
      at <ParentComponent>
      at <App>
```

Figure 4-2. Console warning in development for failed prop validation

For the `default` field, the `Function` type is a function that returns the initial value of the prop. You can't use it to pass data back to the parent component or to trigger data changes on the parent level.

In addition to the built-in types and validation provided by Vue, you can combine a JavaScript `Class` or a function constructor and TypeScript to create your custom prop type. I'll cover them in the next section.

Declaring Props with Custom Type Checking

Using primitive types like `Array`, `String`, or `Object` suits the essential use case. However, as your application grows, primitive types can be too generic to keep your component's type safe. Take a `PizzaComponent` with the following template code:

```
<template>
  <header>Title: {{ pizza.title }}</header>
  <div class="pizza--details-wrapper">
    <img :src="pizza.image" :alt="pizza.title" width="300" />
    <p>Description: {{ pizza.description }}</p>
    <div class="pizza--inventory">
      <div class="pizza--inventory-stock">Quantity: {{pizza.quantity}}</div>
      <div class="pizza--inventory-price">Price: {{pizza.price}}</div>
    </div>
  </div>
</template>
```

This component accepts a mandatory `pizza` prop, which is an `Object` containing some details about the `pizza`:

```
export default {
  name: 'PizzaComponent',
  props: {
    pizza: {
      type: Object,
      required: true
    }
  }
}
```

Straightforward enough. However, by declaring `pizza` as an `Object` type, we assume the parent will always pass the suitable object with the appropriate fields (`title`, `image`, `description`, `quantity`, and `price`) required for a `pizza` to render.

This assumption can lead to a problem. Since `pizza` accepts data of type `Object`, any component that uses `PizzaComponent` can pass any object data to the prop `pizza` without the actual fields needed for a `pizza`, as in Example 4-8.

Example 4-8. Using Pizza component with wrong data

```
<template>
  <div>
    <h2>Bad usage of Pizza component</h2>
    <pizza-component :pizza="{ name: 'Pinia', description: 'Hawaiian pizza' }" />
  </div>
</template>
```

The preceding code results in a broken UI render of `PizzaComponent`, where only a `description` is available, and the rest of the fields are empty (with a broken image), as shown in Figure 4-3.

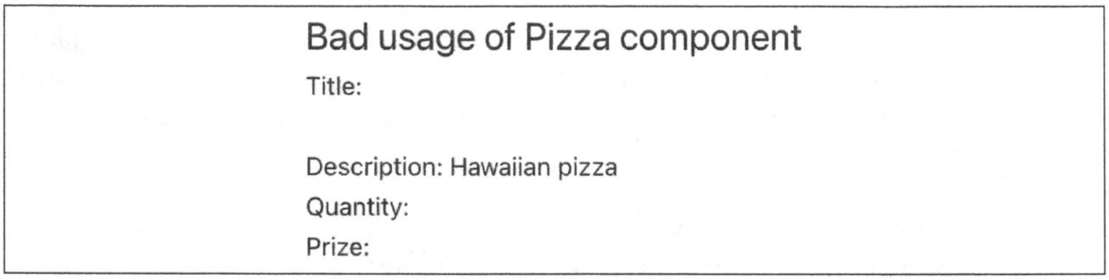

> Bad usage of Pizza component
> Title:
>
> Description: Hawaiian pizza
> Quantity:
> Prize:

Figure 4-3. Broken UI with no image link and missing fields for a pizza

TypeScript won't be able to detect the data type mismatch here either, as it performs the type checking according to the declared type of `pizza`: the generic `Object`. Another potential problem is that passing `pizza` in the wrong nest properties format can cause the app to crash. Therefore, to avoid such accidents, we use custom type declarations.

We can define the `Pizza` class and declare the prop `pizza` of type `Pizza` as shown in Example 4-9.

Example 4-9. Declaring a Pizza custom type

```
class Pizza {
  title: string;
  description: string;
  image: string;
  quantity: number;
  price: number;

  constructor(
    title: string,
    description: string,
    image: string,
    quantity: number,
    price: number
  ) {
    this.title = title
    this.description = description
```

```
      this.image = image
      this.quantity = quantity
      this.price = price
  }
}

export default {
  name: 'PizzaComponent',
  props: {
    pizza: {
      type: Pizza, ❶
      required: true
    }
  }
}
```

❶ Declare the type of `pizza` props as `Pizza` directly

Alternatively, you can use TypeScript's `interface` or `type` to define your custom type instead of `Class`. However, in such scenarios, you must use type `PropType` from the vue package, with the following syntax, to map the declared type to the target prop:

```
type: Object as PropType<Your-Custom-Type>
```

Let's rewrite the `Pizza` class as an `interface` instead (Example 4-10).

Example 4-10. Declaring a Pizza custom type using the TypeScript interface API

```
import type { PropType } from 'vue'

interface Pizza {
  title: string;
  description: string;
  image: string;
  quantity: number;
  price: number;
}

export default {
  name: 'PizzaComponent',
  props: {
    pizza: {
      type: Object as PropType<Pizza>, ❶
      required: true
    }
  }
}
```

❶ Declare the type of `pizza` props as `Pizza` interface with `PropType` help.

When you use `PizzaComponent` with the wrong data format, TypeScript will detect and highlight the error appropriately.

Vue performs type validation during run-time, while TypeScript performs type checking during compile-time. Hence, it is a good practice to use both Vue's type checking and TypeScript's type checking to ensure your code is bug-free.

Declaring Props Using defineProps() and withDefaults()

As we learned in "setup" on page 63, starting with Vue 3.x, Vue offers `<script setup>` syntax for declaring a functional component without the classic Options API. Within this `<script setup>` block, you can use `defineProps()` to declare props, as shown in Example 4-11.

Example 4-11. Props declaration with defineProps() and `<script setup>`

```
<script setup>
import { defineProps } from 'vue'

const props = defineProps({
  name: {
    type: String,
    default: "Hello from the child component."
  }
})
</script>
```

Thanks to TypeScript, we can also declare the accepted type for `defineProps()` per component with type validation on compile-time, as shown in Example 4-12.

Example 4-12. Props declaration with defineProps() and TypeScript type

```
<script setup >
import { defineProps } from 'vue'

type ChildProps = {
  name?: string
}

const props = defineProps<ChildProps>()
</script>
```

In this case, to declare the default value of the `message` prop, we need to wrap the `defineProps()` call with `withDefaults()`, as in Example 4-13.

Example 4-13. Props declaration with defineProps() and withDefaults()

```
import { defineProps, withDefaults } from 'vue'

type ChildProps = {
```

```
    name?: string
}

const props = withDefaults(defineProps<ChildProps>(), {
  name: 'Hello from the child component.'
})
```

Using defineProps() with TypeScript Type Checking

We can't combine run-time and compile-time type checking when using `defineProps()`. I recommend using `defineProps()` in the approach in Example 4-11, for better readability and a combination of both Vue and TypeScript type checking.

We have learned how to declare props for passing raw data in a Vue component, with type checking and validation. Next, we will explore how to pass functions as custom event emitters to a child component.

Communication Between Components with Custom Events

Vue treats data passed to a child component via props as read-only and raw data. One-way data flow ensures that the parent component is the only one that can update the data prop. We often want to update a specific data prop and sync it with the parent component. To do so, we use the `emits` field in the component's options to declare custom events.

Take a to-do list, or `ToDoList` component, for instance. This `ToDoList` will use `ToDoItem` as its child component to render a list of tasks with the code in Example 4-14.

Example 4-14. ToDoList component

```
<template>
  <ul style="list-style: none;">
    <li v-for="task in tasks" :key="task.id">
      <ToDoItem :task="task" />
    </li>
  </ul>
</template>
<script lang="ts">
import { defineComponent } from 'vue'
import ToDoItem from './ToDoItem.vue'
import type { Task } from './ToDoItem'

export default defineComponent({
  name: 'ToDoList',
  components: {
```

```
      ToDoItem
    },
    data() {
      return {
        tasks: [
          { id: 1, title: 'Learn Vue', completed: false },
          { id: 2, title: 'Learn TypeScript', completed: false },
          { id: 3, title: 'Learn Vite', completed: false },
        ] as Task[]
      }
    }
  }
})
</script>
```

And `ToDoItem` is a component that receives a `task` prop and renders an `input` as a checkbox for the user to mark the task as completed or not. This `input` element receives `task.completed` as its initial value for the `checked` attribute. Let's look at Example 4-15.

Example 4-15. ToDoItem component

```
<template>
  <div>
    <input
      type="checkbox"
      :checked="task.completed"
    />
    <span>{{ task.title }}</span>
  </div>
</template>
<script lang="ts">
import { defineComponent, type PropType } from 'vue'

export interface Task {
  id: number;
  title: string;
  completed: boolean;
}

export default defineComponent({
  name: 'ToDoItem',
  props: {
    task: {
      type: Object as PropType<Task>,
      required: true,
    }
  },
})
</script>
```

When a user toggles this `input` checkbox, we want to emit an event called `task-completed-toggle` to inform about the `task.completed` value of the specific task to the parent component. We can do so by first declaring the event in the `emits` field of the component's options (Example 4-16).

Example 4-16. `ToDoItem` component with emits

```
/** ToDoItem.vue */
export default defineComponent({
  //...
  emits: ['task-completed-toggle']
})
```

Then, we create a new method `onTaskCompleted` to emit the `task-completed-toggle` event with the new value of `task.completed` from the checkbox and the `task.id` as the event's payload (Example 4-17).

Example 4-17. `ToDoItem` component with a method to emit `task-completed-toggle` event

```
/** ToDoItem.vue */
export default defineComponent({
  //...
  methods: {
    onTaskCompleted(event: Event) {
      this.$emit("task-completed-toggle", {
        ...this.task,
        completed: (event.target as HTMLInputElement)?.checked,
      });
    },
  }
})
```

We use `defineComponent` to wrap around the component's options and create a TypeScript-friendly component. Using `defineComponent` is not required for simple components, but you need to use it to access other data properties of `this` inside components' methods, hooks, or computed properties. Otherwise, TypeScript will throw an error.

Then we bind the `onTaskCompleted` method to the `input` element's `change` event, as shown in Example 4-18.

Example 4-18. `ToDoItem` *component's updated template*

```
<div>
  <input
    type="checkbox"
    :checked="task.completed"
    @change="onTaskCompleted"
  />
  <span>{{ task.title }}</span>
</div>
```

Now in the parent component `<ToDoList>` of `ToDoItem`, we can bind the `task-completed-toggle` event to a method using @ notation, with the template in Example 4-19.

Example 4-19. `ToDoList` *component's updated template*

```
<template>
  <ul style="list-style: none;">
    <li v-for="task in tasks" :key="task.id">
      <ToDoItem
        :task="task"
        @task-completed-toggle="onTaskCompleted"
      />
    </li>
  </ul>
</template>
```

The `onTaskCompleted` method in the parent component `<ToDoList>` will receive the payload of the `task-completed-toggle` event, and update the `task.completed` value of the specific task in the `tasks` array, as in Example 4-20.

Example 4-20. `ToDoList` *component's script with a method to handle* `task-completed-toggle` *event*

```
//...

export default {
  //...
  methods: {
    onTaskCompleted(payload: { id: number; completed: boolean }) {
      const index = this.tasks.findIndex(t => t.id === payload.id)

      if (index < 0) return

      this.tasks[index].completed = payload.completed
    }
  }
}
```

These code blocks will render the page shown in Figure 4-4.

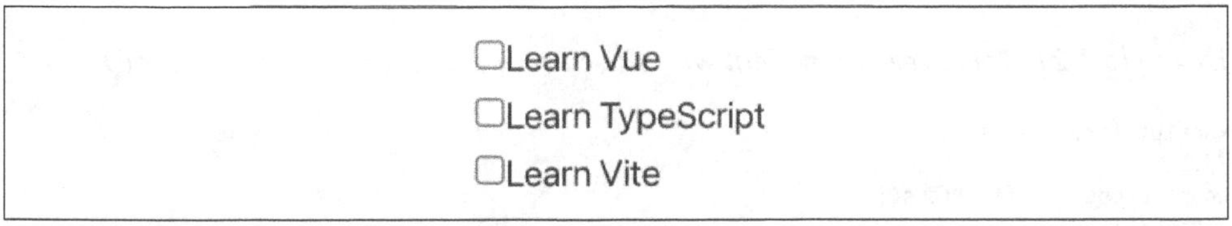

☐Learn Vue

☐Learn TypeScript

☐Learn Vite

Figure 4-4. `ToDoList` component with three items

Vue will update the related data in `ToDoList` and accordingly render the relevant `ToDoItem` component instance. You can toggle the checkbox to mark a to-do item as completed. Figure 4-5 shows we can detect the component's event using the Vue Devtools.

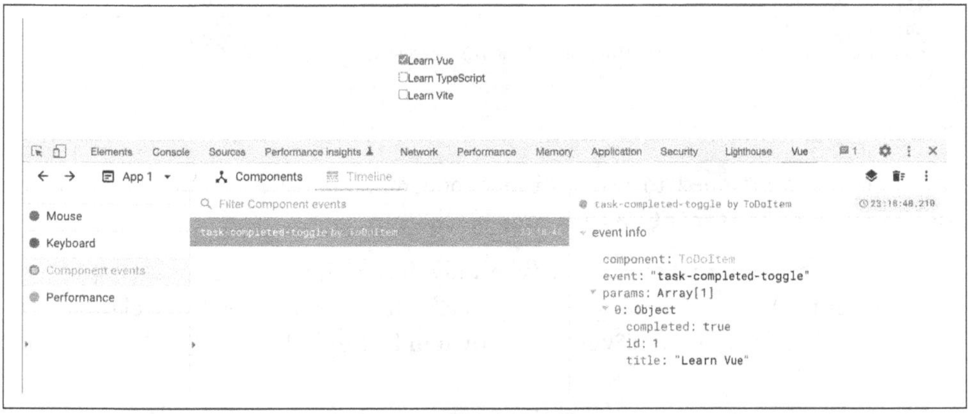

Figure 4-5. Mark a to-do item as completed and debug the event emitted using Vue Devtools

Defining Custom Events Using defineEmits()

Similar to "Declaring Props Using defineProps() and withDefaults()" on page 116, within a `<script setup>` code block, you can use `defineEmits()` to define custom events. The `defineEmits()` function accepts the same input parameter type as `emits` accepts:

```
const emits = defineEmits(['component-event'])
```

It then returns a function instance that we can use to invoke a specific event from the component:

```
emits('component-event', [...arguments])
```

Thus we can write the script section of `ToDoItem` as in Example 4-21.

Example 4-21. ToDoItem component with the custom event using defineEmits()

```ts
<script lang="ts" setup>
//...
const props = defineProps({
  task: {
    type: Object as PropType<Task>,
    required: true,
  }
});

const emits = defineEmits(['task-completed-toggle'])

const onTaskCompleted = (event: Event) => {
  emits("task-completed-toggle", {
    id: props.task.id,
    completed: (event.target as HTMLInputElement)?.checked,
  });
}
</script>
```

Note here we don't need to use `defineComponent` since there is no `this` instance available within the `<script setup>` code block.

For better type checking, you can use type-only declaration for the `task-completed-toggle` event instead of a single string. Let's improve the `emits` declaration in Example 4-21 to use type `EmitEvents` as shown in Example 4-22.

Example 4-22. Custom event using defineEmits() and type-only declaration

```ts
// Declare the emit type
type EmitEvents = {
  (e: 'task-completed-toggle', task: Task): void;
}

const emits = defineEmits<EmitEvents>()
```

This approach helps ensure you bind the correct method to the declared event. As seen for the `task-complete-toggle` event, any event declaration should follow the same pattern:

```ts
(e: 'component-event', [...arguments]): void
```

In the previous syntax, `e` is the event's name, and `arguments` are all the inputs passed to the event emitter. In the case of the `task-completed-toggle` event, its emitter's argument is `task` of type `Task`.

`emits` is a powerful feature that allows you to enable two-way communication between a parent and a child component without breaking the data flow mechanism of Vue. However, `props` and `emits` are only beneficial when you want direct data communication.

You must use a different approach to pass data from a component to its grandchild or descendant. In the next section, we will see how to use the `provide` and `inject` APIs to pass data from a parent component to its child or grandchild component.

Communicate Between Components with provide/inject Pattern

To establish data communication between an ancestor component and its descendants, the `provide/inject` API is a reasonable option. The `provide` field passes data from the ancestor, while `inject` ensures that Vue injects the provided data into any target descendant.

Using provide to Pass Data

The component's option field `provide` accepts two formats: a data object or a function.

`provide` can be an object containing data to inject, with each property representing a (key, value) data type. In the following example, `ProductList` provides a data value, `selectedIds`, with the value `[1]` to all its descendants (Example 4-23).

Example 4-23. Passing `selectedIds` using provide in `ProductList` component

```
export default {
  name: 'ProductList',
  //...
  provide: {
    selectedIds: [1]
  },
}
```

Another format type for `provide` is a function that returns an object containing the data available to inject for descendants. A benefit of this format type is we can access the `this` instance and map dynamic data or a component method to the relevant fields of the return object. From Example 4-23, we can rewrite the `provide` field as a function as shown in Example 4-24.

Example 4-24. Passing `selectedIds` using provide in `ProductList` component as a function

```
export default {
//...
  provide() {
    return {
      selectedIds: [1]
    }
  },
//...
}
</script>
```

 Unlike `props`, you can pass a function and have the target descendant trigger it using the `provide` field. Doing so enables sending data back up to the parent component. However, Vue considers this approach an anti-pattern, and you should use it cautiously.

At this point, our `ProductList` passes some data values to its descendant using `provide`. Next, we must inject the provided values to operate within a descendant.

Using inject to Receive Data

Like `props`, the `inject` field can accept an array of strings, each representing the provided data key (`inject: [selectedId]`) or an object.

When using `inject` as an object field, each of its properties is an object, with the key presenting the local data key used within the component and the following properties:

```
{
  from?: string;
  default: any
}
```

Here, `from` is optional if the property key is the same as the provided key from the ancestor. Take Example 4-23 with the `selectedIds` as the data provided by `Product List` to its descendants, for instance. We can compute a `ProductComp` that receives the provided data, `selectedIds`, from `ProductList` and rename it to `current SelectedIds` to use locally, as shown in Example 4-25.

Example 4-25. Injecting provided data in `ProductComp`

```
<script lang='ts'>
export default {
  //...
  inject: {
    currentSelectedIds: {
```

```
      from: 'selectedIds',
      default: []
    },
  },
}
</script>
```

In this code, Vue will take the value of injected `selectedIds` and assign it to a local data field, `currentSelectedIds`, or use its default value `[]` if there is no injected value.

Within the Components section of the Vue tab in the browser's Developer Tools, when selecting the `ProductComp` from the component tree (the left-side panel), you can debug the indication of the renaming for the injected data (the right-side panel), as shown in Figure 4-6.

```
 ⟦  ⬚   Elements   Console   Sources   Performance insights ⚡   Network   Performance   Memory   Application   Security   Lighthouse   Vue

 ←  →   ⊟ App 1 ▾      ⤬ Components   ▦ Timeline

 Q Find components...              <ProductComp>  Q Filter state...

 ▾ <App>                           ▸ props
   ▾ <ProductList> fragment
       <ProductComp>               ▾ provided

                                      ▾ selectedIds: Array[1]
                                          0: 1

                                   ▾ injected

   ▸                                  ▾ selectedIds → currentSelectedIds: Array[1]
                                          0: 1
```

Figure 4-6. Debug the provided and injected data using Vue Devtools

The equivalent hooks in Composition API for `provide/inject` are `provide()` and `inject()`, respectively.

Now we understand how to use `provide` and `inject` to pass data between components efficiently without props drilling. Let's explore how we can render a specific content section of an element to another location in the DOM with the `<Teleport>` component.

Teleport API

Due to styling constraints, we often need to implement a component that contains elements that Vue should render in a different location in the actual DOM for full visual effect. In such cases, we usually need to "teleport" those elements to the desired place by developing a complex solution, resulting in lousy performance impact, time consumption, etc. To solve this "teleport" challenge, Vue offers the `<Teleport>` component.

The `<Teleport>` component accepts a prop `to`, which indicates the target container, whether an element's query selector or the desired HTML element. Suppose we have a `House` component that will have a section of *Sky and clouds* that needs the Vue engine to teleport it to a designated #sky DOM element, as in Example 4-26.

Example 4-26. House component with `Teleport`

```
<template>
  <div>
    This is a house
  </div>
  <Teleport to="#sky">
    <div>Sky and clouds</div>
  </Teleport>
</template>
```

In our `App.vue`, we add a `section` element with the target id `sky` above the `House` component, as in Example 4-27.

Example 4-27. Template of `App.vue` with `House` component

```
<template>
  <section id="sky" />
  <section class="wrapper">
      <House />
  </section>
</template>
```

Figure 4-7 shows the code outputs.

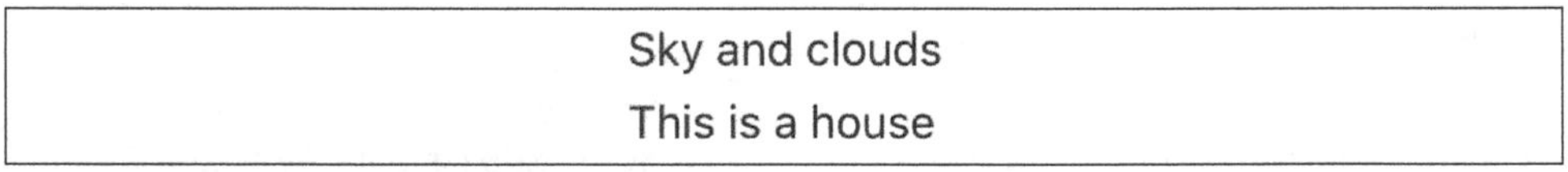

Sky and clouds
This is a house

Figure 4-7. Actual display order when using the `Teleport` component

When you inspect the DOM tree using the Elements tab of the browser's Developer Tools, "Sky and clouds" appears as nested within `<section id="sky">` instead (Figure 4-8).

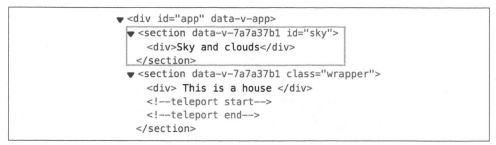

```
▼ <div id="app" data-v-app>
  ▼ <section data-v-7a7a37b1 id="sky">
      <div>Sky and clouds</div>
    </section>
  ▼ <section data-v-7a7a37b1 class="wrapper">
      <div> This is a house </div>
      <!--teleport start-->
      <!--teleport end-->
    </section>
```

Figure 4-8. Actual DOM tree when using the Teleport component

You can also temporarily disable moving the content inside a `<Teleport>` component instance with its Boolean prop `disabled`. This component is handy when you want to keep the DOM tree structure, and Vue should move only the desired content to the target location when needed. An everyday use case for `Teleport` is a modal, which we will implement next.

Wrapping Both Sections Under a Parent

The destination component for teleporting must exist in the DOM before mounting `<Teleport>`. In Example 4-27, if you wrap both instances of `section` under a `main` element, the `<Teleport>` component will not work as expected. See "Rendering Problem Using Teleport" on page 134 for more details.

Implementing a Modal with Teleport and the <dialog> Element

A modal is a dialog window that appears on top of a screen and blocks the user's interaction with the main page. The user must interact with the modal to dismiss it and then returns to the main page.

A modal is very handy in displaying essential notifications that require the user's full attention and should appear only once.

Let's design a basic modal. Similar to a dialog, a modal should contain the following elements (Figure 4-9):

- A backdrop that covers the entire screen where the modal appears on top and blocks the user's interactions with the current page.

- A modal window that contains the modal's content, including a `header` with a title and a close button, a `main` content section, and a `footer` section with a default close button. These three sections should be customizable using slots.

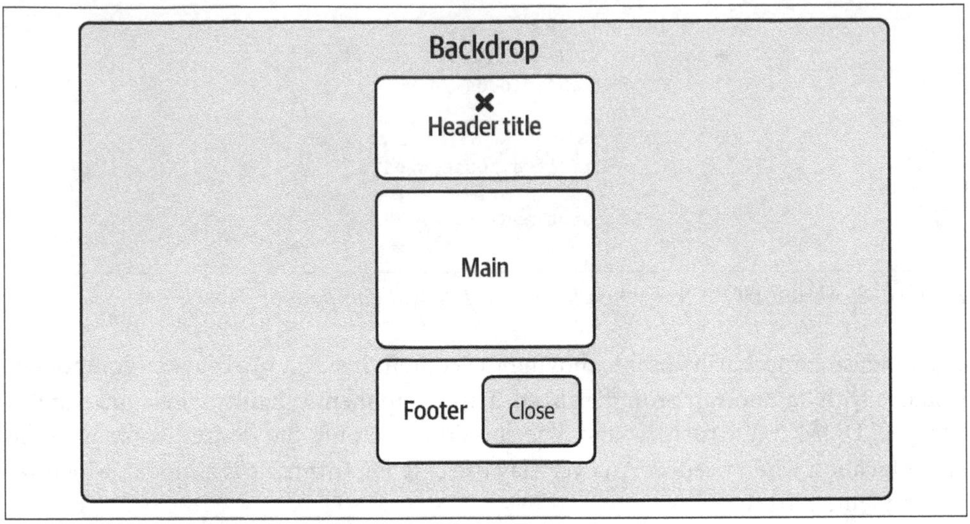

Figure 4-9. Design of a basic modal

Based on the preceding design, we implement a `Modal` component template using the `<dialog>` HTML element in Example 4-28.

Example 4-28. Modal component

```
<template>
  <dialog :open="open">
    <header>
      <slot name="m-header">  ❶
        <h2>{{ title }}</h2>
        <button>X</button>
      </slot>
    </header>
    <main>
      <slot name="m-main" />  ❷
    </main>
    <footer>
      <slot name="m-footer">  ❸
        <button>Close</button>
      </slot>
    </footer>
  </dialog>
</template>
```

In the preceding code, we use three slot sections to allow the user to customize:

❶ The modal's header (`m-header`)

❷ The main content (`m-main`)

❸   The modal's footer (m-footer)

We also bind the <dialog> element's open attribute to a local data prop open for controlling the modal's visibility (visible/hidden). In addition, we render the title prop as the modal's default title. Now, let's implement the Modal component's options, which receive two props: open and title as in Example 4-29.

Example 4-29. Adding props to Modal component

```ts
<script lang="ts">
import { defineComponent } from 'vue'

export default defineComponent({
  name: 'Modal',
  props: {
    open: {
      type: Boolean,
      default: false,
    },
    title: {
      type: String,
      default: 'Dialog',
    },
  },
})
</script>
```

When a user clicks on the modal's close button or the "X" button on the header, it should close itself. Since we control the visibility of the modal using the open prop, we need to emit a closeDialog event with the new value of open from the Modal component to the parent. Let's declare emits and a close method that emits the target event as in Example 4-30.

Example 4-30. Declaring the event closeDialog for Modal to emit

```ts
<script lang="ts">
/** Modal.vue */
import { defineComponent } from 'vue'

export default defineComponent({
  name: 'Modal',
  //...
  emits: ["closeDialog"],  ❶
  methods: {
    close() {  ❷
      this.$emit("closeDialog", false);
    },
  },
})
</script>
```

emits with one event, `closeDialog`

 `close` method that emits the `closeDialog` event with the new value of `open` as `false`

Then we bind it to the relevant action elements in the `<dialog>` element using @ notation, as shown in Example 4-31.

Example 4-31. Binding event listener on click events

```
<template>
  <dialog :open="open" >
    <header>
      <slot name="m-header" >
        <h2>{{ title }}</h2>
        <button @click="close" >X</button> ❶
      </slot>
    </header>
    <main>
      <slot name="m-main" />
    </main>
    <footer>
      <slot name="m-footer" >
        <button @click="close" >Close</button> ❷
      </slot>
    </footer>
  </dialog>
</template>
```

❶ `@click` event handler for the "X" button on the header

❷ `@click` event handler for the default close button on the footer

Next, we need to wrap the `dialog` element with a `<Teleport>` component to move it outside the parent component's DOM tree. We also pass the `to` prop to the `<Teleport>` component to specify the target location: an HTML element with an id, `modal`. Finally, we bind the `disabled` prop to the component's `open` value to ensure Vue moves only the modal component content to the desired location when visible (Example 4-32).

Example 4-32. Using `<Teleport>` component

```
<template>
  <teleport ❶
    to="#modal" ❷
    :disabled="!open" ❸
  >
    <dialog ref="dialog" :open="open" >
      <header>
```

```
      <slot name="m-header">
        <h2>{{ title }}</h2>
        <button @click="close" >X</button>
      </slot>
      </header>
      <main>
        <slot name="m-main" />
      </main>
      <footer>
        <slot name="m-footer">
          <button @click="close" >Close</button>
        </slot>
      </footer>
    </dialog>
  </teleport>
</template>
```

❶ `<Teleport>` component

❷ to prop with the target location with id selector `modal`

❸ `disabled` prop with the condition when component's `open` value is falsy

Now let's try out our `Modal` component in a `WithModalComponent` by adding the following code in Example 4-33 to the `WithModalComponent`.

Example 4-33. Using modal component in `WithModalComponent`

```
<template>
  <h2>With Modal component</h2>
  <button @click="openModal = true">Open modal</button>
  <Modal :open="openModal" title="Hello World" @closeDialog="toggleModal"/>
</template>
<script lang="ts">
import { defineComponent } from "vue";
import Modal from "./Modal.vue";

export default defineComponent({
  name: "WithModalComponent",
  components: {
    Modal,
  },
  data() {
    return {
      openModal: false,
    };
  },
  methods: {
    toggleModal(newValue: boolean) {
      this.openModal = newValue;
    },
  },
});
</script>
```

Finally, add a `<div>` element with id `modal` to the body element in the `index.html` file:

```
<body>
  <div id="app"></div>
  <div id="modal"></div>  ❶
  <script type="module" src="/src/main.ts"></script>
</body>
```

❶ `div` element with id `modal`

By doing so, Vue renders the `Modal` component's content to this `div` with id `modal` whenever the `open` prop is set to `true` (Figure 4-10).

Figure 4-10. Modal component rendered to the `div` with id `modal` when visible

Figure 4-11 shows how it looks on screen:

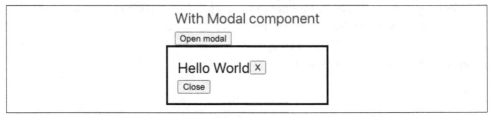

Figure 4-11. Output of the `WithModalComponent` when modal is visible

And when the `open` prop is `false`, the `div` with id `modal` is empty (Figure 4-12), and the modal is invisible on screen (Figure 4-13).

Figure 4-12. Modal component not rendered to the `div` with id `modal` when hidden

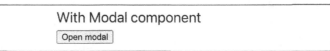

Figure 4-13. Modal component not visible when hidden

At this point, you have a working modal component. However, the visual appearance of the modal isn't exactly as good as we wanted; there should be a dark overlay over the main page content when the modal is visible. Let's fix this issue using CSS stylings for `::backdrop` selector in the `<style>` section of the modal element:

```
<style scoped>
  dialog::backdrop {
    background-color: rgba(0, 0, 0, 0.5);
  }
</style>
```

However, this won't change the appearance of the modal's backdrop. This behavior is because the browser applies the `::backdrop` CSS selector rules to the dialog only when we open the dialog using `dialog.showModal()` method, and not by changing the open attribute. To fix this issue, we need to perform the following modifications in our `Modal` component:

- Add a direct reference to the `<dialog>` element by assigning a "dialog" value to the `ref` attribute:

  ```
  <dialog :open="open" ref="dialog">
    <!--...-->
  </dialog>
  ```

- Trigger `$refs.dialog.showModal()` or `$refs.dialog.close()` on the `dialog` element whenever the open prop changes respectively with `watch`:

  ```
  watch: {
    open(newValue) {
      const element = this.$refs.dialog as HTMLDialogElement;
      if (newValue) {
        element.showModal();
      } else {
        element.close();
      }
    },
  },
  ```

- Remove the original binding for the open attribute of the `<dialog>` element:

  ```
  <dialog ref="dialog">
    <!--...-->
  </dialog>
  ```

- Remove the use of the `disabled` attribute in the `<teleport>` component:

  ```
  <teleport to="#modal">
    <!--...-->
  </teleport>
  ```

When opening the modal using the built-in `showModal()` method, the browser will add a `::backdrop` pseudo-element to the actual `<dialog>` element in the DOM, and dynamically moving the element content to the target location will disable this functionality, leaving the modal without the desired backdrop.

We also reposition the modal to the center of the page and on top of other elements by adding the following CSS rules to the `dialog` selector:

```css
dialog {
  position: fixed;
  z-index: 999;
  inset-block-start: 30%;
  inset-inline-start: 50%;
  width: 300px;
  margin-inline-start: -150px;
}
```

The output will be as shown in Figure 4-14 when the modal is visible.

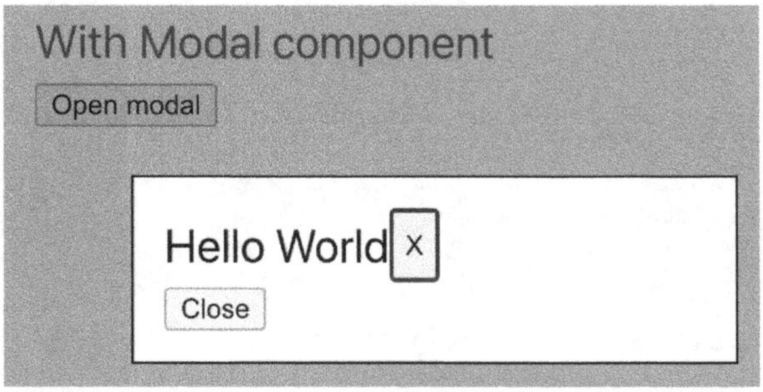

Figure 4-14. Modal component with backdrop and stylings

We have learned how to implement a reusable `Modal` component using `Teleport` and explored different use cases with each of the built-in `<dialog>` element features. We also learned how to use the `::backdrop` CSS selector to style the modal's backdrop.

As you have noticed, we set the target location `div` for the modal to be a direct child of body, outside of the Vue app entry element `<div id="app">`. What happens if we want to move the modal's target `div` to within the entry component `App.vue` of the Vue application? Let's find out in the next section.

Rendering Problem Using Teleport

To understand the problem with using `Teleport` to render the modal inside a child component of the `App.vue` component, let's first move the `<div id="modal"></div>` from `index.html` to `App.vue`, after the `WithModalComponent` instance:

```html
<template>
  <section class="wrapper">
    <WithModalComponent />
  </section>
  <div id="modal"></div>
</template>
```

After running your application, you can see that the browser doesn't render the modal despite how often you click on the `Open modal` button. And the console shows the following error:

```
⊗ ▶Uncaught (in promise) TypeError: Cannot read properties of null (reading
  'insertBefore')
      at insert (runtime-dom.esm-bundler.js:10:16)
      at move (runtime-core.esm-bundler.js:6094:13)
      at moveTeleport (runtime-core.esm-bundler.js:6555:17)
```

Figure 4-15. Console error message when rendering modal inside `App.vue`

Due to the Vue rendering order mechanism, the parent waits for the children to render before rendering itself. The children render in the order of appearance in the parent's `template` section. In this scenario, the `WithModalComponent` renders first. Thus Vue renders the `<dialog>` element and starts moving the component's content to the target location before rendering the `ParentComponent`. However, since the `ParentComponent` is still waiting for `WithModalComponent` to finish its rendering, the `<div id="modal">` element doesn't yet exist on the DOM. As a result, Vue can't locate the target location and perform the right move, and it can't render the `<dialog>` element inside the `<div id="modal">` element, hence the error.

A workaround to bypass this limitation is to put the target element `<div id="modal">` to appear before `WithModalComponent`:

```
<template>
  <div id="modal"></div>
  <section class="wrapper">
    <WithModalComponent />
  </section>
</template>
```

This solution ensures the target `div` is available before Vue renders the `Modal` element and moves the content. Another approach is to use the `disabled` attribute to postpone the content moving process for `Modal` during rendering until the user clicks on the `Open modal` button. Both options have pros and cons, and you should choose the one that best suits your needs.

The most common solution is to insert the target element as a direct child of the body element and isolate it from the Vue rendering context.

A significant benefit of using `<Teleport>` is achieving the maximum visual display effect (such as fullscreen mode, modal, sidebar, etc.) while maintaining the code hierarchy structure, component isolation, and readability.

Summary

This chapter explored the concept of different approaches in components' communication using the built-in Vue features such as props, emits, and provide/inject. We learned how to use these features to pass data and events between components while keeping Vue's data flow mechanism intact. We also learned how to use Teleport API to render an element outside the parent component's DOM tree while keeping its appearance order in the parent component's <template>. <Teleport> is beneficial for building components that require displaying with alignment to the main page element, such as popups, dialogs, modals, etc.

In the next chapter, we will explore more on Composition API and how to use it to compose Vue components together.

CHAPTER 5

Composition API

In the previous chapter, you learned how to compose Vue components using the classic Options API. Despite it being the most common API for composing Vue components since Vue 2, using Options API can lead to unnecessary code complexity, unreadability for large component code, and logic reusability between them. For such use cases, this chapter introduces an alternative approach for composing Vue components, the Composition API.

In this chapter, we will explore the different composition hooks to create a functional stateful element in Vue. We also will learn how to combine Options API and Composition API for better reactive control and to compose our own reusable composable for our application.

Setting Up Components with Composition API

Composing components using the Options API is a common practice in Vue. However, in many cases, we want to reuse part of the component logic without worrying about the overlapping data and methods like in mixins[1], or a component that is more readable and organized. Composition API can be helpful in such scenarios.

Introduced in Vue 3.0, Composition API provides an alternative way to compose stateful and reactive components with the help of the `setup()` hook ("setup" on page 63) or `<script setup>` tag. The `setup()` hook is part of the component's options object and runs *once* before initializing and creating the component instance (before `beforeCreate()` hook).

---

[1] When you use the mixin, you are writing a new component's configurations.

You can *only* use Composition API functions or composables ("Creating Your Reusable Composables" on page 154) within this hook or its equivalent syntax `<script setup>` tag. This combination creates a stateful functional component and provides an excellent place to define the component's reactive state and methods and initialize other lifecycle hooks (see "Using the Lifecycle Hooks" on page 146) with more straightforward code readability.

Let's explore the power of Composition API, starting with `ref()` and `reactive()` functions to handle your component's reactive data.

Handling Data with ref() and reactive()

In Chapter 2, you learned about the `data()` function property in the Options API for initializing the component's data ("Creating Local State with Data Properties" on page 22). All the data properties in the returned object from `data()` are reactive, meaning the Vue engine will automatically watch for changes on each declared data property. However, this default functionality may cause overhead in your component when you have many data properties, most of which are static. In such cases, the Vue engine still enables watchers for these static values, which is unnecessary. To limit the number of excessive data watchers and to have more control over which data properties to observe, Vue introduced the `ref()` and `reactive()` functions in the Composition API.

Using ref()

`ref()` is a function that accepts a single argument and returns a reactive object with that argument as its initial value. We call this returned object the `ref` object:

```
import { ref } from 'vue'

export default {
  setup() {
    const message = ref("Hello World")
    return { message }
  }
}
```

Or in `<script setup>`:

```
<script setup>
import { ref } from 'vue'

const message = ref("Hello World")
</script>
```

We then can access the return object's current value through its single `value` property within the `script` section. For example, the code in Example 5-1 creates a reactive object with the initial value of 0.

Example 5-1. Using ref() to create a reactive message with an initial value of "Hello World"

```
import { ref } from 'vue'

const message = ref("Hello World")

console.log(message.value) //Hello World
```

If you use Options API with setup() hook, you can access message in other part of component's without .value, i.e., message is sufficient.

However, in the template tag section, you can retrieve its value directly without the value property. For example, the code in Example 5-2 will print the same message as Example 5-1, but to the browser.

Example 5-2. Accessing message value in the template section

```
<template>
    <div>{{ message }}</div>
</template>
<script lang="ts" setup>
import { ref } from 'vue'

const message = ref("Hello World")
</script>
```

The ref() function infers types for the return object from the initial value passed. If you explicitly want to define the type of the return object, you can use the TypeScript syntax ref<type>(), such as ref<string>().

Since the ref object is reactive and mutable, we can change its value by assigning a new value to its value property. The Vue engine then will trigger the relevant watchers and update the component.

In Example 5-3, we will re-create the MyMessageComponent (from Example 3-3 with Options API), which accepts input from the user and changes the message displayed.

Example 5-3. Using ref() to create a reactive MyMessageComponent

```
<template>
    <div>
        <h2 class="heading">{{ message }}</h2>
```

```
        <input type="text" v-model="message" />
    </div>
</template>
<script lang="ts" setup>
import { ref } from 'vue'

const message = ref("Welcome to Vue 3!")
</script>
```

When we change the input field's value, the browser will show the updated `message` value accordingly, as shown in Figure 5-1.

My name is
My name is

Figure 5-1. The value displayed changes when we change the input field's value

In the Vue tab of the browser's Developer Tools, we can see ref object `message` listed under the `setup` section, with the indication `Ref` (Figure 5-2).

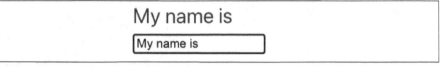

```
<MyMessageComponent>    Q  Filter state...

 ▼ setup
        message: "Welcome to Vue 3!" (Ref)
```

Figure 5-2. The `message` ref object is listed under the `setup` section

If we add another static data `title` to the component (Example 5-4), the Vue tab will show the `title` data property without the indication (Figure 5-3).

Example 5-4. Adding static `title` to `MyMessageComponent`

```
<template>
    <div>
        <h1>{{ title }}</h1>
        <h2 class="heading">{{ message }}</h2>
        <input type="text" v-model="message" />
    </div>
</template>
<script lang="ts" setup>
import { ref } from 'vue'

const title = "My Message Component"
const message = ref("Welcome to Vue 3!")
</script>
```

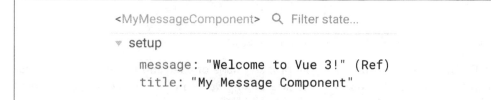

Figure 5-3. The title data property is listed without the indication

The previous code (Example 5-4) is equivalent to Example 5-5 with setup() hook.

Example 5-5. Using setup() hook to create a reactive MyMessageComponent

```ts
<template>
    <div>
        <h2 class="heading">{{ message }}</h2>
        <input type="text" v-model="message" />
    </div>
</template>
<script lang="ts">
import { ref } from 'vue'

export default {
    setup() {
        const message = ref("Welcome to Vue 3!")
        return {
            message
        }
    }
}
</script>
```

You can use the ref() function to create a reactive object for any primitive type (such as string, number, boolean, null, undefined, etc.) and any object type. However, for the object type such as array and object, the ref() returns an intensely reactive object, meaning both the ref object and its nested properties are mutable, as seen in Example 5-6.

Example 5-6. Using ref() to create a deeply reactive object

```
import { ref } from 'vue'

const user = ref({
    name: "Maya",
    age: 20
})

user.value.name = "Rachel"
user.value = {
    name: "Samuel",
```

```
    age: 20
}

console.log(user.value) // { name: "Samuel", age: 20 }
```

In Example 5-6, we can replace the property name of user and the entire user object with a new value. We consider this case a *bad practice* in Vue, which can lead to performance issues for large data structures, and unexpected behaviors. To avoid falling into such a situation, I would recommend that you use the shallowRef() and reactive() functions instead, depending on your use case:

- If you want to create a reactive object-type data and *replace it later on with new value*, use shallowRef(). A good example is integrating the component with asynchronous data fetching with the help of lifecycle composition hooks, as seen in Example 5-7.

- If you want to create a reactive object-type data and *update its properties only*, use reactive(), which we will cover in the next section.

Example 5-7. Using shallowRef() to manage external data fetching

```
<script lang="ts" setup>
import { shallowRef } from "vue";

type User = {
    name: string;
    bio: string;
    avatar_url: string;
    twitter_username: string;
    blog: string;
};

const user = shallowRef<User>({  ❶
    name: "",
    bio: "",
    avatar_url: "",
    twitter_username: "",
    blog: "",
});

const error = shallowRef<Error | undefined>();  ❷

const fetchData = async () => {
    try {
        const response = await fetch("https://api.github.com/users/mayashavin");

        if (response.ok) {
            user.value = (await response.json()) as User;  ❸
        }
    } catch (e) {
        error.value = e as Error;  ❹
```

```
    }
};

fetchData();
</script>
```

❶ Create a reactive `user` variable of type `User` with the initial data using `shallow Ref`.

❷ Create a reactive `error` variable that can be `undefined` or of type `Error` using `shallowRef`.

❸ Replace the value of `user` with the response's data, assuming it is of type `User`.

❹ Update the value of `error` when an error occurred.

Using reactive()

The `reactive()` function is similar to the `ref()` function, except:

- It accepts object-type data as its argument.
- You can directly access the reactive return object without `value` and its properties.

Only the return object's nested properties are mutable, and trying to modify the return object's value directly or using the `value` property will result in an error:

```
import { reactive } from 'vue'

const user = reactive({
    name: "Maya",
    age: 20
})

/*
TypeScript error - property 'value' does not exist
on type '{ name: string; age: number; }'
*/
user.value = {
    name: "Samuel",
    age: 20
}

/*
TypeScript error - cannot reassign a read-only variable
*/
user = {
    name: "Samuel",
    age: 20
}
```

But you can modify user object's properties, such as name and age:

```
import { reactive } from 'vue'

const user = reactive({
    name: "Maya",
    age: 20
})

user.name = "Rachel"
user.age = 30
```

> Behind the scenes, ref() triggers reactive().

One important note is that the reactive() function returns a reactive proxy version of the original passed object. Hence, if we make any change to the reactive return object, it would be reflected on the original object, and vice versa, as seen in Example 5-8.

Example 5-8. Modify both the original object and the reactive object

```
import { reactive } from 'vue'

const defaultUser = {
    name: "Maya",
    age: 20
}

const user = reactive(defaultUser)

user.name = "Rachel"
user.age = 30

console.log(defaultUser) // { name: "Rachel", age: 30 }

defaultUser.name = "Samuel"

console.log(user) // { name: "Samuel", age: 30 }
```

In this example, the properties of both defaultValue and user change when user changes and vice versa. Hence it will be best if you are extra cautious when using the reactive() function. You should use the spread syntax (...) to create a new object before passing to the reactive() instead (Example 5-9).

Example 5-9. Using reactive() with spread syntax

```
import { reactive } from 'vue'

const defaultUser = {
    name: "Maya",
    age: 20
}

const user = reactive({ ...defaultUser })

user.name = "Rachel"
user.age = 30

console.log(defaultUser) // { name: "Maya", age: 20 }

defaultUser.name = "Samuel"

console.log(user) // { name: "Rachel", age: 30 }
```

 The reactive() function enables profound reactivity conversion for the initial object. Thus, it can lead to undesired performance issues for the large data structure. In a scenario where you only want to observe the root object's properties and not their descendant, you should use the shallowReactive() function instead.

You also can combine ref() and reactive(), though I don't recommend it due to its complexity and the reactivity unwrapping mechanism. If there is a need to create a reactive object from another reactive object, you should use computed() instead (see "Using computed()" on page 151).

Table 5-1 summarizes the use cases for ref(), reactive(), shallowRef(), and shallowReactive().

Table 5-1. Use cases for ref(), reactive(), shallowRef() and shallowReactive() functions

Hook	When to use
ref()	Primitive data types for general cases or object-type when there is a need for reassigning both the object and its properties.
shallowRef()	Object type only as a placeholder for later reassigning and no property observation.
reactive()	For property observation of object-type data, including nested properties.
shallowReactive()	For property observation of object-type data, excluding nested properties.

Next, we will look at the lifecycle composition hooks and what they offer.

Using the Lifecycle Hooks

In "Component Lifecycle Hooks" on page 61, we learned the component's lifecycle hooks and how they look in the classic Vue's Options API as properties of the component's options object. With Composition API, the lifecycle hooks are separate functions that we need to import from the vue package before using them to execute logic at specific points in a component's lifecycle.

The Composition API's lifecycle hooks are similar to the ones in the Options API, except the syntax now contains the prefix on (for example, mounted becomes onMounted in Composition API). Table 5-2 shows the mapping from Options API to Composition API for some lifecycle hooks.

Table 5-2. Lifecycle hooks from Options API to Composition API

Options API	Composition API	Description
beforeMount()	onBeforeMount()	Call before the first render of the component.
mounted()	onMounted()	Call after Vue renders and mounts the component to the DOM.
beforeUpdate()	onBeforeUpdate()	Call after the component's update process starts.
updated()	onUpdated()	Call after Vue renders the updated component to the DOM.
beforeUnmount()	onBeforeUnmount()	Call before unmounting the component.
unmounted()	onUnmounted()	Call after Vue removes and destroys the component instance.

You probably noticed here that not all Options API's lifecycle hooks have an equivalent in Composition API, such as beforeCreate() and created(). Instead, we use setup() or <script setup> with other Composition API hooks to achieve the same result and even define the component's logic in a more organized way.

We use the above hooks to register callbacks that Vue will execute when appropriate by passing the callback function as its only argument. For example, to register a callback to beforeMount() hook, we can do this:

```
<script setup lang="ts">
import { onBeforeMount } from 'vue'

onBeforeMount(() => {
    console.log('beforeMount triggered')
})
</script>
```

Since Vue triggers setup() before creating the component instance, there is no access to the this instance, both in setup() and in the hooks registered within it. The following code will print out undefined (Figure 5-4) when in use:

```
import { onMounted } from 'vue'
onMounted(() => {
    console.log('component instance: ', this)
})
```

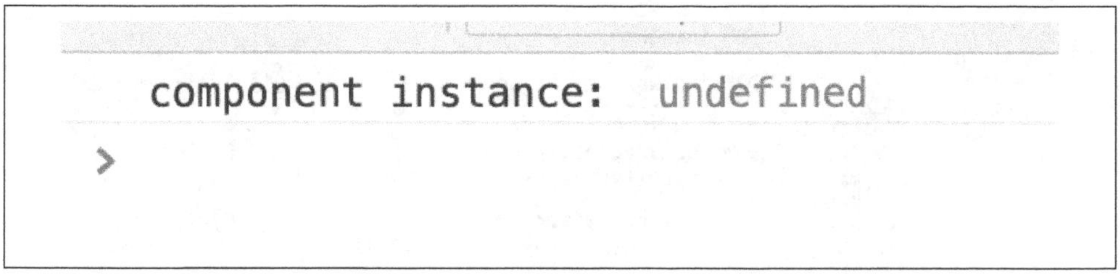

Figure 5-4. Accessing this *in the Composition lifecycle hook yields* undefined

However, you can access the component's DOM instance (like this.$el as in Options API) by using the ref() hook and ref directive, like how we define inputRef in this example:

```
import { ref } from 'vue'

const inputRef = ref(null)
```

Then bind it to the ref directive in the template:

```
<template>
    <input
        ref="inputRef"
        v-model="message" type="text" placeholder="Enter your name"
    />
</template>
```

Finally, we can access the DOM instance in the onMounted() or onUpdated() hook:

```
import { onUpdated, onMounted } from 'vue'

onMounted(() => {
    console.log('DOM instance: ', inputRef.value)
})

onUpdated(() => {
    console.log('DOM instance after updated: ', inputRef.value)
})
```

After mounting the component, inputRef will refer to the input element's correct DOM instance. Every time the user changes the input field, Vue will trigger the onUpdated() hook and update the DOM instance accordingly. Figure 5-5 shows the console log after mounting and the user typing in the input field.

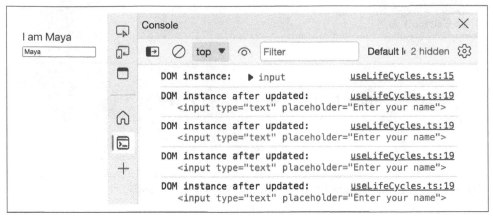

Figure 5-5. Console log after mounting and the user making a change to the input field

Composition API's lifecycle hooks can be helpful in many cases compared to the Options API's lifecycle hooks, especially when you want to keep your functional component's logic concise and organized. You can also combine the lifecycle hooks with other Composition API hooks to achieve more complex logic and create your reusable custom hooks (see "Creating Your Reusable Composables" on page 154). In the next section, we will look at other significant Composition API hooks, starting with `watch()`.

Understanding Watchers in Composition API

Like the Options API's `watch()`, the Composition API's `watch()` hook is used to observe for changes and invoke the callback in reactive data. `watch()` accepts three arguments, as shown in this syntax:

```
watch(
    sources: WatchSource,
    cb: (newValue: T, oldValue: T, cleanup: (func) => void)) => any,
    options?: WatchOptions
): WatchStopHandle
```

- `sources` is the reactive data for Vue to observe. It can be a single piece of reactive data, a getter function that returns reactive data, or an array of those.

- `cb` is the callback function that Vue will execute when any of the `sources` changes. This function accepts two main arguments: `newValue` and `oldValue`, and an optional side effect cleanup function to trigger before the next invoke.

- `options` are the options for the `watch()` hook, which is optional and contains the fields described in Table 5-3.

Table 5-3. The watch() options' fields

Property	Description	Accepted type	Default value	Required?
deep	Indicates whether Vue should observe changes in the nested properties of the target data (if any).	boolean	`false`	No
immediate	Indicates whether to trigger the handler immediately after mounting the component.	boolean	`false`	No
flush	Indicates the timing order of the handler's execution. By default, Vue triggers the handler before updating the Vue component.	pre, post, sync	pre	No
onTrack	For debugging when it tracks the reactive data, *only in development mode*.	Function	undefined	No
onTrigger	For debugging when triggering the callback, *only in development mode*.	Function	undefined	No

And it returns a `WatchStopHandle` function that we can use to stop the watcher anytime.

Let's look at the `UserWatcherComponent` component with the same template presented in Chapter 3's Example 3-17, where we allow modifying `user.name` and `user.age` based on a default `user` object. We will rewrite its `<script>` using Composition API, as in Example 5-10.

Example 5-10. `UserWatcherComponent` component using `setup()` and `ref()`

```
<script setup lang='ts'>
import { reactive } from 'vue'

//...

const user = reactive<User>({
  name: "John",
  age: 30,
});
</script>
```

Then, we add a watcher for the `user` object, as in Example 5-11.

Example 5-11. Using the `watch()` hook for watching `user` data

```
import { reactive, watch } from 'vue'

watch(user, (newValue, oldValue) => {
    console.log('user changed from: ', oldValue, ' to: ', newValue)
})
```

By default, Vue will trigger the callback function only when the user changes. In the previous example, because we use reactive() to create user, Vue will automatically enable deep to watch for its properties. In case you want Vue to only observe a specific property of user, such as user.name, we can create a getter function that returns that property and pass it as the sources argument to watch(), as in Example 5-12.

Example 5-12. Using the watch() hook for watching a specific property of user

```
import { reactive, watch } from 'vue'

watch(
    () => user.name,
    (newValue, oldValue) => {
        console.log('user.name changed from: ', oldValue, ' to: ', newValue)
    }
)
```

When you make a change to the user.name, the console log will display the message shown in Figure 5-6.

```
user.name changed from:  John   to:   Johnn
user.name changed from:  Johnn  to:   Johnnn
user.name changed from:  Johnnn to:   Johnnny
>
```

Figure 5-6. Console log after changing user.name

In case you need to trigger the watcher right after mounting the component, you can pass { immediate: true } as the third argument to watch(), as in Example 5-13.

Example 5-13. Using the watch() hook with immediate option

```
import { reactive, watch } from 'vue'

watch(
    () => user.name,
    (newValue, oldValue) => {
        console.log(
            'user.name changed from: ',
            oldValue,
            ' to: ',
            newValue
        )
    },
    { immediate: true }
)
```

The console log will display the change of user.name from undefined to John right after mounting the component.

You can also pass a sources array of reactive data to watch(), and Vue will trigger the callback function with two collections of new and old values, each of which corresponds to the reactive data in the same order as the sources array, as shown in Example 5-14.

Example 5-14. Using the watch() hook with an array of reactive data

```
import { reactive, watch } from 'vue'

watch(
    [() => user.name, () => user.age],
    ([newName, newAge], [oldName, oldAge]) => {
        console.log(
            'user changed from: ',
            { name: oldName, age: oldAge },
            ' to: ',
            { name: newName, age: newAge }
        )
    }
)
```

The above watcher will be triggered when either user.name or user.age changes and the console log will display the difference accordingly.

If you want to observe and trigger side action to multiple data changes, watchEffect() can be a better option. It will track the reactive dependencies used in the watcher's function, run the function immediately right after the component renders, and rerun it whenever any dependencies change their value. However, you should be cautious using this API as it can lead to performance issues if the list of dependencies is extensive and the updating frequency between them is high.

Using the watch() hook is a great way to create a dynamic observation on specific reactive data or its properties. But if we want to create new reactive data based on the existing ones, we should use computed(), which we will look at next.

Using computed()

Similar to computed properties, we use computed() to create a reactive and cached data value derived from other reactive data. Unlike ref() and reactive(), computed() returns a *read-only* reference object, meaning we can't manually reassign value to it.

Let's take the reserved message example written in Options API in Example 3-11 and rewrite it using the computed() hook as in Example 5-15.

Example 5-15. PalindromeCheck component using computed()

```ts
<script lang="ts" setup>
import { ref, computed } from 'vue'

const message = ref('Hello World')
const reversedMessage = computed<string>(
    () => message.value.split('').reverse().join('')
)
</script>
```

Within the script section, we use the value property of the returned object (reversedMessage.value) to access its value, like ref() and reactive().

The code in Example 5-16 shows how we create another computed data point to check if the message is a palindrome based on the reversedMessage.

Example 5-16. Using computed() to create new reactive isPalindrome data

```ts
<script lang="ts" setup>
import { ref, computed } from 'vue'

//...
const isPalindrome = computed<boolean>(
    () => message.value === reversedMessage.value
)
</script>
```

Notice here we declare the types for reservedMessage and isPalindrome explicitly as string and boolean to avoid type inference errors. You can now use these computed data in your template (Example 5-17).

Example 5-17. Using data created from computed() in the template

```
<template>
  <div>
    <input v-model="message" placeholder="Enter your message"/>
    <p>Reversed message: {{ reversedMessage }}</p>
    <p>Is palindrome: {{ isPalindrome }}</p>
  </div>
</template>
```

This code results in the output shown in Figure 5-7 when the user changes the message input.

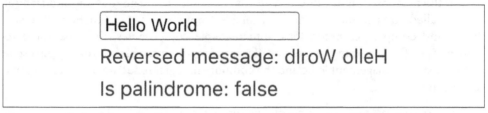

Figure 5-7. Palindrome check component for the message using `computed()`

When you open the Vue tab in the browser's Developer Tools, you can see these computed data values available under the **setup** section of the `PalindromeCheck` component (Figure 5-8).

```
<PalidromeCheck>

<PalidromeCheck>   Q  Filter state...                    ⊙  <>  ≡<  ☑

▼ setup
    isPalindrome: false (Computed)
    message: "Hello World" (Ref)
    reversedMessage: "dlroW olleH" (Computed)
```

Figure 5-8. Computed and reactive data shown in the developer tool for the `PalindromeCheck` component

 By default, `computed()` returns a *read-only* reactive data reference. Still, you can intentionally declare it as a *writable* object by passing an object of { `get`, `set` } as the first argument to `computed()`. This mechanism stays consistent with `computed` properties in the Options API. However, I don't recommend using this feature. You should combine it with `ref()` or `reactive()` instead.

We have learned how to use `computed()` and `watch()` to achieve the same result as the classic `computed` and `watch` option properties. You can use either of them, depending on your preference. You also can use these hooks to create your own hooks, called composables, and reuse them in other components, which we will explore next.

Creating Your Reusable Composables

One of the most exciting features of Vue 3 is the ability to create reusable and stateful hooks, called composables,[2] from the available Composition API functions. We can divide and compose common logic into readable composables, then use them to manage specific data state changes in different components. This approach helps separate the state management logic and the component logic, reducing our components' complexity.

To start composing, you can create a new TypeScript (.ts) file and export a function that returns a reactive data object as your composable, as shown in Example 5-18.

Example 5-18. Creating an example composable, useMyComposable

```
// src/composables/useMyComposable.ts
import { reactive } from 'vue'

export const useMyComposable = () => {
    const myComposableData = reactive({
        title: 'This is my composable data',
    })

    return myComposableData
}
```

In the previous code, we create a new TypeScript file named useMyComposable.ts under the src/composables folder and export a function called useMyComposable. The function returns a reactive data object named myComposableData created using the reactive() function.

> You can place the composable file anywhere in your project, but I recommend putting it under the src/composables folder to keep it organized. Also, it's a good practice to name the composable file with the use prefix, followed by the concise, descriptive name of the composable.

You can then import and use useMyComposable in your component as shown in Example 5-19.

Example 5-19. Using the useMyComposable composable in the a Vue component

```
<script lang="ts" setup>
import { useMyComposable } from '@/composables/useMyComposable'
```

---

2 In general, a composable is a custom hook.

```
const myComposableData = useMyComposable()
</script>
```

Now you can access the `myComposableData` in your component's template, and other parts of the component logic, as its local reactive data.

Let's create a `useFetch` composable to query data from an external API using the `fetch` API, as shown in Example 5-20.

Example 5-20. Create useFetch composable

```
import { ref, type Ref, type UnwrapRef } from "vue";

type FetchResponse<T> = {
    data: Ref<UnwrapRef<T> | null>;
    error: Ref<UnwrapRef<Error> | null>;
    loading: Ref<boolean>;
}

export function useFetch<T>(url: string): FetchResponse<T> {
    const data = ref<T | null>(null);
    const loading = ref<boolean>(false);
    const error = ref<Error | null>(null);

    const fetchData = async () => { ❶
        try {
            loading.value = true;
            const response = await fetch(url);

            if (!response.ok) {
                throw new Error(`Failed to fetch data for ${url}`);
            }

            data.value = await response.json();
        } catch (err) {
            error.value = (err as Error).message;
        } finally {
            loading.value = false;
        }
    };

    fetchData(); ❷

    return { ❸
        data,
        loading,
        error,
    };
};
```

❶ Declare the internal logic for fetching data.

❷ Trigger fetching data during the creation of the component and update the data automatically.

❸ Return the declared reactive variables.

You then can reuse `useFetch` to compose another asynchronous composable, such as `useGitHubRepos`, to query and manage user's repositories data from the GitHub API (Example 5-21).

Example 5-21. Create a useGitHubRepos composable

```ts
// src/composables/useGitHubRepos.ts
import { useFetch } from '@/composables/useFetch'
import { ref } from 'vue'

type Repo = { /**... */ }

export const useGitHubRepos = (username: string) => {
    return useFetch<Repo[]>(
        `https://api.github.com/users/${username}/repos`
    );
}
```

Once done, we can use `useGitHubRepos` in a `GitHubRepos.vue` component (Example 5-22).

Example 5-22. Using useGitHubRepos in a GitHubRepos component

```ts
<script lang="ts" setup>
import { useGitHubRepos } from "@/composables/useGitHubRepos";
const { data: repos } = useGitHubRepos("mayashavin"); ❶
</script>
<template>
    <h2>Repos</h2>
    <ul>
    <li v-for="repo in repos" :key="repo.id"> ❷
      <article>
        <header>{{ repo.name }}</header>
        <p>{{ repo.description }}</p>
      </article>
    </li>
  </ul>
</template>
```

❶ Get the `data` and rename it `repos`.

❷ Iterate `repos` and display each `repo`'s information.

And on the browser, we will see a list of repos displayed after the fetching completes (Figure 5-9).

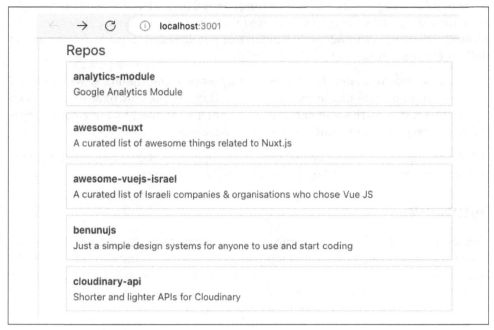

Figure 5-9. Retrieve and display a list of repos using useGitHubRepos composable

 Mapping Data Between Composables

If you need to re-map any reactive data received from another composable, use computed() or watch() to preserve the reactivity. Example 5-23 demonstrates a *non-working* example of useFetch inside useGitHubRepos.

Example 5-23. Using useFetch in the wrong way within useGitHubRepos

```
export const useGitHubRepos = (username: string) => {
  const response = useFetch<Repo[]>(
    `https://api.github.com/users/${username}/repos`
  );

  return {
    repos: response.data,
    loading: response.loading,
    error: response.error,
  };
};
```

With composables, you can create your application's state management logic in a modular and composable way. You can even build your library of composables to reuse in other Vue projects, such as theming control, data fetching, payment management for a store, etc. An excellent resource for composables is VueUse (*https://oreil.ly/pKJmK*), where you can find many helpful, ready-to-use, and tested Vue composition utilities for your needs.

Since all the reactive states get initialized only when using the hook, we can avoid data overlapping issues like in mixins. Also, testing components have become more straightforward, whereby you can test each composable used in the element separately and keep the component's logic small and maintainable.

After learning about Composition API and composables, how about creating your own composables system and using them in your components?

Summary

This chapter explored how to rewrite our components from the Options API to use Composition API functions such as setup function, reactivity, and lifecycle hooks. We also learned to create our custom composable based on the existing ones, enhancing code reusability. Based on this foundation, we now understand the pros and cons of each API, hence their use cases for better development.

You are ready to move to the next chapter, where you will learn how to incorporate external data from an API or database resource into your Vue application.

CHAPTER 6

Incorporating External Data

The previous chapters prepared you for the essentials of working with components, including passing data between components and handling data changes and events within components. You are now ready to use Vue components to incorporate and represent your application's data on the screen to your users.

In most cases, an application will not have data available within the application itself. Instead, we usually request the data from an external server or database, then populate the proper UI with the received data for our application. This chapter covers this aspect of developing a robust Vue application: how to communicate and handle external data from an external resource using Axios as the HTTP request tool.

What Is Axios?

For making HTTP requests to external resources, various options are available for Vue developers, including the built-in `fetch` method, the classic `XMLHttpRequest`, and third-party libraries such as Axios. While the built-in `fetch` is a good option for making HTTP requests for fetching data only, Axios, in the long term, provides extra functionalities that come in handy when working with more complex external resources' API handling.

Axios is a JavaScript open source lightweight library for making HTTP requests. Like `fetch`, it is a promise-based HTTP client and isomorphic, supporting both node (server-side) and browser side.

Some significant advantages of using Axios are the ability to intercept and cancel HTTP requests and its built-in cross-site request forgery protection for the client side. Another advantage of Axios is that it automatically transforms the response data to JSON format, giving you a better developer experience in working with the data than using the built-in `fetch`.

The official website for Axios (*https://oreil.ly/WxSN3*) includes API documentation, installation, and primary use cases for reference (Figure 6-1).

Figure 6-1. Axios official website

Installing Axios

To add Axios to your Vue project within your project's root directory, use the following command in your terminal:

```
yarn add axios
```

Once Axios is installed, you can import the Axios library into your component where needed with the following code:

```
import axios from 'axios';
```

You then can use `axios` to start querying for your application's data. Let's explore how to combine Axios with lifecycle hooks to load and display data.

Load Data with Lifecycle Hooks and Axios

As you learned in Chapter 3, you can use the `beforeCreate`, `created`, and `before Mounted` lifecycle hooks to perform side calls such as data fetching. However, in a scenario where you need to load external data and use it within the component and use Options API, `beforeCreate` is not an option. Vue ignores any data assignment using `beforeCreate` since it hasn't initialized any reactive data yet. Using `created` and `beforeMounted` is a better choice in this case. However, `beforeMounted` is not available in server-side rendering, and if we want to use the Composition API (covered in Chapter 5), there is no equivalent lifecycle function in Composition API to the `created` hook.

A better option for loading external data is to use `setup()` or `<script setup>` with the respective reactive composition functions.

Let's make an asynchronous GET request to get the public information about my GitHub profile through the URL *https://api.github.com/users/mayashavin* by using the `axios.get()` method, as seen in the following code:

```
/**UserProfile.vue */
import axios from 'axios';
import { ref } from 'vue';

const user = ref(null);

axios.get('https://api.github.com/users/mayashavin')
    .then(response => {
        user.value = response.data;
    });
```

`axios.get()` returns a promise, which can use the promise chaining method `then()` to handle the response data when it resolves. Axios automatically parses the response data from the HTTP response body into the appropriate JSON format. In this example, we assign the received data to the `user` data property of the component. We can also rewrite this code to use `await/async` syntax:

```
/**UserProfile.vue */
//...

async function getUser() {
    const response = await axios.get(
        'https://api.github.com/users/mayashavin'
    );
    user.value = response.data;
}

getUser();
```

We also should wrap the code in a `try/catch` block to handle any errors that may occur during the request. Hence, our code becomes:

```
/**UserProfile.vue */
import axios from 'axios';
import { ref } from 'vue';

const user = ref(null);
const error = ref(null); ❶

async function getUser() {
    try { ❷
        const response = await axios.get('https://api.github.com/users/mayashavin');
```

```
        user.value = response.data;
    } catch (error) {
        error.value = error; ❸
    }
}

getUser();
```

❶   Add an `error` data property to store any error received from the request.

❷   Wrap the code in a `try/catch` block to handle any errors that occur during the request.

❸   Assign the error to the `error` data property, for displaying an error message to the user in the browser.

GitHub responds to our request with a JSON object containing the primary fields shown in Example 6-1.

Example 6-1. `UserProfile` type

```
type User = {
  name: string;
  bio: string;
  avatar_url: string;
  twitter_username: string;
  blog: string;
  //...
};
```

With this response data, we now have the necessary information to display the user's profile on the screen. Let's add the following code to our component's `template` section:

```
<div class="user-profile" v-if="user">
    <img :src="user.avatar_url" alt="`${user.name} Avatar`" width="200"  />
    <div>
        <h1>{{ user.name }}</h1>
        <p>{{ user.bio }}</p>
        <p>Twitter: {{ user.twitter_username }}</p>
        <p>Blog: {{ user.blog }}</p>
    </div>
</div>
```

Note here we add `v-if="user"` to ensure the Vue renders the user profile only when `user` is available.

Finally, as in Example 6-2, we need to add some modifications to our component's `script` section to make the code fully TypeScript compatible, including mapping the response data to be the User data type before assigning it to the user property, as well as the `error`.

Example 6-2. UserProfile component

```
<template>
    <div class="user-profile" v-if="user">
        <!-- ... -->
    </div>
</template>
<script lang="ts" setup>
import axios from 'axios';
import { ref } from 'vue';

type User = { /**... */ }

const user = ref<User | null>(null) ❶
const error = ref<Error | null>(null)

async function getUser () {
    try {
        const response = await axios.get<User>(
            "https://api.github.com/users/mayashavin"
        )

        user.value = await response.data ❷
    } catch (err) {
        error.value = err as Error ❸
    }
}

getUser();
</script>
```

❶ Add the User type declaration to the user.

❷ Assign the response data to the user property.

❸ Cast the error to be Error type before assigning it to the error property.

When the request is successfully resolved, you will see my GitHub profile information displayed on the screen, as shown in Figure 6-2.

Figure 6-2. Sample output for a successful GitHub profile information request

Similarly, you can also add a section with `v-else-if="error"` condition to display an error message to the user when the request fails:

```
<template>
<div class="user-profile" v-if="user">
    <!--...-->
</div>
<div class="error" v-else-if="error">
    {{ error.message }}
</div>
</template>
```

At this point, you may wonder what happens behind the scenes when we perform an asynchronous request while the component is in the middle of creation. The component's lifecycle operates synchronously, meaning Vue still proceeds in creating the component despite the status of the asynchronous request. That brings us to the challenge of handling different data requests in various components during run-time, which we will explore next.

Async Data Requests in Run-Time: the Challenge

Similar to how the JavaScript engine works, Vue also works synchronously. If there is any asynchronous request along the way, Vue will not wait for the request to complete before proceeding to the next step. Instead, Vue finishes the component's creation process, then returns to handle the asynchronous request when it resolves/rejects according to the execution order.

Let's take a step back, add some console logs to the onBeforeMounted, onMounted, and onUpdated hooks in our component and see the order of execution:

```
//<script setup>
import { onBeforeMount, onMounted, onUpdated } from "vue";

//...
async function getUser() {
  try {
    const response = await axios.get<User>(
        'https://api.github.com/users/mayashavin'
    );
    user.value = response.data;

    console.log('User', user.value.name) ❶
  } catch (err) {
    error.value = err;
  }
}

onBeforeMount(async () => {
    console.log('created') ❷
    getUser();
})

onMounted(() => {
    console.log("mounted"); ❸
});

onUpdated(() => {
    console.log("updated"); ❹
})
```

❶ Log the details of **user** when finished fetching to the console.

❷ Log the lifecycle state: before mounting

❸ Log the lifecycle state: mounted

❹ Log the lifecycle state: component is updated

Looking at the browser's console log, we see the order displayed as in Figure 6-3.

created	UserProfile.vue:37
mounted	UserProfile.vue:50
User Maya Shavin	UserProfile.vue:44
updated	UserProfile.vue:53

Figure 6-3. Order of execution with an asynchronous request

Once the asynchronous request is resolved/rejected and there are component data changes, the Vue renderer will trigger the update process for the component. The component is not yet with the response data when Vue mounts it to the DOM. Thus, we still need to handle the component's loading state before receiving the server's data.

To do so, we can add another loading property to the component's data and disable the loading state after the request is resolved/rejected, as in Example 6-3.

Example 6-3. UserProfile component with loading state and error state

```
//...
const loading = ref<boolean>(false); ❶

async function getUser() {
    loading.value = true; ❷

    try {
        const response = await axios.get<User>(
            "https://api.github.com/users/mayashavin"
        )

        user.value = await response.data
    } catch (err) {
        error.value = err as Error
    } finally {
        loading.value = false; ❸
    }
}

getUser();
```

❶ Create a reactive loading variable.

❷ Set loading to true before fetching the data.

❸ Set loading to false after the request is resolved/rejected.

And then add a `v-if="loading"` condition to the component's `template` section for a loading message, as in Example 6-4.

Example 6-4. UserProfile component template with loading state and error state

```
<template>
    <div v-if="loading">Loading...</div>
    <div class="user-profile" v-else-if="user">
        <!--...-->
    </div>
    <div class="error" v-else-if="error">
        {{ error.message }}
</div>
</template>
```

This code renders a loading message while the asynchronous request is in progress and displays the user's profile information when the request resolves or otherwise sends an error message.

You can also create your reusable wrapper component to handle different states for components with the asynchronous data request, such as a skeleton placeholder component when a list of components is loading (Figure 6-4) or a fetch component (covered next).

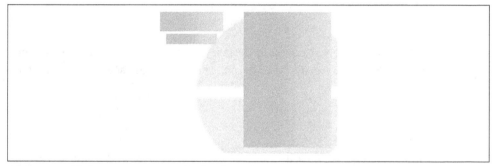

Figure 6-4. Skeleton component for loading state

Creating Your Reusable Fetch Component

Handling states in a Vue component for its asynchronous data request is a common challenge. The UI for these states usually follows the same pattern: a spinner or loading message for the loading state, an error message, or a more stylish error component when a data request rejects. Thus, we can create one common component for handling such cases, which we call `FetchComponent`.

FetchComponent has a `template` section divided into three main areas using `slot` and `v-if`:

#loading *slot for displaying a loading message*
> The condition for this slot to render is if the component is in the `isLoading` state.

#error *slot for displaying an error message*
> We also pass the `error` object as the slot props for customization if needed while ensuring Vue renders this slot only if `error` is available.

#default *slot for displaying the component's content, when there is* `data` *received*
> We also pass the `data` to the slot as props.

We also use a named `slot` to allow customizing the error and loading the component instead of the default messages:

```
<template>
  <slot name="loading" v-if="isLoading">
    <div class="loadin-message">Loading...</div>
  </slot>
  <slot :data="data" v-if="data"></slot>
  <slot name="error" :error="error" v-if="error">
    <div class="error">
      <p>Error: {{ error.message }}</p>
    </div>
  </slot>
</template>
```

In our `script setup` section, we need to declare our data type `FetchComponentData` for the component to contain the `isLoading`, `error`, and `data` properties of type generics `Object`:

```
const data = ref<Object | undefined>();
const error = ref<Error | undefined>();
const loading = ref<boolean>(false);
```

The component receives two props: a `url` for the request URL and a `method` for the request method with the default value of GET:

```
//...

const props = defineProps({
    url: {
        type: String,
        required: true,
    },
    method: {
        type: String,
        default: "GET",
    },
});
//...
```

Finally, we make the asynchronous request and update the component's state when Vue creates the component:

```
async function fetchData () {
    try {
        loading.value = true;
        const response = await axios(props.url, {
            method: props.method,
            headers: {
                'Content-Type': 'application/json',
            },
        });
        data.value = response.data;
    } catch (error) {
        error.value = error as Error;
    } finally {
        loading.value = false;
    }
};

fetchData();
```

> If you know the types of data in advance, you should use them instead of any or Object to ensure full TypeScript type check coverage. Don't use any unless there is no other way.

Now we can rewrite Example 6-2 to use the new `FetchComponent` component as in Example 6-5.

Example 6-5. UserProfile component using the `FetchComponent`

```
<template>
    <FetchComponent url="https://api.github.com/users/mayashavin"> ❶
        <template #default="defaultProps"> ❷
            <div class="user-profile"> ❸
                <img
                    :src="(defaultProps.data as User).avatar_url"
                    alt="`${defaultProps.data.name} Avatar`"
                    width="200"
                />
                <div>
                    <h1>{{ (defaultProps.data as User).name }}</h1>
                    <p>{{ (defaultProps.data as User).bio }}</p>
                    <p>Twitter: {{(defaultProps.data as User).twitter_username }}</p>
                    <p>Blog: {{ (defaultProps.data as User).blog }}</p>
                </div>
            </div>
        </template>
    </FetchComponent>
</template>
<script lang="ts" setup> ❹
```

```
import FetchComponent from "./FetchComponent.vue";
import type { User } from "../types/User.type";
</script>
```

 Use the `FetchComponent` component and pass the `url` prop as the target URL for the request (*https://api.github.com/users/mayashavin*).

 Wrap the main content of the component inside the `template` for the main slot, `#default`. We also bind the props this slot receives to the `defaultProps` object. Since `defaultProps.data` is of `Object` type, we cast it to `User` to pass TypeScript validation.

❸ Use the `defaultProps.data` to access the data received from the request and display it on the UI.

❹ Remove all the related original logic code for fetching.

Here we pass `data` to this slot from our `FetchComponent` implementation, which in our case stands for our original `user` property. Thus, we replace the occurrences of `user` from the previous implementation with `defaultProps.data`. The output remains the same.

Implementing FetchComponent with Composition API

You can rewrite the `FetchComponent` with `useFetch()` (see Example 5-20) in `setup()` function (or `<script setup>` tag) instead.

Now you understand how to create a simple `FetchComponent` to fetch and handle data request states on the UI for your Vue components. You may want to extend it to handle more complex data requests, such as POST requests. By isolating the data request and controlling logic in a single place, you can reduce the complexity and reuse it in other components more quickly.

Connect Your Application with an External Database

At this point, you can handle external data requests and errors on the UI of your Vue components. However, fetching data every time Vue creates a component may not be the best practice, especially if the component's data is not likely to change frequently.

A perfect illustration is switching between pages in a web application, where we need to fetch the page's data only once when loading the view for the first time. In this case, we can cache the data using the browser's local storage as an external local database or using a state management service such as Vuex and Pinia (more in Chapter 9).

To use local storage, we can use the built-in browser localStorage API. For example, to save the user's GitHub profile data to local storage, we can write:

```
localStorage.setItem('user', JSON.stringify(user));
```

Note the browser's localStorage saves the item as a string, so we need to convert the object to a string before saving it. When we need it, we can use this code:

```
const user = JSON.parse(localStorage.getItem('user'));
```

You can add the previous code to your UserProfile component (Example 6-2) as follows:

```
<script lang="ts">
import axios from 'axios';

//...

async function getUser() {
    try {
        const user = JSON.parse(localStorage.getItem('user'));
        if (user) return user.value = user;

        const response = await axios.get<User>(
            'https://api.github.com/users/mayashavin'
        );

        user.value = response.data;
        localStorage.setItem('user', JSON.stringify(user.value));
    } catch (error) {
        error.value = error as Error;
    }
}

getUser();
</script>
```

It will trigger the asynchronous call only when loading the page for the first time. When the page is loaded again, if we have saved the data successfully, it will load directly from local storage.

Using localStorage in Real-World Application

I don't recommend this approach for a real-world application. It has several limitations, such as your browser will reset any local storage data for private/incognito sessions, or users can disable the use of local stage on their end. The better approach is to use state management tools like Vuex or Pinia (see Chapter 9).

Summary

This chapter introduced techniques for handling asynchronous data in a Vue component, with the help of the Axios library and Composition API. We learned how to create a reusable component to fetch and handle data request states on the UI for your Vue applications while keeping the code clean and readable. We also explored connecting your application to an external database service such as local storage.

The next chapter will introduce more advanced rendering concepts of Vue, including using functional components, registering custom plugins globally in your Vue application, and using dynamic rendering to compose layouts conditionally and dynamically.

CHAPTER 7

Advanced Rendering, Dynamic Components, and Plugin Composition

In the previous chapters, you learned how Vue works, how to compose components with Options API and Composition API, and how to incorporate data from an external resource into your Vue application using Axios.

This chapter will introduce a more advanced aspect of rendering in Vue. We will explore how to compute functional components using the rendering function and JSX and how to dynamically and conditionally render elements using Vue's component tag. We will also learn how to register a custom plugin for use within the application.

The Render Function and JSX

With the Vue compiler API, Vue processes and compiles all the HTML templates used for a Vue component into the Virtual DOM upon rendering. When data of a Vue component are updated, Vue triggers the internal render function to send the latest value to the Virtual DOM.

Using `template` is the most common approach to creating a component. However, we need to bypass the HTML template parser process in specific scenarios, such as optimizing performance, working on a server-side rendering application, or working on a dynamic component library. By returning the rendered virtual node from the Virtual DOM directly and skipping the template compiling process, `render()` is the solution for such cases.

Using the Render Function

In Vue 2, the `render()` function property receives a `createElement` callback parameter. It returns a valid VNode[1] by triggering `createElement` with the appropriate arguments. We usually denote `createElement` as an h function.[2]

Example 7-1 illustrates creating a component in Vue 2 syntax.

Example 7-1. Use the render function in Vue 2

```
const App = {
 render(h) {
  return h(
   'div',
   { id: 'test-id' },
   'This is a render function test with Vue'
  )
 }
}
```

This code equals writing the following template code:

```
const App = {
  template: `<div id='test-id'>This is a render function test with Vue</div>`
}
```

In Vue 3, the syntax of `render` changes significantly. It no longer accepts an h function as a parameter. Instead, the `vue` package exposes a global function, h, for creating VNodes. Hence, we can rewrite the code in Example 7-1 to that shown in Example 7-2.

Example 7-2. Use the render function in Vue 3

```
import { createApp, h } from 'vue'

const App = {
 render() {
  return h(
   'div',
   { id: 'test-id' },
   'This is a render function test with Vue'
  )
 }
}
```

The output stays the same.

---

1 Virtual node

2 Stands for hypescript, meaning using JavaScript code to create HTML

Supporting Multi-Root Nodes with the Render Function

Since Vue 3 supports multiple root nodes for a component template, render() can return an array of VNodes, each of which will be injected into the DOM at the same level as the others.

Using the h Function to Create a VNode

Vue designs the h function to be very flexible with three input parameters in different types, as shown in Table 7-1.

Table 7-1. Different parameters for the h function

Parameter	Required?	Acceptable data type	Description
Component	Yes	String, object, or function	It accepts a string as a text or HTML tag element, a component function, or an options object.
props	No	Object	This object contains all components' props, attributes, and events received from its parent, similar to how we write in the template.
Nested children	No	String, array, or object	This parameter includes a list of VNodes, or a string for a text-only component, or an object with different slots (see Chapter 3) as children for the component.

The syntax of the h function is as follows:

```
h(component, { /*props*/ }, children)
```

For example, we want to create a component that uses a div tag as a root element and has a id, an inline border style, and one input child element. We can call h as in this code:

```
const inputElem = h(
  'input',
  {
    placeholder: 'Enter some text',
    type: 'text',
    id: 'text-input'
  })

const comp = h(
  'div',
  {
    id: 'my-test-comp',
    style: { border: '1px solid blue' }
  },
  inputElem
)
```

In the actual DOM, the output of the component will be:

```
<div id="my-test-comp" style="border: 1px solid blue;">
Text input
<input placeholder="Enter some text" type="text" id="text-input">
</div>
```

You can play with the following complete working code and experiment with different configurations for the h function:

```
import { createApp, h } from 'vue'

const inputElem = h(
  'input',
  {
    placeholder: 'Enter some text',
    type: 'text',
    id: 'text-input'
  })

const comp = h(
  'div',
  {
    id: 'my-test-comp',
    style: { border: '1px solid blue' }
  },
  inputElem
)

const App = {
  render() {
    return comp
  }
}

const app = createApp(App)

app.mount("#app")
```

Writing JavaScript XML in the Render Function

JavaScript XML (JSX) is a JavaScript extension introduced by the React framework to allow developers to write HTML code within JavaScript. HTML and JavaScript code in a JSX format looks like this:

```
const JSXComp = <div>This is a JSX component</div>
```

The previous code outputs a component that renders a div tag with the text "This is a JSX component." All that's left to do is to return this component in the render function directly:

```
import { createApp, h } from 'vue'

const JSXComp = <div>This is a JSX component</div>

const App = {
```

```
  render() {
    return JSXComp
   }
  }

const app = createApp(App)

app.mount("#app")
```

Vue 3.0 supports writing with JSX out of the box. The syntax for JSX is different from the Vue template. To bind a dynamic data, we use single curly braces {}, as in Example 7-3.

Example 7-3. Writing a simple Vue component using JSX

```
import { createApp, h } from 'vue'

const name = 'JSX'
const JSXComp = <div>This is a {name} component</div>

const App = {
 render() {
  return JSXComp
 }
}

const app = createApp(App)

app.mount("#app")
```

We bind dynamic data with the same approach. There is no need to wrap the expression with ''. The following example shows how we attach a value to the id attribute of the div:

```
/**... */
const id = 'jsx-comp'
const JSXComp = <div id={id}>This is a {name} component</div>
/**... */
```

However, unlike JSX in React, we don't transform attributes such as class to class Name with Vue. Instead, we keep these attributes' original syntax. The same goes for elements' event listeners (onclick instead of onClick in React, etc.).

You can also register a JSX component as part of components like other Vue components written in Options API. It can be handy in combining with the render function in writing dynamic components and offers better readability in many cases.

Next, we will discuss how we can write a functional component.

Functional Component

A functional component is a stateless component and bypasses the typical component lifecycle. Unlike a standard component, which works with Options API, a functional component is a function, denoting the render function for that component.

Since it is a stateless component, there is no access to the this instance. Instead, Vue exposes the component's external props and context as function arguments. The functional component must return a virtual node instance created using the global function h() from the vue package. Hence, the syntax will be:

```
import { h } from 'vue'

export function MyFunctionComp(props, context) {
  return h(/* render function argument */)
}
```

context exposes the component's context properties, including emits for the component's event emitters, attrs for passed attributes to the component from the parent, and slots containing the component's nested elements.

For example, the functional component myHeading displays any text passed to it within a heading element. We give the heading's level as level props. If we want to display the text "Hello World" as heading level 2 (<h2>), we use myHeading as follows:

```
<my-heading level="2">Hello World</my-heading>
```

And the output should be:

```
<h2>Hello World</h2>
```

To do this, we use the render function h from the vue package and perform the code shown in Example 7-4.

Example 7-4. Using the h function to create a custom heading component

```
import { h } from 'vue';

export function MyHeading(props, context) {
  const heading = `h${props.level}`

  return h(heading, context.$attrs, context.$slots);
}
```

Vue will skip the template render process for the functional component and add the virtual node declaration directly to its renderer pipeline. This mechanism results in no nested slots or attributes available for functional components.

Defining Props and Emits for Functional Component

You can explicitly define the functional component's acceptable `props` and `emits` by following the syntax:

```
MyFunctionComp.props = ['prop-one', 'prop-two']
MyFunctionComp.emits = ['event-one', 'event-two']
```

Without defining, `context.props` will have the same value as `context.attrs`, containing all the attributes passed to the component.

A functional component is powerful when you want to control how to render your component programmatically, especially for component library authors who need to provide low-level flexibility for their components for users' requirements.

 Vue 3 offers an additional way to write components using `<script setup>`. This is relevant only if you write components in *SFC* format, discussed in "setup" on page 63.

Next, we will explore how to add external functionality to a Vue application using plugins.

Adding Custom Functionality Globally with Vue Plugins

We use plugins to add third-party libraries or extra custom functionality for global usage in our Vue application. A Vue plugin is an object that exposes a single method, `install()`, containing the logic code, and it is responsible for installing the plugin itself. Here is an example plugin:

```
/* plugins/samplePlugin.ts */
import type { App  } from 'vue'

export default {
 install(app: App<Element>, options: Object) {
  // Installation logic
 }
}
```

In this code, we define our sample plugin code within the `samplePlugin` file, located in the `plugins` directory. `install()` receives two argument: an `app` instance, and some `options` as the plugin's configurations.

For example, let's compose a `truncate` plugin that will add a new global function property, `$truncate`. `$truncate` will return a truncated string if its length is over `options.limit` characters, as shown in Example 7-5.

Example 7-5. Compose a truncate plugin

```
/* plugins/truncate.ts */
import type { App } from 'vue';

export default {
  install(app: App<Element>, options: { limit: number }) {
    const truncate = (str: string) => {
      if (str.length > options.limit) {
        return `${str.slice(0, options.limit)}...`;
      }

      return str;
    }
    app.config.globalProperties.$truncate = truncate;
  }
}
```

To use this plugin in our application, we call the `app.use()` method on the created app instance in the `main.ts`:

```
/* main.ts */
import { createApp } from 'vue'
import truncate from './plugins/truncate'

const App = {}

//1. Create the app instance
const app = createApp(App);

//2. Register the plugin
app.use(truncate, { limit: 10 })

app.mount('#app')
```

The Vue engine will install the `truncate` plugin and initialize it with a `limit` of 10 characters. The plugin will be available in every Vue component within the `app` instance. You can call this plugin using `this.$truncate` in the `script` section or just `$truncate` in the `template` section:

```
import { createApp, defineComponent } from 'vue'
import truncate from './plugins/truncate'

const App = defineComponent({
  template: `
  <h1>{{ $truncate('My truncated long text') }}</h1>
  <h2>{{ truncatedText }}</h2>
  `,
  data() {
    return {
      truncatedText: this.$truncate('My 2nd truncated text')
    }
  }
});

const app = createApp(App);
```

```
app.use(truncate, { limit: 10 })
app.mount('#app')
```

The output should look like Figure 7-1.

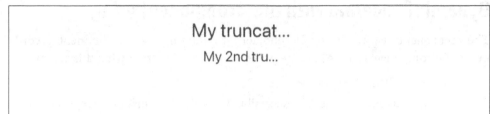

Figure 7-1. Component output texts are truncated

However, `$truncate` is available only if you use it in the `<template>` section or as `this.$truncate` with Options API in the `script` section. Accessing `$truncate` inside `<script setup>` or `setup()` is *not* possible. To do so, we need the provide/inject pattern (see "Communicate Between Components with provide/inject Pattern" on page 123), starting with adding the following code to the plugin's `install` function, located in the `plugins/truncate.ts` file:

```
/* plugins/truncate.ts */
export default {
  install(app: App<Element>, options: { limit: number }) {
    //...
    app.provide("plugins", { truncate });
  }
}
```

Vue will pass `truncate` as part of the `plugins` object to all the application's components. With that, we can use `inject` to receive our desired plugin `truncate` and move on to computing the `truncatedText`:

```
<script setup lang="ts">
import { inject } from 'vue';

const { truncate } = inject('plugins');
const truncatedText = truncate('My 2nd truncated text');
</script>
```

Plugins are very helpful in organizing global methods and making them available for reuse in other applications. It is also beneficial in writing your logic during an installation of an external library, such as *axios* for fetching external data, *i18n* for localization, etc.

Registering Pinia and Vue Router in Our Application

During the scaffolding of our application, Vite adds Pinia and Vue Router as application plugins using the same approach reflected in the original generated code in `main.ts`.

The next section will look at rendering the dynamic component in run-time using the Vue <component> tag.

Dynamic Rendering with the <component> Tag

The <component> tag acts as the placeholder for rendering a Vue component, according to the component reference name passed to its is props, following this syntax:

```
<component is="targetComponentName" />
```

Suppose your target component is accessible from the Vue instance (registered as a component of the app or the parent component when <component> is nested); the Vue engine will know how to look up the target component based on the name string and replace the tag with the target component. The target component will also inherit all the extra props passed to <component>.

Say we have a HelloWorld component that renders the text "Hello World":

```
<template>
  <div>Hello World</div>
</template>
```

We register this component to the App, then render it dynamically using the <component> tag, as follows:

```
<template>
  <component is="HelloWorld" />
</template>
<script lang="ts">
import HelloWorld from "@/components/HelloWorld";
import { defineComponent } from "vue";

export defineComponent({
 components: { HelloWorld },
});
</script>
```

You can also bind the component as a reference to the is props using the v-bind directive (denoted by : short syntax). We can shorten the two previous code blocks into a single App component by rewriting the code as follows:

```
<template>
  <component :is="myComp" />
</template>
<script lang="ts">
import HelloWorld from "@/components/HelloWorld";
import { defineComponent } from "vue";

export defineComponent({
 data() {
  return {
   myComp: {
    template: '<div>Hello World</div>'
```

```
      }
     }
    }
  });
  </script>
```

Note here the component reference myComp follows Options API syntax. You can also pass an imported SFC component instead. The output of both cases should be the same.

The <component> tag is powerful. For example, if you have a gallery component, you can choose to render each gallery item as a Card component or a Row component, using <component> to switch parts conditionally.

However, switching components means Vue unmounts the current element completely and erases all the component's current data states. Switching back to that component equals creating a new instance with a new data state. To prevent that behavior and maintain the states of a passive element for a future switch, we use the <keep-alive> component.

Keeping Component Instance Alive with <keep-alive>

<keep-alive> is a built-in Vue component for wrapping around a dynamic element and preserving the component's states in inactive mode.

Assume we have two components, StepOne and StepTwo. In the StepOne component, there is a string input field that has two-way binding to a local data property name using v-model:

```
<!--StepOne.vue-->
<template>
  <div>
    <label for="name">Step one's input</label>
    <input v-model="name" id="name" />
  </div>
</template>
<script setup lang="ts">
import { ref } from 'vue';

const name = ref<string>("");
</script>
```

While the StepTwo component renders a static string:

```
<!--StepTwo.vue-->
<template>
  <h2>{{ name }}</h2>
</template>
<script setup lang="ts">
const name = "Step 2";
</script>
```

In the main App template, we will use component tag to render a local data property: activeComp as a component reference. The initial value of activeComp is StepOne, and we have a button to move between StepOne to StepTwo, and vice versa:

```
<template>
  <div>
    <keep-alive>
      <component :is="activeComp" />
    </keep-alive>
    <div>
      <button @click="activeComp = 'StepOne'" v-if="activeComp === 'StepTwo'">
      Go to Step Two
      </button>
      <button @click="activeComp = 'StepTwo'" v-else>Back to Step One</button>
    </div>
  </div>
</template>
<script lang="ts">
import { defineComponent } from "vue";
import StepOne from "./components/StepOne.vue";
import StepTwo from "./components/StepTwo.vue";

export default defineComponent({
  components: { StepTwo, StepOne },
  data() {
    return {
      activeComp: "StepOne",
    };
  },
});
</script>
```

Whenever you switch between StepOne and StepTwo, Vue preserves any value of the name property received from the input field. When switching back to StepOne, you can continue with the previous value rather than starting from the initial value.

You can also define the maximum instances for keep-alive to the cache using its max props:

```
<keep-alive max="2">
  <component :is="activeComp" />
</keep-alive>
```

This code defines the maximum number of instances keep-alive should hold as two by setting max="2". Once the number of cached instances exceeds the limit, Vue removes the least recently used (LRU) instance from the cached list, allowing for caching new instances.

Summary

This chapter explored how to control the component rendering with JSX and functional components, register Vue custom plugins globally, and dynamically and conditionally render a component using the <component> tag.

The next chapter will introduce Vue Router, the official routing management library for Vue, and discuss how to handle the navigation between different routes in our application using Vue Router.

CHAPTER 8

Routing

In previous chapters, we have learned the fundamentals of Vue components and different approaches to composing a Vue component. We proceeded to create reusable component logic as standalone composable using Composition API. We also learned about more advanced concepts of rendering and custom plugin creation.

This chapter will explore a different aspect of building a Vue application, routing, by introducing you to the concept of a routing system with Vue Router, the official routing management library for the Vue application, and its core API. We then learn how to configure the app's routes, pass and handle data between the application's paths using router guards, and build dynamic and nested routes for our application.

What is Routing?

When users navigate around the web, they enter a Uniform Resource Locator (URL) in the browser's address bar. A URL is the address of a resource within the web. It contains many parts, which we can divide into the following significant sections (Figure 8-1):

Location
> Includes the protocol, the application's domain name (or IP address of the web server), and the port used to access the requested resource.

Path
> The path to the requested resource. In web development, we use it to determine the page component to render on the browser side based on a predefined path pattern.

Query parameters

A set of key-value pairs for passing additional information to the server, separated by an & symbol. We mainly use query parameters to pass data between pages.

Anchor

Any text after the # symbol. We use anchors to navigate to a specific element on the same page, often with matched id value with the matched id or a time-lapse for a media element.

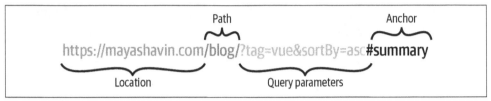

Figure 8-1. URL structure

Upon receiving the URL from the user, the browser then communicates with the server based on the received URL, which returns the requested resource, if any. The resource can be a static file, such as an image or a video, or a dynamic page, such as a web page or a web application.

With single-page applications (SPAs), we perform the routing mechanism on the browser side instead, thus allowing smooth page navigation without refreshing the browser. As a URL is a page's address, we use a routing system to connect its path pattern to a specific component representing it in our application.

Frontend frameworks like Vue provide the layout for building components for an SPA but not the routing services. To create a complete user navigation experience, we must design and develop the application's routing ourselves, including solving the SPA's issues such as history keeping and bookmarking.

Or we can use Vue Router as our primary engine for routing.

Using Vue Router

As the official routing service for Vue applications, Vue Router offers a control mechanism for handling page navigation in a Vue application. We use Vue Router to set up our application's routing systems, including configuring the mapping between components and pages, delivering a good user experience on the client side for the SPA's flow.

The official Vue Router documentation is available at the Vue Router website (*https://oreil.ly/AwUZo*), containing information on installation, APIs, and primary use cases for reference.

Since Vue Router is a standalone package from the Vue framework, we need to perform additional steps to have it installed and ready to use in our application, which we will discuss next.

Installing Vue Router

The most straightforward way to install Vue Router for a new Vue project using Vite is to choose Yes when being asked to install Vue Router during the setup (see "Create a New Vue Application" on page 9). Vite then will take care of installing the Vue Router package and scaffold your project with related files and folders (Figure 8-2), as in the following structure:

- The router folder with one file, index.ts, containing the routes configurations for the app.
- The views folder has two sample Vue components, AboutView and HomeView. Each component is the view for the related URL paths, which we will discuss shortly.

```
src
  assets
  components
  router
    index.ts
  views
    AboutView.vue
    HomeView.vue
  App.vue
main.ts
```

Figure 8-2. Project structure after scaffolding with Vite with Vue Router enabled

Vite will also inject some code into the main.ts file to initialize Vue Router. Hence, the created app will enable the primary router enabled and make it ready to use.

However, to fully understand how Vue Router works, we will skip the scaffolding option and add Vue Router to our existing project manually by using the following command:

```
yarn add -D vue-router@4
```

In this book, we use Vue Router 4.1.6, the latest version at the time of writing. You can replace the version number after @ with the latest version from the Vue Router NPM page (*https://oreil.ly/h6Q0V*).

For Vue 3 projects, you should use version 4 and above.

To demonstrate the Vue Router's capabilities, we will build an SPA representing a pizza ordering system. The application header will have the following page links: Home, About, Pizzas, Contact, and Login (see Figure 8-3).

Home   About   Pizzas   Contact   Login
[Main View of Pizza House]

Figure 8-3. Pizza House application with navigation header

Each application link leads to a page represented by a Vue component. For each application page, we create a placeholder component and keep it under the `views` folder. Our Pizza House codebase now contains the following view components:

`HomeView`
Our application's home page contains a welcome message and a list of pizzas.

`AboutView`
The about page, which will contain a short description of the application.

`PizzasView`
Displaying a list of pizzas for ordering.

`ContactView`
Displaying a contact form.

`LoginView`
Displaying the login form for the user.

We need to map these components to the appropriate page links, demonstrated in Table 8-1.

Table 8-1. Table of the available routes with their corresponding components and page URLs in Pizza House

Page link	Component	Route path pattern
https://localhost:4000	HomeView	`/`
https://localhost:4000/about	AboutView	`/about`
https://localhost:4000/pizzas	PizzasView	`/pizzas`
https://localhost:4000/contact	Contact	`/contact`
https://localhost:4000/login	LoginView	`/login`

Table 8-1 also shows the corresponding route patterns for each page link. We will use these patterns to define the routes in our application.

The port `4000` for `localhost` is the local port number for the development server by Vite. It can change depending on your Vite configuration and the available ports when you run your project locally.

Defining Routes

A route is a path pattern in response to a page URL. We define a route in Vue Router based on a configuration object using the interface `RouteRecordRaw`. This configuration object contains the following properties described in Table 8-2.

Table 8-2. Properties for a route configuration object

Property	Type	Description	Required?
`path`	`string`	The pattern to check against the browser's location (browser URL)	Yes
`component`	`Component`	The component to render when the browser's location matches the route's path pattern	No
`name`	`string`	The name of the route. We can use it to avoid hard-coded URLs in the code.	No
`components`	`{ [name: string]: Component }`	A collection of components to render based on the matched route's name	No
`redirect`	`string` or `Location` or `Function`	The redirect path	No
`props`	`boolean` or `Object` or `Function`	The props to pass to the component	No
`alias`	`string` or `Array<string>`	The alias path	No
`children`	`Array<RouteConfig>`	The child routes	No

Property	Type	Description	Required?
beforeEnter	Function	The navigation guard callback	No
meta	any	The route's metadata. We can use this for passing additional information not visible on the URL.	No
sensitive	Boolean	Whether the route should be case sensitive. By default, all routes are case insensitive; for example, /pizzas and /Pizzas are the same route.	No
strict	Boolean	Whether we should allow trailing slash (like /about/ or /about)	No

We often don't use all the available fields to define a route. For instance, take the default application path (/). It's sufficient to define the following home route object with the path property set to / and the component property set to HomeView:

```
/**router/index.ts */
//import the required component modules

const homeRoute = {
  path: '/',
  name: 'home',
  component: HomeView
}
```

Vue Router in the previous code maps the default entry URL (such as *https://local-host:4000*) to the / case unless strict mode is enabled. If there is no indicator after the slash /, Vue Router will render the HomeView component as the default view. This behavior applies in both cases: when a user visits *https://localhost:4000*, or *https://localhost:4000/*.

Now we can proceed to configure our app's routes as an array of RouteRecordRaw configuration objects in the index.ts file under the router folder, as in the following code:

```
/**router/index.ts */
import { type RouteRecordRaw } from "vue-router";
//import the required component modules

const routes:RouteRecordRaw[]  = [
  {
    path: '/',
    name: 'home',
    component: HomeView
  },
  {
    path: '/about',
    name: 'about',
    component: AboutView
  },
  {
    path: '/pizzas',
    name: 'pizzas',
```

```
    component: PizzasView
  },
  {
    path: '/contact',
    name: 'contact',
    component: ContactView
  },
  {
    path: '/login',
    name: 'login',
    component: LoginView
  }
]
```

Using Named Routes

This chapter uses the named route with the name property. I recommend using this approach in your application, making the code more readable and maintainable.

That's straightforward enough. We have defined the necessary routes for our Pizza House. But we need more than this for our route system to work. We must create a router instance from the given routes and plug it into our Vue application on initialization. We will do this next.

Creating a Router Instance

We can create the router instance using the createRouter method from the vue-router package. This method takes a configuration object of type RouterOptions as an argument, with the following main properties:

history
> The history mode object can be hash-based or web-based (HTML history mode). The web-based method utilizes the HTML5 history API to make the URL readable, allowing us to navigate without reloading the page.

routes
> The array of routes to use in the router instance.

linkActiveClass
> The class name for the active link. By default, it is router-link-active.

linkExactActiveClass
> The class name for the active link. By default, it is router-link-exact-active.

Other less common properties for the `RouterOptions` interface are available at the RouterOptions documentation (*https://oreil.ly/ pcSqw*).

We use the `createWebHistory` method from the `vue-route` package to create a web-based `history` object. This method takes a string that represents the base URL as its optional argument:

```
/**router/index.ts */
import {
  createRouter,
  createWebHistory,
  type RouteRecordRaw
} from 'vue-router';

const routes: RouteRecordRaw[] = [/**... */]

export const router = createRouter({
  history: createWebHistory("https://your-domain-name"),
  routes
})
```

However, passing the base URL as a static string is not a good practice. We want to keep the base URL configurable and isolated for different environments like development and production. For this purpose, Vite exposes the environment object `import.meta.env`, which contains a `BASE_URL` property. You can set the value for `BASE_URL` in a dedicated environment file, often denoted by the `.env` prefix, or through the command line when running the Vite server. Vite then extracts the relevant value for `BASE_URL` and injects it into the `import.meta.env` object, and we can use it in our code, as follows:

```
/**router/index.ts */
import {
  createRouter,
  createWebHistory,
  type RouteRecordRaw
} from 'vue-router';

const routes: RouteRecordRaw[] = [/**... */]

export const router = createRouter({
  history: createWebHistory(import.meta.env.BASE_URL),
  routes
})
```

Using BASE_URL from the Environment File

You don't have to set the BASE_URL value in the .env file for development. Vite will map it to the local server URL automatically.

Most modern hosting platforms, such as Netlify, will set the BASE_URL value for you during deployment, often to your application's domain name.

We have created the router instance from the given `routes` and the desired `history` mode. Our next step is to plug this instance into our Vue application.

Plugging the Router Instance Into the Vue Application

In the `main.ts` file where we initialize the application instance `app`, we will import the created `router` instance and pass it as the argument to the `app.use()` method:

```
/**main.ts */
import { createApp } from 'vue'
import App from './App.vue'
import { router } from './router'

const app = createApp(App)

app.use(router)

app.mount('#app')
```

Our application now has a routing system for the navigation between pages. However, if you run the application now, you will see that the `AboutView` component is still not rendered when navigating to the `/about` path. We must modify our `App.vue` component to display the suitable component that binds to the route's path in its configurations. Let's do that next.

Rendering the Current Page with the RouterView Component

To dynamically generate the desired view for a particular URL path, Vue Router provides `RouterView` (or `router-view`) as the placeholder component. During running, Vue Router will replace it with the element that matches the current URL pattern based on the configuration provided. We can use this component in our `App.vue` component to render the current page:

```
/**App.vue */
<script setup lang="ts">
import { RouterView } from 'vue-router'
</script>
<template>
  <RouterView />
</template>
```

When running the application, the default home page is now the `HomeView` (Figure 8-4). When navigating to `/about` using the browser's location bar, you will see that the `AboutView` component is rendered (Figure 8-5).

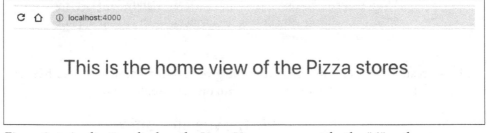

Figure 8-4. Application displays the HomeView component for the "/" path

Figure 8-5. Application displays the AboutView component for the "/about" path

Since `RouterView` is a Vue component, we can pass props, attributes, and event listeners to it. `RouterView` will then pass them to the rendered view to handle. For instance, we can add a class using the `RouterView`:

```
/**App.vue */
<template>
  <RouterView class="view" />
</template>
```

The rendered component—`AboutView`, for example—will then receive the `class` as the primary container element (see Figure 8-6), and we can use it for CSS styling accordingly.

```
▼<div id="app" data-v-app> grid
    <h1 data-v-7a7a37b1 class="view">About this Pizza store</h1>
  </div>
```

Figure 8-6. `AboutView` receives the `class` attribute from the `RouterView` component

At this point, we have seen how to set up the routes for our application and render the current page using the RouterView component. However, navigating by manually setting the URL path on the browser's address bar does not seem to be very convenient for users. To enhance the user experience for our app, we can compose a header with navigation links using the a element and the full path. Or we can use the built-in RouterLink component to build the links to our routes, which we will discuss next.

Build a Navigation Bar with the RouterLink Component

Vue Router provides the RouterLink (or router-link) component to generate an interactive and navigable element from a set of given props, such as to, for a specific route's path. The route path can be a string that has the same value as path in the route configuration, as in the following example for the link to navigate to the about page:

```
<router-link to="/about">About</router-link>
```

Alternatively, we can pass an object representing the route's location object, including the name and the params for the route parameters:

```
<router-link :to="{ name: 'about' }">About</router-link>
```

By default, this component renders an anchor element (a) with an href and classes for the active link, such as router-link-active and router-link-exact-active. We can change the default element to any other element using the Boolean custom prop and v-slot, usually another interactive element such as button, as in the following example:

```
<router-link custom to="/about" v-slot="{ navigate }" >
  <button @click="navigate">About</button>
</router-link>
```

This code will render a button element instead of the default a element, binding with the navigate function to navigate the given route when clicking.

Using custom Prop

If you use the custom prop, you must bind the navigate function as a click handler or the href link to the custom element. Otherwise, the navigation will not work.

Also, no class names such as router-link-active or router-link-exact-active will be added to the custom element when in action.

Let's build our navigation bar, NavBar, using RouterLink as shown in Example 8-1.

Example 8-1. NavBar component

```
/**NavBar.vue */

<template>
  <nav>
    <router-link :to="{ name: 'home' }">Home</router-link>
    <router-link :to="{ name: 'about' }">About</router-link>
    <router-link :to="{ name: 'pizzas' }">Pizzas</router-link>
    <router-link :to="{ name: 'contact' }">Contact</router-link>
    <router-link :to="{ name: 'login' }">Login</router-link>
  </nav>
</template>
```

We also add some CSS styles to the navigation bar and the active link:

```
/**NavBar.vue */

<style scoped>
nav {
  display: flex;
  gap: 30px;
  justify-content: center;
}

.router-link-active, .router-link-exact-active {
  text-decoration: underline;
}
</style>
```

Using activeClass and exactActiveClass Props

You can use the activeClass and exactActiveClass props of RouterLink to customize the class names for the active link instead of using the default ones.

Once we add NavBar to the App component, we will see the navigation bar at the top of the page (Figure 8-7).

| Home | About | Pizzas | Contact | Login |

This is the home view of the Pizza stores

Figure 8-7. Navigation bar of the application

Now our users can navigate between pages using the navigation bar. However, we still need to handle the data flow between the pages. In the upcoming sections, we will see how to pass data between routes with route parameters.

Passing Data Between Routes

To pass data between routes, we can use the `query` field in the router object passed to `to`:

```
<router-link :to="{ name: 'pizzas', query: { id: 1 } }">Pizza 1</router-link>
```

The `query` field is an object that contains the query parameters we want to pass to the route. Vue Router will translate it into a complete `href` path with query parameters, starting with ? syntax:

```
<a href="/pizzas?id=1">Pizza 1</a>
```

We can then access the query parameters in the route component, `PizzasView`, using the `useRoute()` function:

```
<template>
  <div>
    <h1>Pizzas</h1>
    <p v-if="pizzaId">Pizza ID: {{ pizzaId }}</p>
  </div>
</template>
<script lang="ts" setup>
import { useRoute } from "vue-router";

const route = useRoute();
const pizzaId = route.query?.id;
</script>
```

This code will render the following page, where the browser's URL is *http://localhost: 4000/pizzas?id=1* (Figure 8-8).

Figure 8-8. Pizzas page with the query parameter

You can also pass the query parameters in the browser's address bar, and the router instance will decouple it from the route.query object accordingly. This mechanism is handy in many scenarios. Take our PizzasView page, for instance. This page displays a list of pizzas taken from a usePizzas hook, using the PizzaCard component as shown in Example 8-2.

Example 8-2. PizzasView component

```
<template>
  <div class="pizzas-view--container">
    <h1>Pizzas</h1>
    <ul>
      <li v-for="pizza in searchResults" :key="pizza.id">
        <PizzaCard :pizza="pizza" />
      </li>
    </ul>
  </div>
</template>
<script lang="ts" setup>
import PizzaCard from "@/components/PizzaCard.vue";
import { usePizzas } from "@/composables/usePizzas";

const { pizzas } = usePizzas();
</script>
```

Now we want to add a search feature, where the user can search for a pizza by its title using a query params search and get the filtered list of pizzas. We can add a use Search hook, which receives the value of route.query.search as its initial value and returns the filtered list of pizzas as well as the reactive search value, as shown in Example 8-3.

Example 8-3. Implementing useSearch hook

```
import { computed, ref, type Ref } from "vue";

type UseSearchProps = {
  items: Ref<any[]>;
  filter?: string;
  defaultSearch?: string;
};

export const useSearch = ({
  items,
  filter = "title",
  defaultSearch = "",
}: UseSearchProps) => {
  const search = ref(defaultSearch);
  const searchResults = computed(() => {
    const searchTerm = search.value.toLowerCase();

    if (searchTerm === "") {
```

```
      return items.value;
    }

    return items.value.filter((item) => {
      const itemValue = item[filter]?.toLowerCase()
        return itemValue.includes(searchTerm);
      });
  });

  return { search, searchResults };
};
```

Then we use the useSearch hook in the PizzasView component and change the iteration to be over searchResults instead of pizzas:

```
<template>
  <!--...other code -->
    <li v-for="pizza in searchResults" :key="pizza.id">
      <PizzaCard :pizza="pizza" />
    </li>
  <!--...other code -->
</template>
<script lang="ts" setup>
/**...other imports */
import { useRoute } from "vue-router";
import { useSearch } from "@/composables/useSearch";
import type { Pizza } from "@/types/Pizza";

/**...other code */
const route = useRoute();

type PizzaSearch = {
  search: Ref<string>;
  searchResults: Ref<Pizza[]>;
};

const { search, searchResults }: PizzaSearch = useSearch({
  items: pizzas,
  defaultSearch: route.query?.search as string,
});
</script>
```

Now when you go to /pizzas?search=hawaii, the list will show only the pizza with the title Hawaii (Figure 8-9).

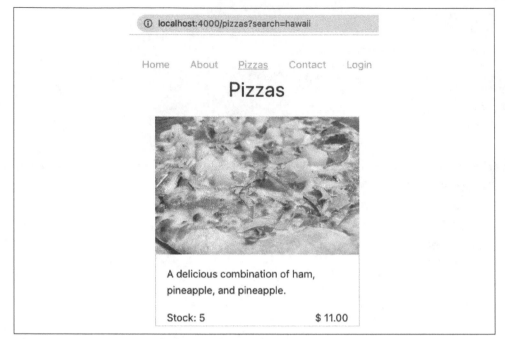

Figure 8-9. Pizzas page with the search term from query parameter

How about allowing the user to search while on the page and then syncing the updated search term with the query parameter? For that, we need to perform the following changes:

- Add an input field to the `template` and bind it to the `search` variable:

```
<template>
  <!--...other code -->
  <input v-model="search" placeholder="Search for a pizza" />
  <!--...other code -->
</template>
```

- Get the `router` instance using the `useRouter()` method:

```
/**...other imports */
import { useRoute, useRouter } from "vue-router";

/**...other code */
const router = useRouter();
```

- Use the `watch` function to watch for changes in the `search` value and update the query parameter using `router.replace`:

```
/**...other imports */
import { watch } from 'vue';
```

```
/**...other code */
watch(search, (value, prevValue) => {
  if (value === prevValue) return;
  router.replace({ query: { search: value } });
});
```

When you type in the search field, the router instance will update the URL with the new query value.

 If you use Vue 2.x and below or Options API (without setup()), you can access the router and route instances using this.$router and this.$route, respectively.

At this point, we have learned how to retrieve the query params with the route instance. Using the route instance in every component that needs to access the query params can be tedious. Instead, we can decouple the query params using props, which we will learn next.

Decoupling Route Parameters Using Props

In the route configuration object, we can define the static props to pass to the view component as an object with static values or a function that returns the props. For example, in the following code, we change our pizzas route configuration to pass the searchTerm prop, whose value is from route.query.search, to the PizzaView component:

```
import {
  type RouteLocationNormalizedLoaded,
  type RouteRecordRaw,
} from "vue-router";

const routes: RouteRecordRaw = [
  /** other routes */
  {
    path: "/pizzas",
    name: "pizzas",
    component: PizzasView,
    props: (route: RouteLocationNormalizedLoaded) => ({
      searchTerm: route.query?.search || "",
    }),
  },
];
```

In the PizzasView component, we can remove the use of useRoute and access the searchTerm prop using the props object:

```
const props = defineProps({
  searchTerm: {
```

```
      type: String,
      required: false,
      default: "",
    },
  });

  const { search, searchResults }: PizzaSearch = useSearch({
    items: pizzas,
    defaultSearch: props.searchTerm,
  });
```

The behavior of the application stays the same as before.

You can also use `props: true` to pass the `route.params` object to the view component as props, without caring about any specific props. When the route changes, we
can combine this approach with navigation guards to perform side effects for the
route's parameters. More about navigation guards in the next section.

Understanding Navigation Guards

Navigation guards are functions to help us control the navigation flow better. We can
also use them to perform side effects when the route changes or before the navigation
happens. There are three types of navigation guards and hooks: global, component-
level, and route-level.

Global Navigation Guards

For every router instance, Vue Router exposes a set of global-level navigation guards,
including:

`router.beforeEach`
> Called *before* every navigation

`router.beforeResolve`
> Called *after* Vue Router has resolved all async components in the route and all in-
> component guards (if any), but *before* confirming the navigation

`router.afterEach`
> Called *after* confirming the navigation and *before* the next update of the DOM
> and the navigation

The global guards help perform validation before navigating to a specific route. For
example, we can use the `router.beforeEach` to check if the user is authenticated
before navigating to the `/pizzas` route. If not, we can redirect the user to the `/login`
page:

```
const user = {
  isAuthenticated: false,
};
```

```
router.beforeEach((to, from, next) => {
  if (to.name === "pizzas" && !user.isAuthenticated) {
    next({ name: "login" });
  } else {
    next();
  }
});
```

In this code, to is the destination route object to navigate to, from is the current route object, and next is a function to call to resolve the hook/guard. We need to trigger next() at the end, either without any argument to continue to the original destination or with a new route object as its argument to redirect the user to a different route. Otherwise, Vue Router will block the navigation flow.

 Alternatively, we can use the router.beforeResolve to perform the same validation. The critical difference between router.beforeEach and router.beforeResolve is that Vue Router triggers the latter after resolving all in-component guards. However, invoking the callback after settling everything will be less valuable when you want to avoid loading the suitable async component before confirming the navigation.

How about the router.afterEach? We can use this hook to perform actions like saving some page's data as cache, tracking page analytics, or authenticating our user when navigating away from the login page:

```
router.afterEach((to, from) => {
  if (to.name === "login") {
    user.isAuthenticated = true;
  }
});
```

While the global guards help perform side effects and control the redirecting of the whole application, in some cases we only want to achieve side effects for a specific route. In this case, using route-level guards is a good option.

Route-Level Navigation Guards

For every route, we can define a callback for the beforeEnter guard, which Vue Router triggers when entering a path from a different one. Take our /pizzas route, for instance. Instead of mapping the props field with a function, we can achieve mapping the search query as a prop to the view by manually setting the to.params.searchTerm field to to.query.search before entering the route:

```
const routes: RouteRecordRaw = [
  /** other routes */
  {
    path: "/pizzas",
    name: "pizzas",
```

```
    component: PizzasView,
    props: true,
    beforeEnter: async (to, from, next) => {
      to.params.searchTerm = (to.query.search || "") as string;

      next()
    },
  },
];
```

Note that we have set `props: true` in the pizzas route. The UI will still display the same list of pizzas as before (Figure 8-10).

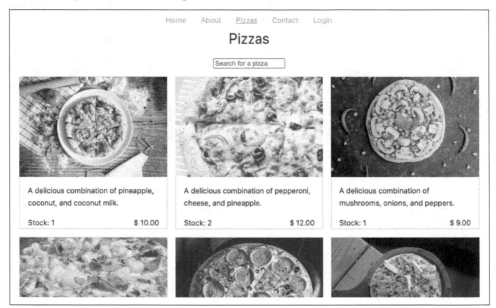

Figure 8-10. Pizzas list

We can manually modify the `to.query.searchTerm` within this guard. However, the changes won't reflect on the URL path in the browser's address bar. If we want to update the URL path, we can use the `next` function to redirect the user to a new route object with the desired query parameters.

Passing an Array of Callbacks to beforeEnter

`beforeEnter` also accepts an array of callbacks, which Vue Router triggers in sequence. Hence we can perform multiple side effects for a specific route before entering it.

Like other global guards, the beforeEnter guard is handy when you want to perform authentication to specific routes, additional modification to the route parameters before passing them to the view component, etc. Next, we will learn how to leverage the component-level guards to perform side effects for a specific view.

Component-Level Router Guards

From Vue 3.x on, Vue Router also provides composable guards at the component level to help control the flow of route leaving and updating, as onBeforeRouteLeave and onBeforeRouteUpdate. While Vue Router triggers onBeforeRouteLeave when the user navigates away from the current path view, it invokes onBeforeRouteUpdate when the user navigates to the same path view but with different parameters.

We can use onBeforeRouteLeave to display a message to confirm the user's navigation away from the Contact page with the following code:

```
import { onBeforeRouteLeave } from "vue-router";

onBeforeRouteLeave((to, from, next) => {
  const answer = window.confirm("Are you sure you want to leave?");

  next(!!answer);
});
```

Now when you are on the Contact page and try to navigate to another page, you will see a confirmation popup asking you to confirm your navigation, as in Figure 8-11. Clicking on the Cancel button will prevent navigation, and clicking the OK button will continue the navigation.

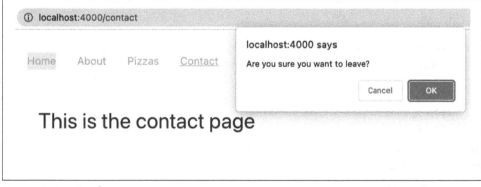

Figure 8-11. Confirmation popup

If you use Options API for your components, beforeRouteLeave and beforeRouteUpdate guards would be available on the options object to achieve the same functionality.

There is also a beforeRouteEnter hook, which the router triggers before Vue initialize the view component. This guard is similar to the setup() hook; hence, Vue Router's API has no equivalent composable.

We have explored the available navigation guards in different levels of a routing system and their order of execution, shown in Figure 8-12.

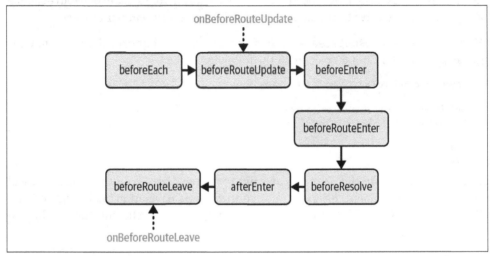

Figure 8-12. Order of triggering navigation guards and their equivalent composable

Understanding the navigation flow and the order of execution of the guards is crucial to building a robust routing system. Next, we will learn how to create nested routes for our application.

Creating Nesting Routes

At this point, we have built a basic one-level routing system for our application. In reality, most routing systems are more complex. Sometimes, we want to create subpages for a specific page, such as a Frequently Asked Questions (FAQs) page, and a Form page for the Contact page:

```
/contact/faq
/contact/form
```

The default UI for the /contact page will be the ContactView page, and the user can navigate to the Form page by clicking on a link presented on this page. In this case, we need to create nested routes for the /contact page using the children field of the route configuration object.

First create the ContactFaqView and ContactFormView components, so the router can render them when matched, and then modify our /contact route:

```
const routes = [
  /**...other routes */
  {
    path: "/contact",
    name: "contact",
    component: ContactView,
    children: [
      {
        path: "faq",
        name: "contact-faq",
        component: ContactFaqView,
      },
      {
        path: "form",
        name: "contact-form",
        component: ContactFormView,
      },
    ],
  },
];
```

We must also stub the placeholder component RouterView inside the ContactView to render the nested routes. As an example, let's add the following code to the Contact View:

```
<template>
  <div class="contact-view--container">
    <h1>This is the contact page</h1>
    <nav>
      <router-link to="/contact/faq">FAQs</router-link>
      <router-link to="/contact/form">Contact Us</router-link>
    </nav>
    <router-view />
  </div>
</template>
```

Now this Contact component will render ContactFaqView when the user navigates to *http://localhost:4000/contact/faq* (Figure 8-13) and ContactFormView when the user navigates to *http://localhost:4000/contact/form*, respectively.

Figure 8-13. Example output when navigating to http://localhost:4000/contact/faq

This approach proves beneficial when we want to create a specific UI layout for a page containing nested views with nested routes.

We have seen how to create a nested route within a parent layout. However, in some cases we want to make a nested way without a parent layout, so we must declare the default path for the parent's route as its nested route object. For example, instead of claiming the parent /contact route's name and component, we can move it to the nested path with an empty path pattern:

```
const routes = [
  /**...other routes */
  {
    path: "/contact",
    children: [
      /**... other children */,
      {
        path: "",
        name: "contact",
        component: ContactView,
      }
    ],
  },
];
```

This way, when the user navigates to *http://localhost:4000/contact/faq*, only the ContactFaqView component will be rendered as a separate page, without the content of the ContactView (Figure 8-14).

```
          ⓘ  localhost:4000/contact/faq


                                    Home    About    Pizzas    Contact    Login

          Frequent Asked Questions
```

Figure 8-14. Example output when navigating to http://localhost:4000/contact/faq

> As you can see in the screenshot, the Contact link is still active in the navigation bar. This behavior happens because the link element of the Contact page still has the class `router-link-active`, but not `router-link-exact-active`. We can fix this styling issue by defining CSS rules for only the exact active link instead.

Using nested routes is very common in real-world applications; in fact, our `routes` array is already nested children for the router instance of the application. Declaring nested routes is a great way to organize routing structure and create dynamic routes, which we will explore next.

Creating Dynamic Routes

One of the most beneficial features of Vue Router is the ability to set up dynamic routes with routing parameters (routing params), which are variables extracted from a URL path. Routing params come in handy when we have a dynamic data-driven route structure. Each route shares a typical pattern and differs only by a unique identifier, such as a user or product id.

Let's revise our routes for the Pizza House and add a dynamic path for displaying one pizza at a time. One option is to define a new route, `/pizza`, and pass the pizza's id as its query parameter as `/pizza?id=my-pizza-id` as we learned in "Passing Data Between Routes" on page 199. The better option, however, is to modify the `/pizzas` route and add a new nested route to it with the path pattern `:id`, as follows:

```
const routes = [
  /**...other routes */
  {
    path: "/pizzas",
    /**...other configurations */
```

```
        children: [{
            path: ':id',
            name: 'pizza',
            component: PizzaView,
        }, {
            path: '',
            name: 'pizzas',
            component: PizzasView,
        }]
        },
    ]
```

By using :id, Vue Router will match any path that has a similar format, like *pizzas/1234-pizza-id*, and save the extracted id (like 1234-pizza-id) as the route.par
ams.id field.

Since we learned about the props field in the route configuration object, we can set its value to true, enabling the automatic mapping of route parameters to the Pizza View's props:

```
const routes = [
  /**...other routes */
  {
    path: "/pizzas",
    /**...other configurations */
    children: [{
        path: ':id',
        name: 'pizza',
        component: PizzaView,
        props: true,
    },
    /**...other nested routes */
    ],
  },
]
```

In the bound PizzaView component, we declare id as the component's props with defineProps() and retrieve the pizza's details from the pizzas array using the use Route hook and this id prop:

```
import { usePizzas } from "@/composables/usePizzas";

const props = defineProps({
  id: {
    type: String,
    required: true,
  },
});

const { pizzas } = usePizzas();

const pizza = pizzas.value.find((pizza) => pizza.id === props.id);
```

We can display the details of pizza in the PizzaView component as follows:

```
<template>
  <section v-if="pizza" class="pizza--container">
    <img :src="pizza.image" :alt="pizza.title" width="500" />
    <div class="pizza--details">
      <h1>{{ pizza.title }}</h1>
      <div>
        <p>{{ pizza.description }}</p>
        <div class="pizza-stock--section">
          <span>Stock: {{ pizza.quantity || 0 }}</span>
          <span>Price: ${{ pizza.price }}</span>
        </div>
      </div>
    </div>
  </section>
  <p v-else>No pizza found</p>
</template>
```

Now when you navigate to **/pizzas/1**, with 1 as the id of an existing pizza in the list, the PizzaView component will display the pizza's details, as shown in Figure 8-15.

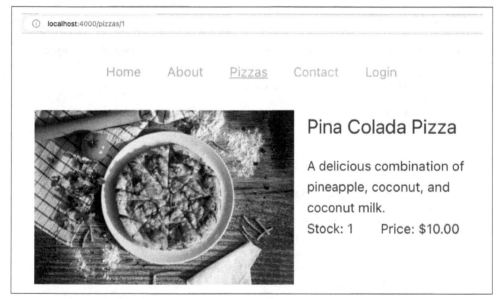

Figure 8-15. Pizza details page

Fetching Data from the Server

Ideally, you should avoid fetching data again from the server, such as pizzas in the PizzaView component. Instead, you should use data store management such as Pinia (Chapter 9) to store fetched pizzas and retrieve them from the store whenever needed.

Thus far, we have explored how to create nested and dynamic routes and decoupled the route's parameters into props. In the next section, we will learn how to implement custom back and forward buttons for our application with Vue Router.

Going Back and Forward with the Router Instance

Implementing a custom back button is a common feature in web applications in addition to using the native browser's back button. We can use the `router.back()` method to navigate to the previous page in the history stack, where `router` is the app's router instance received from `useRouter()`:

```ts
<template>
  <button @click="router.back()">Back</button>
</template>
<script setup lang="ts">
import { useRouter } from "vue-router";

const router = useRouter();
</script>
```

To move forward in the history stack, we can use the `router.forward()` method:

```ts
<template>
  <button @click="router.forward()">Forward</button>
</template>
<script setup lang="ts">
import { useRouter } from "vue-router";

const router = useRouter();
</script>
```

Using router.go() To Navigate to a Specific Page in the History Stack

You can also use the `router.go()` method, which accepts an argument as the number of steps in the history stack to go back or forward. For instance, `router.go(-2)` will navigate to the page two steps back, while `router.go(2)` will jump two steps forward (if they exist).

We have explored the basics of Vue Router and created a basic routing system for our application with all the pages we need. But there is one thing we need to handle: if you try to navigate a path that doesn't exist, you will see a blank page. This scenario happens because Vue Router can't find a matched component to render when the user tries to navigate to a path that doesn't exist. This will be our next topic.

Handling Unknown Routes

In most scenarios, we can't control all the paths users will try to navigate while using our application. For instance, a user may attempt to access *https://localhost:4000/pineapples,* for which we haven't defined a route. We can display a 404 page to the user in such cases by using the regular expressions (regex) pattern /:pathMatch(.) as path in a new error route:

```
/**router/index.ts */

const routes = [
  /**... */
  {
    path: '/:pathMatch(.*)*',
    name: 'error',
    component: ErrorView
  }
]
```

Vue Router will match the unfound paths against the pattern /:pathMatch(.) accordingly and then store the matched path value in the pathMatch parameter of the route location object.

Using Regex to Match Unknown Paths

You can replace pathMatch with any other name you want. Its purpose is to let Vue Router knows where to store the matched path value.

In the ErrorView component, we can display a message to the user:

```
<!--ErrorView.vue -->

<template>
  <h1>404 - Page not found</h1>
</template>
```

Now when we try to visit *https://localhost:4000/pineapples* or any unknown path, we will see the 404 page rendered.

Furthermore, we can use the useRoute() method of the vue-router package to access the current route location and display its path's value:

```
<!--ErrorView.vue -->

<template>
  <h1>404 - Page not found</h1>
  <p>Path: {{ route.path }}</p>
</template>
<script lang="ts" setup>
import { useRoute } from 'vue-router'
```

```
const route = useRoute()
</script>
```

This code will display the path of the current route, which is, in this case, /pineap ples (Figure 8-16).

Figure 8-16. The 404 page

Alternatively, we can use the redirect property in the route configuration to redirect users to a specific route, such as the home page, when they visit an unknown path. For example, we can rewrite our error route as:

```
/**router/index.ts */

const routes = [
  /**... */
  {
    path: '/:pathMatch(.*)*',
    redirect: { name: 'home' }
  }
]
```

When we visit an unknown path, the router instance will automatically redirect us to the home page, and we no longer need an ErrorView component.

Summary

In this chapter, we have explored how we can build a routing system for our Vue application using different APIs provided by Vue Router in our application.

Moving between routes requires the data flow to be consistent, like handling data flow between components that aren't in a direct parent-children relationship. To solve this challenge, we need an efficient data management system for our application. The next chapter introduces Pinia, the official data management library for Vue, and how we can build an efficient, reusable data management system using Pinia APIs.

CHAPTER 9

State Management with Pinia

The previous chapter guided us through building our application's routings using Vue Router, including nested routes, route guards, and dynamic route navigation.

In this chapter, we will learn state management and how to manage the data flow within our Vue application using Pinia, the officially recommended state management library for Vue. We will also explore how to build our application's reusable and efficient data state management system.

Understanding State Management in Vue

Data makes an application come to life and connects components. And components interact with users and with others using data states. State management is crucial for building an application that works with actual data, regardless of size and complexity. For example, we can display only a gallery of product cards with a list of pizzas and their details. Once a user adds a product to the cart within this gallery component, we need to update the cart's data and display the updated cart's data in the cart component at the same time as updating the chosen product's remaining stock.

Take our Pizza House application, for example. In the main view (`App.vue`), we have a header component (`HeaderView`) and a gallery of pizza cards (`PizzasView`). The header contains a cart icon that displays the number of items in the cart, while the gallery includes a list of pizza cards, each with a button allowing the user to add the selected item to the cart. Figure 9-1 illustrates the hierarchical structure of the components from the main view.

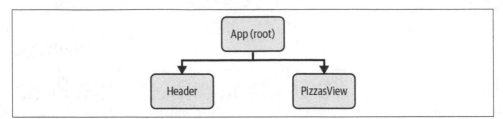

Figure 9-1. Hierarchy structure of the components from the main view of Pizza House

When a user adds a pizza to the cart, the cart icon will display the updated number of items. To enable data communication between the header component and the gallery component, we can have the `App` manage the `cart` data and pass its data to the header as props while communicating with the gallery using an event `updateCart`, as seen in Figure 9-2.

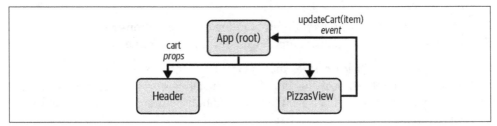

Figure 9-2. Data flow between the gallery and header with the App as the middleman

This approach works well for small applications. However, suppose we want to split `PizzasView` into subcomponents, such as `PizzasGallery`, and have `PizzasGallery` render the `PizzaCard` component for each pizza. For each new parent-child layer, we will need to propagate the `updateCart` event to ensure the propagation of the data flow between the gallery and the header, as in Figure 9-3.

It will become more complicated when we have more components and layers, leaving a lot of unnecessary props and events. As a result, this approach could be less scalable and maintainable when our application grows.

To reduce this overhead and manage the state flows within the application, we need a global state management system, a centralized place to store and manage the data states of the application. This system is responsible for managing the data states and distributing the data to the necessary components.

One of the most popular approaches to provide developers with a smooth experience is using a state management library, such as Pinia.

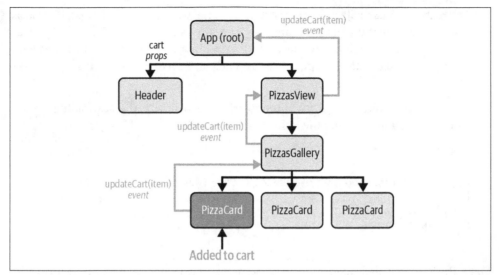

Figure 9-3. Data flow between the gallery with children and header, with the App as the middleman

Understanding Pinia

Inspired by Vuex[1] and Vue Composition API, Pinia is Vue's current official state management library. Nevertheless, you can always use other state management JavaScript libraries that support Vue, such as Vuex, MobX and XState.

Pinia follows the store pattern of Vuex but with a more flexible and scalable approach.

> The official Pinia documentation is available at the Pinia website (*https://oreil.ly/JoOwm*), with information on installation, APIs, and primary use cases for reference.

Instead of having a single system for all data sets used across the application, with Pinia, we can split each data set into its state module (or store). We then can access relevant data in a store from any component using a custom composable, following the Composition API pattern.

---

1 Vuex was previously the official state management for Vue applications.

When creating a Vue project from scratch using Vite, we can choose to install Pinia as the state management during the scaffolding process (see "Create a New Vue Application" on page 9). Vite will create our project with Pinia installed and configured with an example `counter` store, exposed as `useCounterStore`, located in `src/stores/counter.ts`.

However, to fully understand how Pinia works, we will skip the scaffolding option and add Pinia manually using the following command:

```
yarn add pinia
```

 In this book, we use Pinia 2.1.3, the latest version at the time of writing. You can replace the version number after @ with the newest version from the Pinia NPM page (*https://oreil.ly/zCUCg*).

Once Pinia is installed, navigate to `src/main.ts` and import `createPinia` from the `pinia` package, use it to create a new Pinia instance, and plug it into the application:

```
import { createApp } from 'vue'
import { createPinia } from 'pinia'  ❶

import App from './App.vue'
import router from './router'

const app = createApp(App)
const pinia = createPinia()  ❷

app.use(pinia)  ❸

app.mount('#app')
```

❶ Import `createPinia` from the `pinia` package

❷ Create a new Pinia instance

❸ Plug the Pinia instance into the application for use

With Pinia installed and plugged in, we will create the first store for our application: a `pizzas` store to manage the available pizzas for the application.

Creating a Pizzas Store for Pizza House

As Pinia follows the store pattern of Vuex, a store in Pinia contains the following fundamental properties:

State

The reactive data (state) of the store, created by using `ref()` or `reactive()` methods from Composition API.

Getters

The computed and read-only properties of the store, created by using the `computed()` method.

Actions

The methods to update the store's state or perform custom logic on the store's data (state).

Pinia provides a `defineStore` function to create a new store, which accepts two arguments: the store's name and properties, and the methods available for use in other components. The store's properties and methods can be an object with the key fields `state`, `getters`, `actions` following Options API (Example 9-1), or a function that uses Composable API and return an object with the fields to expose (Example 9-2).

Example 9-1. Defining a store using an object configuration

```
import { defineStore } from 'pinia'

export const useStore = defineStore('storeName', () => {
    return {
        state: () => ({
            // state properties
            myData: { /**... */}
        }),
        getters: {
            // getters properties
            computedData: () => { /**... */ }
        },
        actions: {
            // actions methods
            myAction(){ /**... */ }
        }
    }
})
```

Example 9-2. Defining a store using a function

```
import { defineStore } from 'pinia'
import { reactive, computed } from 'vue'

export const useStore = defineStore('storeName', () => {
    //state properties
    const myData = reactive({ /**... */ })

    // getters properties
    const computedData = computed(() => { /**... */})
```

```
    // actions methods
    const myAction = () => { /**... */ }

    return {
        myData,
        computedData,
        myAction
    }
})
```

 This chapter will focus on using Pinia stores with Vue 3.x Composition API, usually known as *setup stores*.

Let's go back to our `pizzas` store. We add a new file, `src/stores/pizzas.ts`, with the code shown in Example 9-3.

Example 9-3. Pizzas store

```
/** src/stores/pizzas.ts */
import { defineStore } from 'pinia'
import type { Pizza } from '../types/Pizza';
import { ref } from 'vue'

export const usePizzasStore = defineStore('pizzas', () => { ❶
    const pizzas = ref<Pizza[]>([]); ❷

    const fetchPizzas = async () => { ❸
        const response = await fetch(
            'http://exploringvue.com/.netlify/functions/pizzas'
        );
        const data = await response.json();
        pizzas.value = data;
    }

    return {
        pizzas,
        fetchPizzas
    }
})
```

Then in `PizzasView` (based on the previous chapter's Example 8-2 component), we will use the `pizzas` and `fetchPizzas` properties from the `pizzas` store to fetch and display the list of pizzas from our API as in Example 9-4.

Example 9-4. `PizzasView` component using the pizzas store

```
<template>
  <div class="pizzas-view--container">
```

```
    <h1>Pizzas</h1>
    <ul>
      <li v-for="pizza in pizzasStore.pizzas" :key="pizza.id"> ❶
        <PizzaCard :pizza="pizza" />
      </li>
    </ul>
  </div>
</template>
<script lang="ts" setup>
/**.... */
import { watch, type Ref } from "vue";
import { usePizzasStore } from "@/stores/pizzas";

//...
const pizzasStore = usePizzasStore(); ❷

pizzasStore.fetchPizzas(); ❸
</script>
```

❶ Render the list of pizzas using `pizzasStore.pizzas`.

❷ Import the `usePizzasStore` function from the `pizzas` store and use it to get the `pizzasStore` instance.

❸ Fetch the pizzas from the API when the component is mounted asynchronously.

With the previous code, our `PizzasView` component is now using the `pizzas` store to fetch and display the list of pizzas from our API (Figure 9-4).

Figure 9-4. `PizzasView` component using the pizzas store

Great. Nevertheless, notice that we no longer have the search functionality, which uses the `useSearch()` composable from the previous chapter's Example 8-3. If we pass `pizzasStore.pizzas` directly to the `useSearch()` composable as `items`, it will lose the reactivity, and `searchResults` won't get recalculated after `pizzasStore.fetchPizzas()` resolves. To fix this issue, we use `storeToRefs()` from `pinia` to extract `pizzas` from the `pizzasStore` and keep its reactivity when passing to `useSearch()` (Example 9-5).

Example 9-5. `useSearch()` composable working with pizzas store

```
/** src/views/PizzasView.vue */
import { useSearch } from '@/composables/useSearch';
import { storeToRefs } from 'pinia';

//...
const pizzasStore = usePizzasStore();
const { pizzas } = storeToRefs(pizzasStore);
const { search, searchResults }: PizzaSearch = useSearch({
  items: pizzas,
  defaultSearch: props.searchTerm,
});

//...
```

Now our template uses the `searchResults` instead of `pizzasStore.pizzas` and we can bring the search input field back (Example 9-6).

Example 9-6. `PizzasView` component with a search using the pizzas store

```
<template>
  <div class="pizzas-view--container">
    <h1>Pizzas</h1>
    <input v-model="search" placeholder="Search for a pizza" />
    <ul>
      <li v-for="pizza in searchResults" :key="pizza.id">
        <PizzaCard :pizza="pizza" />
      </li>
    </ul>
  </div>
</template>
```

Next, we will create a cart store to manage the current user's cart data, including the list of items added.

Creating a Cart Store for Pizza House

To create our `cart` store, we define our `cart` store with the following properties:

- A list of `items` added to the cart; each item contains the `id` and `quantity` of the pizza
- The `total` items of the cart
- An `add` method to add an item from the cart

To create our `cart` store, we add a new file, `src/stores/cart.ts`, with the code shown in Example 9-7.

Example 9-7. Cart store

```
import { defineStore } from 'pinia'

type CartItem = { ❶
    id: string;
    quantity: number;
}

export const useCartStore = defineStore('cart', () => {
    const items = reactive<CartItem[]>([]); ❷
    const total = computed(() => { ❸
        return items.reduce((acc, item) => {
            return acc + item.quantity
        }, 0)
    })

    const add = (item: CartItem) => { ❹
        const index = items.findIndex(i => i.id === item.id)
        if (index > -1) {
            items[index].quantity += item.quantity
        } else {
            items.push(item)
        }
    }

    return {
        items,
        total,
        add
    }
})
```

❶ Define the type of the cart item

❷ Initialize the `items` state with an empty array

❸ Create a `total` getter to calculate the total items in the cart

❹ Create an `add` action to add an item to the cart. If the item is already in the cart, the quantity will update instead of adding a new item.

With the `cart` store created, we can now use it in our application.

Using the Cart Store in a Component

Let's create a new component, `src/components/Cart.vue`, to display the cart's total items. Within the `<script setup()>` section, we import the `useCartStore()` method and call it to get the `cart` instance. Then in the template, we display the total items in the cart by using the `cart.total` getter, as seen in Example 9-8.

Example 9-8. Cart component

```
<template>
    <div class="cart">
        <span class="cart__total">Cart: {{ cart.total }}</span>
    </div>
</template>
<script setup lang="ts">
import { useCartStore } from '@/stores/cart'

const cart = useCartStore();
</script>
<style scoped>
.cart__total {
    cursor: pointer;
    text-decoration: underline;
}
</style>
```

We then see the cart displayed with the initial value of 0 (Figure 9-5) when we use the `<Cart />` component in our `App.vue` as in the following code:

```
<!-- App.vue -->
<template>
    <header>
        <div>Pizza House</div>
        <Cart />
    </header>
    <RouterView />
</template>
```

| Pizza House | Cart: 0 |

Pizzas

Search for a pizza

Figure 9-5. Cart component displayed in the header of the application

Next, let's enable adding items to the cart from our pizzas gallery for each pizza rendered by `PizzaCard`.

Adding Items to the Cart from the Pizzas Gallery

In `PizzaCard`, we will add a button with the `click` event handler calling the `cart.add()` action to add the pizza to the cart. The `PizzaCard` component will look like Example 9-9.

Example 9-9. `PizzaCard` component

```ts
<template>
  <article class="pizza--details-wrapper">
    <img :src="pizza.image" :alt="pizza.title" height="200" width="300" />
    <p>{{ pizza.description }}</p>
    <div class="pizza--inventory">
      <div class="pizza--inventory-price">$ {{ pizza.price }}</div>
    </div>
    <button class="pizza--add" @click="addToCart">Add to cart</button> ❶
  </article>
</template>
<script setup lang="ts">
import { useCartStore } from "@/stores/cart";
import type { Pizza } from "@/types/Pizza";
import type { PropType } from "vue";

const props = defineProps({
  pizza: {
    type: Object as PropType<Pizza>,
    required: true,
  },
});

const cart = useCartStore(); ❷
const addToCart = () => {
  cart.add({ id: props.pizza.id, quantity: 1 }); ❸
};
</script>
```

❶ Add a button to add the pizza to the cart

❷ Get the `cart` instance from the `useCartStore()` method

❸ Call the `cart.add()` action to add the pizza to the cart within the `addToCart()` method

With the previous code, in the browser, we can add a pizza to the cart by clicking on the "Add to cart" button and see the cart's total items updated (Figure 9-6).

Figure 9-6. *Pizza card with adding option and updated cart total*

We can also use the `cart.items` to detect whether the current pizza is already in the cart, and display its status on the pizza card, as in Example 9-10.

Example 9-10. *PizzaCard component with status*

```
<template>
  <article class="pizza--details-wrapper">
    <!--...-->
    <div class="pizza--inventory">
      <!--...-->
      <span v-if="isInCart">In cart</span> ❶
    </div>
    <button class="pizza--add" @click="addToCart">
        Add to cart
    </button>
  </article>
</template>
<script setup lang="ts">
//...

const isInCart = computed((():boolean => { ❷
  return !!cart.items.find((item) => item.id === props.pizza.id);
});
</script>
```

The "In cart" status is displayed on the pizza card if the pizza is already in the cart (Figure 9-7).

A delicious combination of pineapple, coconut, and coconut milk.

$ 10.00   In cart

Add to cart

A delicious combination of pepperoni, cheese, and pineapple.

$ 12.00

Add to cart

Figure 9-7. Pizza card with status

We have successfully created a cart store and used it in our Pizza House. The Cart and the PizzaCard component now synchronize and communicate through the cart store.

At this point, the Cart component currently displays only the total items in the cart, which, most of the time, is not enough for users to understand what they have added. In the next section, we will improve this experience by displaying the cart items when users click on the cart.

Displaying Cart Items with Actions

In Cart.vue, we will add a section displaying the list of cart items and a showCart Details variable to control the list's visibility. We will toggle the visibility of the list when users click on the cart text, as shown in Example 9-11.

Example 9-11. Cart component with cart items

```
<template>
    <div class="cart">
        <span
            class="cart__total"
            @click="showCartDetails.value = !showCartDetails.value;" ❶
        >
```

```
                Cart: {{ cart.total }}
            </span>
            <ul class="cart__list" v-show="showCartDetails"> ❷
                <li v-for="item in cart.items" :key="item.id" class="cart__list-item"> ❸
                    <span>Id: {{ item.id }}</span> |
                    <span>Quantity: {{ item.quantity }}</span>
                </li>
            </ul>
        </div>
    </template>
<script setup lang="ts">
import { useCartStore } from '@/stores/cart'
import { ref } from 'vue'

const cart = useCartStore();
const showCartDetails = ref(false); ❹
</script>
```

❶ Toggle the visibility of the cart items list when users click on the cart text

❷ Display the cart items list when `showCartDetails` is `true`

❸ Loop through the cart items and display the item id and quantity

❹ Initialize a `showCartDetails` variable using the `ref()` method

We also add some CSS styles to the `Cart` component to position the list to look like a dropdown:

```
.cart {
    position: relative; ❶
}

.cart__list {
    position: absolute; ❷
    list-style: none;
    border: 1px solid #e3e0e0;
    padding: 10px;
    inset-inline-end: 0; ❸
    box-shadow: 2px 2px 3px #e3e0e0; ❹
    background-color: white;
    min-width: 200px;
}
```

❶ Set the position of the `.cart` container to `relative` to make the `absolute` list container float within the container.

❷ Set the position of the list container to `absolute` to make it float concerning the `relative` positioned `.cart` container.

❸ Set the `inset-inline-end` property to 0 to make the list container float to the right of the `.cart` container.

❹ Add box shadow and border to the list container to make it look like a dropdown.

When we click on the cart text, the cart items list will be displayed (Figure 9-8).

Figure 9-8. Cart items list displayed when clicking on the cart text

But wait, there is a problem. The list displays only the items `id` and `quantity`, which needs to be more descriptive for users to understand what item they have added as well as the total cost. We also need to display the item's name and price. To do so, we can modify the `cart.items` to keep the item's title and price, but this would make the `cart` store's structure complex and would require additional logic fixes.

Instead, we can create a computed `detailedItems` list with the help of the pizzas store.

Within the `cart.ts` store, we will add a `detailedItems` computed property, which will be the joined array from `items` and from the `pizzasStore.pizzas` of the pizzas store, as in Example 9-12.

Example 9-12. Cart store with `detailedItems` computed property

```
import { defineStore } from 'pinia';
import { usePizzasStore } from './pizzas';

export const useCartStore = defineStore('cart', () => {
    //...

    const detailedItems = computed(() => {
        const pizzasStore = usePizzasStore(); ❶

        return items.map(item => { ❷
            const pizza = pizzasStore.pizzas.find(
                pizza => pizza.id === item.id
            )
```

```
        const pizzaPrice = pizza?.price ? +(pizza?.price) : 0;

        return { ❸
            ...item,
            title: pizza?.title,
            price: pizza?.price,
            total: pizzaPrice * item.quantity
        }
    })
})

return {
    //...
    detailedItems ❹
}
});
```

❶   Get the initial list of pizzas from the store using `usePizzaStore`

❷   Filter the relevant pizzas presented in the cart

❸   Format the cart items' information to return

❹   Return the filtered and formatted array `detailedItems`

In `Cart.vue`, we will replace the `cart.items` with `cart.detailedItems` in the `v-for` loop, as shown in Example 9-13.

Example 9-13. Using `detailedItems` to display more information

```
<ul class="cart__list" v-show="showCartDetails">
    <li
        v-for="(item, index) in cart.detailedItems" ❶
        :key="item.id"
        class="cart__list-item">
        <span>{{index + 1}}. {{ item.title }}</span>
        <span>${{ item.price }}</span> x
        <span>{{ item.quantity }}</span>
        <span>= ${{ item.total }}</span>
    </li>
</ul>
```

❶   Iterate the `cart.detailedItems` array to display cart's items

Now, when we click on the cart text, the cart items list will display the item's name, price, quantity, and total cost per item (Figure 9-9).

Pizz   1. Pina Colada Pizza $10.00 x 1 = $10

2. Pepperoni Pizza $12.00 x 3 = $36

Search for a pi...

Figure 9-9. Cart items list displayed with more information

We have successfully displayed the cart items' details. Next we can add the ability to be able to remove items from the cart.

Removing Items from the Cart Store

For each item in the cart's list, we will add a *Remove* button to be able to remove it from the cart. We will also add a *Remove all* button to remove all items from the cart. The `template` section of `Cart.vue` will look like Example 9-14.

Example 9-14. Cart component with Remove and Remove all buttons

```
<div class="cart__list" v-show="showCartDetails">
    <div v-if="cart.total === 0">No items in cart</div>
    <div v-else>
        <ul>
            <li
                v-for="(item, index) in cart.detailedItems"
                :key="item.id" class="cart__list-item"
            >
                <span>{{index + 1}}. {{ item.title }}</span>
                <span>${{ item.price }}</span> x
                <span>{{ item.quantity }}</span>
                <span>= ${{ item.total }}</span>
                <button @click="cart.remove(item.id)">Remove</button> ❶
            </li>
        </ul>
        <button @click="cart.clear">Remove all</button> ❷
    </div>
</div>
```

❶ The Remove button binds to the `cart.remove` method, which takes the item's `id` as an argument

❷ The Remove all button binds to the `cart.clear` method

In `cart.ts`, we will add the `remove` and `clear` methods, as shown in Example 9-15.

Example 9-15. Cart store with `remove` and `clear` methods

```
//...
export const useCartStore = defineStore('cart', () => {
    //...
    const remove = (id: string) => {
        const index = items.findIndex(item => item.id === id)
        if (index > -1) {
            items.splice(index, 1)
        }
    }

    const clear = () => {
        items.length = 0
    }

    return {
        //...
        remove,
        clear
    }
})
```

And that's it! Vue removes the item from the cart when we click the *Remove* button. And it will empty the cart when we click the *Remove all* button; see Figure 9-10.

Pizza House   Cart: 2

              1. Pína Colada Pizza $10.00   x   1   = $10   [Remove]

              2. Pepperoni Pizza $12.00   x   1   = $12   [Remove]

[Remove all]

Figure 9-10. Cart items with Remove and Remove all buttons

 If you are building the `cart` store using Options API, you can use `cart.$reset()` to reset the store's state to its initial state. Otherwise, you must manually reset the store's state, as we did in the `clear` method.

We can also use the Vue Devtool tab ("Vue Developer Tools" on page 6) in the browser's Developer Tools to inspect the `cart` store's state and getters. The `cart` and `pizzas` store will be listed under the `Pinia` tab (Figure 9-11).

Figure 9-11. Cart and pizzas stores in Vue Devtools

We have explored how to build stores using Pinia and Composition API. We have also explored different approaches, such as combining stores and using the store's state in external composables. What about testing Pinia stores? Let's explore that in the next section.

Unit Testing Pinia Stores

Unit testing a store is similar to regular unit testing a function. For Pinia, before running the actual tests, we need to create a Pinia instance using `createPinia` and activate it with the `setActivePinia()` method from the `pinia` package. Example 9-16 shows how we write the test of adding an item to a cart for our `cart` store.

Example 9-16. Cart store test suite for adding items

```
import { setActivePinia, createPinia } from 'pinia';
import { useCartStore } from '@/stores/cart';

describe('Cart store', () => {
    let cartStore;

    beforeEach(() => { ❶
        setActivePinia(createPinia());
        cartStore = useCartStore();
    });

    it('should add item to cart', () => {
        cartStore.add({ id: '1', quantity: 1 });
        expect(cartStore.items).toEqual([{ id: '1', quantity: 1 }]);
    });
});
```

❶ We create and activate a new Pinia instance before each test run.

This code follows the common testing syntax supported by Jest and `Vitest` testing frameworks. We will explore more details on writing and running unit tests in "Vitest as a Unit Testing Tool" on page 253. For now, we will explore how to subscribe to store changes and add side effects to store actions.

Subscribing Side Effects on Store Changes

One significant advantage of Pinia is the ability to extend the store's functionalities and implement side effects using plugins. With this ability, we can easily subscribe to changes in all the stores or in a specific store to perform additional actions like synchronizing data with the server when needed.

Take the following `cartPlugin`, for instance:

```
//main.ts
import { cartPlugin } from '@/plugins/cartPlugin'
//...

const pinia = createPinia()
pinia.use(cartPlugin)

app.use(pinia)
//...
```

The `cartPlugin` is a function that receives an object containing a reference to the `app` instance, the `pinia` instance, the `store` instance, and an options object. Vue will trigger this function once for every store in our application. To make sure we are subscribing only to the `cart` store, we can check the store's id (see Example 9-17).

Example 9-17. Cart plugin

```
//src/plugins/cartPlugin.ts
export const cartPlugin = ({ store}) => {
    if (store.$id === 'cart') {
        //...
    }
}
```

Then we can subscribe to the cart store changes using the `store.$subscribe` method, as in Example 9-18.

Example 9-18. Cart plugin subscribing to store changes

```
//src/plugins/cartPlugin.ts
export const cartPlugin = ({ store}) => {
    if (store.$id === 'cart') {
        store.$subscribe((options) => {
            console.log('cart changed', options)
        })
    }
}
```

When we add an item to the cart, the cartPlugin will log the message to the console (Figure 9-12).

```
cart changed                                                                main.ts:17
▼ Object i
  ▼ events:
    ▶ effect: ReactiveEffect {active: true, deps: Array(17), parent: undefined, fn: f, scheduler: f,
      key: "1"
    ▶ newValue: {id: '1', quantity: 1}
      oldTarget: undefined
      oldValue: undefined
    ▶ target: (2) [{…}, {…}]
      type: "add"
    ▶ [[Prototype]]: Object
      storeId: "cart"
      type: "direct"
    ▶ [[Prototype]]: Object
```

Figure 9-12. Log the store changes using plugin

The options object received by the $subscribe method contains the events object, which contains the current event's type (add), the previous value (oldValue), the current values passed to the event (newValue), the storeId, and the type of the event (direct).

Similarly, we can add a side effect to the cart store's add action using store.$on Action (Example 9-19).

Example 9-19. Cart plugin subscribing to store's adding action

```
//src/plugins/cartPlugin.ts

export const cartPlugin = ({ store}) => {
    if (store.$id === 'cart') {
        store.$onAction(({ name, args }) => {
            if (name === 'add') {
                console.log('item added to cart', args)
            }
        })
    }
}
```

When we add an item to the cart, the cartPlugin will log the new item added to the cart (Figure 9-13).

```
item added to cart  ▼ Array(1) i
                    ▶ 0: {id: '2', quantity: 1}
                      length: 1
                    ▶ [[Prototype]]: Array(0)
```

Figure 9-13. Cart plugin logging store's adding action

With $subscribe and $onAction, we can add side effects such as logging and communicating with external API services such as updating the user's cart in the server, etc. Additionally, if we have an $onAction and $subscribe in the same plugin, Vue will trigger the $onAction first, followed by the relevant $subscribe.

Using Side Effects

It's crucial to note that Vue triggers every side effect we add to the store. For example, for Example 9-19, Vue will activate the side effect function for every action executed in the store. Hence, we must be very cautious when adding side effects to the store to avoid performance issues.

Summary

In this chapter, we learned how to use Pinia to build stores and use them in our application with the help of Composition API. We also learned how to destructure and pass the store's state to external composables with reactivity and how to subscribe to store changes and add side effects to store actions. You are now ready to create a complete data flow from building a centralized data store, using it in different components, and connecting between components through the store.

The next chapter will explore a different aspect of Vue's capabilities in enhancing the user experience: adding animations and transitions to our application and components.

CHAPTER 10

Transitioning and Animation in Vue

We have explored all the crucial aspects of building a working Vue application, including handling routes and data flow with proper state management. This chapter will explore a unique Vue feature for enhancing the user experience: animation and transitions, using transition components, hooks, and CSS.

Understanding CSS Transitions and CSS Animations

CSS animations are the visual effects of a state change on a specific element or component, with no limit on the number of states. A CSS animation can start automatically and go into a loop without explicit triggering. In contrast, CSS transition is an animation that responds to a change *between two states only*, from average to hover for a button or from hidden to visible for a tooltip. To define a CSS animation, we often use the `@keyframes` rule and then apply it to the target element using the `animation` property. For example, we can define a simple animation effect for a button:

```
@keyframes pulse {
  0% {
    box-shadow: 0 0 0 0px rgba(0, 0, 0, 0.5);
  }
  100% {
    box-shadow: 0 0 0 20px rgba(0, 0, 0, 0);
  }
}

.button {
  animation: pulse 2s infinite;
  box-shadow: 0px 0px 1px 1px #0000001a;
}
```

We defined a simple animation effect, pulse, and applied it to any element with but ton class, where the box shadow will expand and shrink in a loop, lasting two seconds. This effect will run infinitely if the element exists in the DOM.

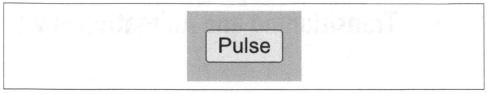

Figure 10-1. Indefinite pulse animation effect

Meanwhile, we can use the transition property to define a transition effect for a specific element when the user hovers over it:

```
.button {
  transition: background-color 0.5s ease-in-out;
}

.button:hover {
  background-color: #ff0000;
}
```

In this code, we created a simple transition effect for the button element: the background color will change from the default color to red on hovering, with a delay of 0.5 seconds, with a smoothing effect of ease-in-out. Alternatively, we can also use JavaScript and other animation libraries to define transition and animation programmatically using JavaScript.

Transition and animation offer users a significantly smoother experience when using the application. However, working with transition and animation can sometimes be challenging. As a framework focusing on the view layer, Vue provides a set of APIs to help us create smooth, beautiful animations and transition effects for components and routes, with CSS and/or JavaScript, in a more straightforward manner. One is the transition component, which we will discuss in the following section.

Transition Component in Vue.js

The transition component is a wrapper component that allows us to create a transition for a single element with two available transition states: enter and leave. The component provides a prop name as the name of the desired transition effect. Vue will compute the relevant transition classes with the name as their prefix and the direction state of the transition (to, active, or from) as their suffix, as seen here:

```
<name>-[enter | leave]-<transition-direction-state>
```

For example, we can use a slidein transition effect on an element:

```
<transition name="slidein">
    <ul class="pizza-list">
        /** code for rendering pizza's card... */
    </ul>
</transition>
```

Vue will generate a set of classes, which are described in Table 10-1.

Table 10-1. Generated transition classes for the slide-in transition effect

Classes	Description
.slidein-enter-from	Class selector for the starting state of the entering transition
.slidein-enter-active	Class selector for defining the duration and delay of transition when the element is actively entering transition
.slidein-enter-to	Class selector for the ending state of the entering transition
slidein-leave-from	Class selector for the starting state of the leaving transition
slidein-leave-to	Class selector for the ending state of the leaving transition
slidein-leave-active	Class selector for defining the duration and delay of transition when the element is active in the middle of leaving transition

The *enter state* means the element starts the process of transitioning to visible mode in the browser's display, while the *leave state* indicates the opposite. We can combine with v-show, which toggles the element's CSS display property, or v-if attribute, which inserts the piece to the DOM conditionally. We will add the v-show to the ul component of our code example:

```
<transition name="slidein">
    <ul class="pizza-list" v-show="showList">
        /** code for rendering pizza's card... */
    </ul>
</transition>
```

Now we can use the previous classes to define the transition named slidein with the CSS transition property and the target CSS property or properties to perform the effect.

The following is an example implementation for the slide-in transition effect:

```
.slidein-enter-to {
  transform: translateX(0);
}

.slidein-enter-from {
  transform: translateX(-100%);
}

.slidein-leave-to {
  transform: translateX(100%);
}
```

```
.slidein-leave-from {
  transform: translateX(0);
}

.slidein-enter-active,
.slidein-leave-active {
  transition: transform 0.5s;
}
```

In this code, before the entering transition, the browser will reposition the ul element horizontally to the left of the viewport using translateX(-100%), then move it back to the correct position with translateX(0) in slidein-enter-to. The same applies to the leaving transition, except that the element will move to the viewport's right instead of the left. Both changes will be on the transform property, with a duration of 0.5 seconds, as stated in the slidein-enter-active and slidein-leave-active classes.

To see the effect in action, we can add a small timeout to change the value of the searchResults data property:

```
import { ref } from "vue";

const showList = ref(false);

setTimeout(() => {
  showList.value = true;
}, 1000);
```

The Vue engine will add or remove each class as appropriate. We add another timeout to change the value of showList back to false, and Vue will trigger the transition effect again, except it is for the leave state (Figure 10-2).

We have implemented a simple effect using the transition component with a single impact of slidein. How about combining different effects, such as slidein for the entering state and rotate for the leaving state? For such cases we use custom transition class attributes, which we will discuss in the next section.

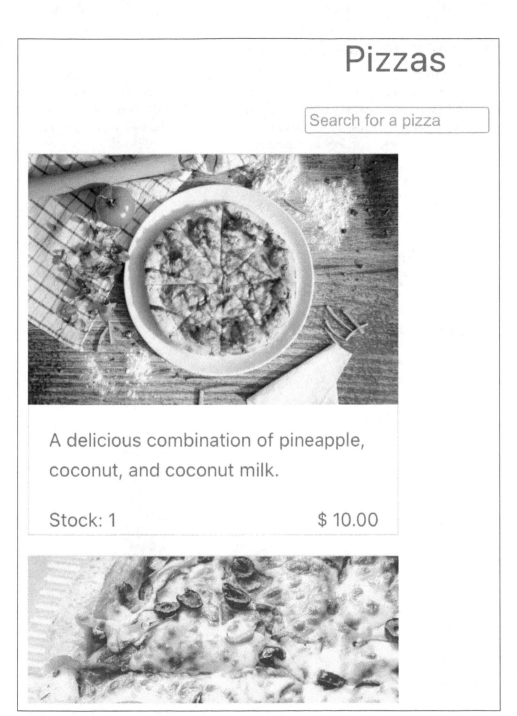

Figure 10-2. Transition effect for the pizza list when showList is true

Using Custom Transition Class Attributes

Besides auto-generating the classes according to the `name` attribute, Vue also lets us specify the custom classes for each transition class using the following relevant props: `enter-class`, `enter-active-class`, `enter-to-class`, `leave-class`, `leave-active-class`, and `leave-to-class`. For example, we can define the custom classes for the `rotate` transition effect on leaving the state:

```
<transition name="slidein" leave-active-class="rotate">
    <ul class="pizza-list" v-show="showList">
        /** code for rendering pizza's card... */
    </ul>
</transition>
```

In the `style` section, we use `@keyframes` controls to define the animation effect for the `rotate` transition with keyframe offsets of 0%, 50%, 90% and 100%:

```
@keyframes rotate {
  0% {
    transform: rotate(0);
  }
  50% {
    transform: rotate(45deg);
  }
  90% {
    transform: rotate(90deg);
  }
  100% {
    transform: rotate(180deg);
  }
}
```

Then we can assign the animation effect `rotate` to `animation` property of the `rotate` class, at a duration of 0.5 seconds:

```
.rotate {
  animation: rotate 0.5s;
}
```

Let's set the initial value of `showList` to `true` and a timeout of `1000` milliseconds to change it to `false`. While the effect on entering for the ul element is still `slidein`, the effect on leaving is now an animation of rotation starting from 45 degrees, then 90 degrees, and finally 180 degrees. See Figure 10-3 for an illustration.

```
import { ref } from "vue";

const showList = ref(true);

setTimeout(() => {
  showList.value = false;
}, 1000);
```

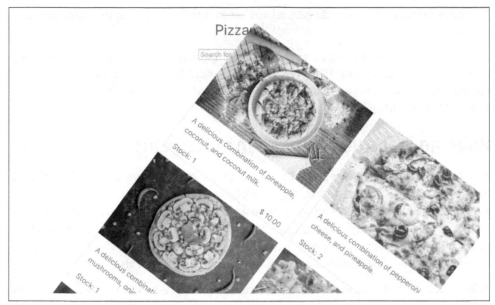

Figure 10-3. Rotating effect on transition using keyframes

You can assign multiple classes to these props, separated by a single space, to apply various effects to a specific transition state. This feature is helpful when you want to integrate animation from external CSS libraries, such as Bootstrap, Tailwind CSS, or Bulma, with their classes.

Our component now has the transition effect whenever toggling the value of show List. However, we often want to animate the element when it appears on the screen after the page is loaded and without additional interaction. To do so, we can use the appear prop.

Adding Transition Effect on the Initial Render with appear

When we set the appear prop to true on the transition element, Vue will automatically add the enter-active and enter-to classes to the component when mounting to the DOM, triggering the transition effect. For instance, to have the slidein impact applied on the initial render of the ul component, we only need to add appear prop to the transition element:

```
<transition name="slidein" appear>
    <ul class="pizza-list">
        /** code for rendering pizza's card... */
    </ul>
</transition>
```

The browser now will apply the slidein effect on the UI's initial appearance of the ul element.

We have learned how to use the transition component to create a smooth transition effect for a single element. However, this component is not useful when we want to animate multiple parts simultaneously and in an orderly fashion. To do this, we have transition-group, which we will discuss next.

Building Transition for a Group of Elements

The transition-group component is a particular version of the transition, aiming to provide animation support to a group of elements. It accepts the same props as transition and is handy when we want to animate each item in a list, such as a list of pizzas or users. Nevertheless, unlike the transition element, transition-group supports rendering a wrapper element using the tag prop, and all the child elements will receive the same transition classes but not the wrapper (if one exists).

Take our list of pizzas, for instance. We can use the transition-group to animate each pizza card with the fadein effect when it appears on screen and wrap the cards under a ul element:

```
<transition-group name="fadein" tag="ul" appear>
    <li v-for="pizza in searchResults" :key="pizza.id">
        <PizzaCard :pizza="pizza" />
    </li>
</transition-group>
```

Using key Attribute

You must use the key attribute on each list element for Vue to track the changes in the list and apply the transition effect accordingly.

Vue will add the relevant classes fadein-enter-active, fadein-enter-to, fadein-leave-active, fadein-leave-to to each li element, which we define with the following CSS rules:

```
.fadein-enter-active,
.fadein-leave-active {
  transition: all 2s;
}

.fadein-enter-from,
.fadein-leave-to {
  opacity: 0;
  transform: translateX(20px);
}
```

That's it. Each pizza card in our list now appears with a fading effect and a slight slide-in transition from the right when loading the component for the first time. Whenever we filter the list using the search box, the new cards will appear with the same effect, while the old cards will disappear with the opposite effect: fading out and sliding out to the right (Figure 10-4).

Figure 10-4. Fading effect on searching in list

Adding More Effects on the Movement

You can also add more effects to the moving items using the `<effect>-move` class (like `fadein-move`). This solution can be smoother when things move around in the list.

So far so good. We have explored how to use `transition` and `transition-group` components. The next step is to learn how to combine these components with the `router-view` element to create a smooth transition when navigating between routes.

Creating Route Transitions

Beginning with Vue Router 4.0, we no longer can wrap the `router-view` component with the `transition` element. Instead, we combine the usage of the `Component` prop exposed by the `v-lot` API from the `router-view`, and the dynamic component, as shown in the following code:

```
<router-view v-slot="{ Component }">
    <transition name="slidein">
        <component :is="Component" />
    </transition>
</router-view>
```

The `Component` prop refers to the target component that Vue renders in place of the `router-view` placeholder. We can then use the `component` element to generate the component dynamically and wrap it with the `transition` element to apply the `slidein` effect. By doing so, whenever we navigate a different route, there will be an animation effect: sliding in for the page entering and sliding out for the page leaving.

There is a minor issue here, however. When we navigate a different route, note that the new page's content may appear before the previous page's content finishes the animation for leaving and disappears. In such cases, we can use `mode` prop with the value `out-in` to ensure the new content will enter and start animating only after the previous content has disappeared entirely from the screen:

```
<router-view v-slot="{ Component }">
    <transition name="slidein" mode="out-in">
        <component :is="Component" />
    </transition>
</router-view>
```

Now, whenever we navigate to a different route, such as moving from / to /about, the About view will appear only after the Home view disappears.

To this point, we have explored how to create transition effects using `name` and custom transition classes. While these are sufficient to create smooth transition effects with custom animation classes for our application in most scenarios, we may find other cases where we want to use third-party JavaScript animation libraries for better transition effects. We need a different approach for such cases, allowing us to plug in custom animation control using JavaScript. We will learn how to do that in the next section.

Using Transition Events to Control Animation

In contrast to the custom classes, Vue exposes some appropriate transition events for both transition components to emit. These events are `before-enter`, `enter`, `after-enter`, and `enter-cancelled` for the entering state of an element, and `before-leave`,

leave, after-leave, and leave-cancelled for its leaving form. We can bind these events to the desired callbacks and control the transition effect using JavaScript.

For instance, we can use the before-enter, enter, afterEnter events to control the animation of the slidein effect on a page transitioning:

```
<router-view v-slot="{ Component }">
    <transition
    @before-enter="beforeEnter"
    @enter="enter"
    @after-enter="afterEnter"
    :css="false"
    >
        <component :is="Component" />
    </transition>
</router-view>
```

Using the css Prop

When using the callbacks approach, we can use the css prop to disable the default and any possible overlapping CSS transition classes.

In the script section, we can define the callbacks for each event:

```
import { gsap } from 'gsap'

const beforeEnter = (el: HTMLElement) => {
  el.style.transform = "translateX(20px)";
  el.style.opacity = "0";
};

const enter = (el: HTMLElement, done: gsap.Callback) => {
  gsap.to(el, {
    duration: 1,
    x: 0,
    opacity: 1,
    onComplete: done,
  });
};

const afterEnter = (el: HTMLElement) => {
  el.style.transform = "";
  el.style.opacity = "";
};
```

In this code, we use the gsap (GreenSock Animation Platform) library to animate the element when it enters the DOM. We define the following:

beforeEnter
  Callback to set the initial state of the element, including setting the opacity to hidden and repositioning the element 20px from the origin

`enter`

Callback to animate the element using `gsap.to` function[1]

`afterEnter`

Callback to set the element's visibility state and the position after the animation finishes

Similarly, we can use the `before-leave`, `leave`, and `after-leave` events to animate the element when it leaves the DOM (such as a sliding-out effect) with the animation library of our choice.

Summary

In this chapter, we learned how to use the transition component and the available hooks to create smooth transition effects from one route to another. We also learned how to make group transitions and use the transition component to animate elements within a segment.

In the next chapter, we will discover another significant aspect of web development: testing. We will learn how to test composables with Vitest and components with the Vue Test Utils library and then develop a complete end-to-end testing plan with Playwright for our application.

---

1 This function receives a target element and optional object containing all properties for animation. See *https://oreil.ly/XNgFb*.

CHAPTER 11

Testing in Vue

To this point, we have learned about developing a complete Vue application from scratch with different Vue APIs. Our application is now ready for deployment, but before we do that, we need to make sure that our application is bug-free and ready for production. This is where testing comes in.

Testing is crucial to any application development, as it helps to increase code confidence and quality before releasing it to production. In this chapter, we will learn about the different types of testing and how to use them in Vue applications. We will also explore the various tools, such as Vitest and Vue Test Utils, for unit testing and PlaywrightJS for end-to-end (E2E) testing.

Introduction to Unit Testing and E2E Testing

Software development has both manual and automated testing practices and techniques to ensure your application works as expected. While manual testing requires a tester to interact with the software manually and can be expensive, automated testing is mainly about executing a predefined test script containing a set of tests in an automated manner. The collection of automated tests can validate simple to more complex application scenarios, from a single function to a combination of different parts.

Automated testing is more reliable and scalable than manual testing, assuming we write the tests correctly, and performs the following testing processes:

Unit testing

The most common and lowest level of testing in software development. We use unit testing to validate a unit of code (or code block) that performs a specific action, such as functions, hooks, and modules. We can combine unit testing with test-driven development (TDD)[1] as a standard development practice.

Integrating testing

This testing type validates the integration of different unit blocks of code. Integrating testing aims to assert the flow of logic functions, components, or modules. Component testing integrates testing with its internal logic as a unit test. We also mock most upstream services and other functions outside the test scope to ensure testing quality.

End-to-end (E2E) testing

The highest level of testing in software development. We use E2E testing to validate the entire application flow from the client side to the backend, usually by simulating actual user behaviors. There would not be any mocked services or functions in E2E testing, as we want to test the entire application flow.

> Test-driven development (TDD) means you design and write the test cases first (red phase), work on the code to pass the tests (green phase), and improve the code implementation (refactor phase). It helps to verify the logic and design before actual development.

These three testing types form a pyramid of testing, as shown in Figure 11-1, where the focus should be mainly on the unit tests, then integration testing, leaving the smallest number to E2E testing as it is primarily for sanity and can be expensive to trigger. Since we create an application from any components, services, and modules, performing unit testing for each isolated function or feature can be sufficient for keeping your codebase's quality at the minimum cost and effort.

And as the primary ground for the testing system in our application, we start with unit tests using Vitest.

---

1 If you are new to TDD, start with *Learning Test-Driven Development* by Saleem Siddiqui (O'Reilly).

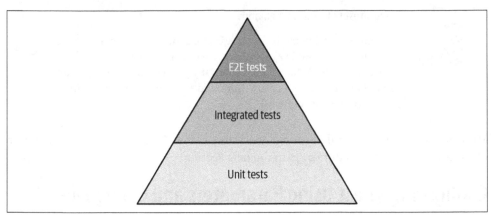

Figure 11-1. Pyramid of testing

Vitest as a Unit Testing Tool

Vitest (*https://oreil.ly/1upy0*) is the test runner for unit testing built on Vite for Vite-powered projects. Its API is similar to Jest and Chai while offering a more modular approach to testing. Focusing on speed and developer experience, Vitest offers several significant features, including multithreading workers, TypeScript and JSX support, and component testing for frameworks such as Vue and React.

To use Vitest, we need to install it as a dev dependency in our project:

```
yarn add -D vitest
```

Then in the `package.json` file, we can add a new script command to run our tests in the watch mode:

```
"script": {
    "test": "vitest"
}
```

Alternatively, during the Vue project initialization, we can choose to install Vitest as a unit testing tool ("Create a New Vue Application" on page 9), and Vite will take care of the rest, including some sample tests as the starter.

Once we run the command `yarn test` in the terminal (or command line), Vitest will automatically detect the test files whose name contains the pattern `.spec.` or `.test.` in the project directory. For example, a test file for the `useFetch` hook will be either `useFetch.spec.ts` or `useFetch.test.ts`. Whenever you change any test file, Vitest will rerun the test in your local environment.

Using vitest with Extra Commands

You can specify the mode for the `vitest` command, such as `vitest watch` for watch mode explicitly or `vitest run` for a one-time run on all the tests. Vite will automatically switch to the single run mode when using the `vitest` command alone in a continuous integration (CI) environment.

We can further customize the settings for Vitest using the command parameters or the Vite config file `vite.config.js` in the next section.

Configuring Vitest Using Parameters and Config File

By default, Vitest will scan for tests starting from the project folder as its current directory. We can specify a target folder for Vitest to check by passing the folder path as an argument to the test command, such as the `tests` folder within the source `src` directory:

```
"script": {
    "test": "vitest --root src/tests"
}
```

In this chapter, we will put our tests under the `tests` folder, with the test file name convention `<test-file-name.test>.ts` (such as `myComponent.test.ts`).

We can also specify the test files to run by passing the file path as an argument to the `yarn test` command:

```
yarn test src/tests/useFetch.test.ts
```

This command is handy when working on a file and wanting to enable the watch mode for that test file exclusively.

We also need to set the `environment` parameter to `jsdom` (JSDOM[2]) as the DOM environment runner for our Vue project:

```
"script": {
    "test": "vitest --root src/tests --environment jsdom"
}
```

Without setting the environment, Vitest will use the default environment `node`, which is unsuitable for testing UI components and interactions.

---

2 JSDOM is an open source library that acts as a headless browser that implements the web standards, providing a simulated environment for testing any web-related code.

Instead of using the command parameters, we can also modify the `vite.config.js` file to configure our Vitest runner, using the field `test` with the relevant properties `root` and `environment`:

```
export default defineConfig({
  /**other settings */
  test: {
    environment: 'jsdom',
    root: 'src/tests
  }
})
```

You also need to add the reference to Vitest using the `<reference>` tag within this file by adding the following line to the top of the `vite.config.ts` file:

```
/// <reference types="vitest" />
```

As a result, Vite will know that we are using Vitest as the test runner and will provide the relevant type definitions for the `test` field in the config file for TypeScript type checking.

We also can turn on the global mode for the Vitest APIs across the entire project, so we don't need to import any function explicitly from the `vitest` package into our test files. We can do this by enabling the `globals` flag of the `test` object in the `vite.config.ts`:

```
/// <reference types="vitest" />
/*...imports...*/

export default defineConfig({
  /**other settings */
  test: {
    environment: 'jsdom',
    root: 'src/tests
    globals: true,
  }
})
```

Once `globals` is enabled, for TypeScript to be able to detect the availability of Vitest APIs as global, we still have one more step to perform: adding `vitest/globals` type definitions to the `types` array in the `tsconfig.json` file:

```
//tsconfig.json
"compilerOptions": {
  "types": ["vitest/globals"]
}
```

With these settings, we are now ready to start writing our tests.

Writing Your First Test

Following the TDD approach, let's start with a simple test to check if a function to filter an array based on a given string and an array element's property key is working as expected.

We will create a new file, `filterArray.test.ts`, in the `src/tests` folder and another one, `filterArray.ts` in the `src/utils` folder. The `filterArray.ts` should export a function `filterArray`, which takes three arguments (the original array to filter of type `ArrayObject`, a `string` property key, and the `string` term to filter with) and returns the filtered elements of type `ArrayObject`:

```
type ArrayObject = { [key: string]: string };

export function filterArray(
  array: ArrayObject[],
  key: string,
  term: string
): ArrayObject[] {
  // code to filter the array
  return [];
}
```

`{ [key: string]: string }` is a type for an object with a `string` key and a `string` value. Specify using type instead of the generic `Object` (similar to using any) to avoid the potential bug of passing the wrong object type to the function.

In the `filterArray.test.ts` file, we will import the `filterArray` function and model its functionality. We will use the `it()` method and `expect()` from the `@vitest` package to define a single test case, and to assert the expected result, respectively:

```
import { it, expect } from '@vitest'
import { filterArray } from '../utils/filterArray'

it('should return a filtered array', () => {
  expect()
})
```

We can remove the `import { it, expect } from @vitest` line if we have `globals` set to `true` in the `vite.config.ts` file or the command line with the `--globals` parameter.

The it() method takes a string representing the test case's name (should return a filtered array), a function containing the test logic to run, and an optional timeout for waiting for the test to complete. By default, we have five seconds for the test's timeout.

We can now implement the test logic for our first test case. We also assume that we have a list of pizzas that we need to filter by title containing Hawaiian:

```
import { it, expect } from '@vitest'
import { filterArray } from '../utils/filterArray'

const pizzas = [
  {
    id: "1",
    title: "Pina Colada Pizza",
    price: "10.00",
    description:
      "A delicious combination of pineapple, coconut, and coconut milk.",
    quantity: 1,
  },
  {
    id: "4",
    title: "Hawaiian Pizza",
    price: "11.00",
    description:
      "A delicious combination of ham, pineapple, and pineapple.",
    quantity: 5,
  },
  {
    id: "5",
    title: "Meat Lovers Pizza",
    price: "13.00",
    description:
      "A delicious combination of pepperoni, sausage, and bacon.",
    quantity: 3,
  },
]

it('should return a filtered array', () => {
  expect(filterArray(pizzas, 'title', 'Hawaiian'))
})
```

expect() returns a test instance that has various modifiers such as not, resolves, rejects, and matcher functions like toEqual and toBe. While toEqual performs a deep comparison for equality on the target object, toBe performs an additional check to the target value's instance reference in the memory. In most scenarios, using toEqual is good enough for validating our logic, such as checking the returned value to match our desired array. We will define our target result array as follows:

```
const result = [
  {
    id: "4",
    title: "Hawaiian Pizza",
    price: "11.00",
    description:
      "A delicious combination of ham, pineapple, and pineapple.",
    quantity: 5,
  },
]
```

Let's modify our `pizzas` to ensure it contains elements of `result` before passing it to the `filterArray` function:

```
const pizzas = [
  {
    id: "1",
    title: "Pina Colada Pizza",
    price: "10.00",
    description:
      "A delicious combination of pineapple, coconut, and coconut milk.",
    quantity: 1,
  },
  {
    id: "5",
    title: "Meat Lovers Pizza",
    price: "13.00",
    description:
      "A delicious combination of pepperoni, sausage, and bacon.",
    quantity: 3,
  },
  ...result
]
```

Then we use `.toEqual()` to assert the expected result:

```
it('should return a filtered array', () => {
  expect(filterArray(pizzas, 'title', 'Hawaiian')).toEqual(result)
})
```

Let's run our tests in the watch mode using the `yarn test` command. The test will fail, and Vitest will display the failure's details, including the expected result and the actual result, as seen in Figure 11-2.

```
┌─────────────────────── Failed Tests 1 ───────────────────────┐

 FAIL  tests/filterArray.test.ts > filterArray > should return a filtered array
AssertionError: expected [] to deeply equal [ { id: '4', …(4) } ]
 ❯ tests/filterArray.test.ts:35:54
     33| describe('filterArray', () => {
     34|   it('should return a filtered array', () => {
     35|     expect(filterArray(pizzas, 'title', 'Hawaiian')).toEqual(result)
       |                                                      ^
     36|   })
     37| });

 - Expected  - 9
 + Received  + 1

 - Array [
 -   Object {
 -     "description": "A delicious combination of ham, pineapple, and pineapple.",
 -     "id": "4",
 -     "price": "11.00",
 -     "quantity": "5",
 -     "title": "Hawaiian Pizza",
 -   },
 - ]"
 + "Array []"

 ─────────────────────────────────────────────────────────────[1/1]─

Test Files  1 failed (1)
```

Figure 11-2. Test failure details

Part of the TDD approach is to define the tests and watch them fail before implementing the actual code. The next step is working on the `filterArray` function to
make the test pass with the minimum code required.

Here is an example implementation of `filterArray` using `filter()` and `toLower`
`Case()`:

```
type ArrayObject = { [key: string]: string };

export function filterArray(
  array: ArrayObject[],
  key: string,
  term: string
): ArrayObject[] {
  const filterTerm = term.toLowerCase();

  return array.filter(
    (item) => item[key].toLowerCase().includes(filterTerm)
  );
}
```

With this code, our test should pass (Figure 11-3).

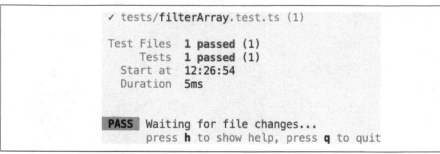

Figure 11-3. Test passes

At this point, you can create more tests to cover the rest of the function's scenarios. For example, when the key doesn't exist in the array's element (item[key] is undefined), or when the term is case-insensitive:

```
it("should return a empty array when key doesn't exist", () => {
  expect(filterArray(pizzas, 'name', 'Hawaiian')).toEqual([])
})

it('should return matching array when term is upper-cased', () => {
  expect(filterArray(pizzas, 'name', 'HAWAIIAN')).toEqual(result)
})
```

In the terminal, you will see the tests displayed with the relevant name (Figure 11-4) in a flat order.

```
RERUN   tests/filterArray.test.ts x1

❯ tests/filterArray.test.ts (3)
  ✓ should return a filtered array
  ✓ should return a empty array when key doesn't exist
  ✗ should return matching array when term is upper-cased
```

Figure 11-4. Displaying the tests in a flat order

As the number of tests in a file and the number of test files grow, the flat order can be hard to read and understand. To make it readable per functionality, use describe() to group the tests into logical blocks, each with the appropriate block name:

```
describe('filterArray', () => {
  it('should return a filtered array', () => {
    expect(filterArray(pizzas, 'title', 'Hawaiian')).toEqual(result)
  })
  it(`should return a empty array when key doesn't exist`, () => {
    expect(filterArray(pizzas, 'name', 'Hawaiian')).toEqual([])
  })

  it('should return matching array when term is upper-cased', () => {
```

```
    expect(filterArray(pizzas, 'name', 'HAWAIIAN')).toEqual(result)
  })
})
```

Vitest will display the tests in a more organized hierarchy, as seen in Figure 11-5.

```
❯ tests/filterArray.test.ts (3)
  ❯ filterArray (3)
    ✓ should return a filtered array
    ✓ should return a empty array when key doesn't exist
    ✗ should return matching array when term is upper-cased
```

Figure 11-5. Displaying the tests per group

We can move `pizzas` and `result` inside the `describe` block. This ensures the scope of these variables is relevant only within the `fil terArray` test group. Otherwise, once this test suite runs, these two variables will be available in the global test scope and can overlap other variables with the same name, causing unwanted behavior.

At this point, we have learned how to write tests for a function with the TDD approach using `it()`, `expect()`, and grouping them with `expect()`. While TDD is handy if we understand all the desired scenarios for our function, it can be challenging for beginners to adapt and follow. Consider combining TDD and other approaches rather than following a single process.

You can also use `test()` for `it()`, `assert()`, and for `expect()` as their alternatives. While its name should start with "should do something" representing a coherent sentence (such as "it should return a filtered array"), `test` can be any meaningful name.

Since composables in Vue are JavaScript functions that use Vue's Composition API, using Vitest to test them is simple. Next, we will explore how to write tests for composables, starting with the non-lifecycle ones.

Testing Non-Lifecycle Composables

We will start with a composition function, `useFilter`, that returns an object containing the following variables:

`filterBy`
    The key to filtering by

`filterTerm`
    The term to filter by

filteredArray
> The filtered array

order
> The order of the filtered array, with the default value of asc

It accepts a reactive array, arr, a key, and a term as initial values for the filtered array, the filter key, and the filter term.

The implementation for useFilter is as follows:

```
/** composables/useFilter.ts */
import { ref, computed, type Ref } from 'vue'

type ArrayObject = { [key: string]: string };

export function useFilter(
  arr: Ref<ArrayObject[]>,
  key: string,
  term: string
) { ❶
  const filterBy = ref(key) ❷
  const filterTerm = ref(term)
  const order = ref('asc')

  const filteredArray = computed(() => ❸
    arr.value.filter((item) =>
      item[filterBy.value]?.toLowerCase().includes(
        filterTerm.value.toLowerCase())
    ).sort((a, b) => {
      if (order.value === 'asc') {
        return a[filterBy.value] > b[filterBy.value] ? 1 : -1
      } else {
        return a[filterBy.value] < b[filterBy.value] ? 1 : -1
      }
    })
  );

  return {
    filterBy,
    filterTerm,
    filteredArray,
    order,
  }
}
```

❶ Declare arr as a reactive Ref type of ArrayObject and key and term as string types

❷ Create filterBy, filterTerm, and order as ref() with the initial values

❸ Create filteredArray as computed(), reacting to changes of filterBy, filter Term, order, and arr

In the `tests/` folder, we create a file `useFilter.test.ts` to test `useFilter`, with the following setup:

```
import { useFilter } from '@/composables/useFilter'

const books = [
  {
    id: '1',
    title: 'Gone with the wind',
    author: 'Margaret Mitchell',
    description:
    'A novel set in the American South during the Civil War and Reconstruction',
  },
  {
    id: '2',
    title: 'The Great Gatsby',
    description:
      'The story primarily concerns the mysterious millionaire Jay Gatsby',
    author: 'F. Scott Fitzgerald',
  },
  {
    id: '3',
    title: 'Little women',
    description: 'The March sisters live and grow in post-Civil War America',
    author: 'Louisa May Alcott',
  },
]

describe('useFilter', () => {
})
```

Since `books` is a constant array and not a Vue-reactive object, in our test case we will wrap it with `ref()` to enable its reactivity before passing it to the function for testing:

```
import { useFilter } from '@/composables/useFilter'
import { ref } from 'vue'

const books = ref([
  //...
]);

const result = [books.value[0]]
```

We also declare the expected `result` based on the books array value. Now we can write our first reactivity test case, where we assert the `useFilter` function to return the updated filtered array when changing `filterTerm`:

```
it(
  'should reactively return the filtered array when filterTerm is changed',
  () => {
  const { filteredArray, filterTerm } = useFilter(books, 'title', '');

  filterTerm.value = books.value[0].title;
  expect(filteredArray.value).toEqual(result);
})
```

When we run the test, it should pass with the output shown in Figure 11-6.

```
✓ tests/useFilter.test.ts (1)

Test Files  1 passed (1)
      Tests  1 passed (1)
   Start at  12:28:32
   Duration  628ms (transform 36ms, setup 0ms, collect 58ms, tests 2ms)
```

Figure 11-6. All the tests for useFilter pass

We can continue writing the test cases for filterBy and order in the same approach and have useFilter fully test-covered. In this example of useFilter, we asserted a composable that uses ref and computed under the hood. We can apply the same asserting practice to composables with similar APIs like watch, reactive, provide, etc. However, for composables that use onMounted, onUpdated, onUnmounted, etc., we use a different approach to test them, discussed next.

Testing Composables with Lifecycle Hook

The following composable, useFetch, uses onMounted to fetch data from an API:

```
/** composables/useFetch.ts */
import { ref, onMounted } from 'vue'

export function useFetch(url: string) {
  const data = ref(null)
  const error = ref(null)
  const loading = ref(true)

  const fetchData = async () => {
    try {
      const response = await fetch(url);

      if (!response.ok) {
        throw new Error(`Failed to fetch data for ${url}`);
      }

      data.value = await response.json();
    } catch (err: any) {
      error.value = err.message;
    } finally {
      loading.value = false;
    }
  };

  onBeforeMount(fetchData);

  return { data, error, loading }
}
```

The function receives a `url` parameter; fetches data from the given `url` before mount-ing the component; updates data, errors, and loading values accordingly; and returns them. Since this composable relies on `onBeforeMount` of a component's lifecycle to fetch data, we must create a Vue component and simulate the mounting process to test it.

We can do this by using `createApp` from the `vue` package and creating a component/app that uses `useFetch` in its `setup` hook:

```
/** tests/useFetch.test.ts */
import { createApp, type App } from 'vue'

function withSetup(composable: Function): [any, App<Element>] {
    let result;

    const app = createApp({
        setup() {
            result = composable();
            return () => {};
        },
    });

    app.mount(document.createElement("div"));

    return [result, app];
}
```

The `withSetup` function takes a `composable` and returns an array of `result` of the composable execution and the `app` instance created. We can then use `withSetup` in all our test cases to mimic the creation process of a component that uses `useFetch`:

```
import { useFetch } from '@/composables/useFetch'

describe('useFetch', () => {
  it('should fetch data from the given url', async () => {
    const [result, app] = withSetup(() => useFetch('your-test-url'));

    expect();
  });
});
```

However, there is one issue here. `useFetch` is using `fetch` API to fetch data; it is not a good practice to use the actual API in the test for these reasons:

- The test will fail if the API is down or the URL is invalid.
- The test will fail if the API is slow.

Thus, we need to mock the `fetch` API to simulate the response by using the `vi.spyOn` method:

```
import { vi } from 'vitest'

const fetchSpy = vi.spyOn(global, 'fetch');
```

We can place the `fetchSpy` declaration within the `describe` section to ensure the isolation of this spy from other test suites. And in the `beforeEach` hook, we need to reset every mocked implementation and value before running the test case with the `mockClear()` method:

```
describe('useFetch', () => {
  const fetchSpy = vi.spyOn(global, 'fetch');

  beforeEach(() => {
    fetchSpy.mockClear();
  });

  it('should fetch data from the given url', async () => {
    //...
  });
});
```

Let's write our test. We will first mock the `fetch` API to return a successful response with the `mockResolvedValueOnce` method:

```
it('should fetch data from the given url', async () => {
  fetchSpy.mockResolvedValueOnce({
    ok: true,
    json: () => Promise.resolve({ data: 'test' }),
  } as any);

  const [result, app] = withSetup(() => useFetch('your-test-url'));
});
```

After that, we can assert the `data` value of the `result` to be equal to the mocked data:

```
it('should fetch data from the given url', async () => {
  //...

  const [result, app] = withSetup(() => useFetch('your-test-url'));

  expect(result?.data.value).toEqual({ data: 'test' });
});
```

We can also expect calling the `fetch` with the given `url` with the `toHaveBeenCalledWith` method:

```
it('should fetch data from the given url', async () => {
  //...

  expect(fetchSpy).toHaveBeenCalledWith('your-test-url');
});
```

And finally, we need to unmount the app to clean up the test environment:

```
it('should fetch data from the given url', async () => {
  //...
  await app.unmount();
});
```

At this point, we expect the test to pass successfully. Unfortunately, the test will still fail. The reason is that while the `fetch` API is asynchronous, the component's lifecycle hook `beforeMount` isn't. The hook execution can finish before the `fetch` API is resolved, causing the `data` value to stay unchanged (Figure 11-7).

```
FAIL  tests/useFetch.test.ts > useFetch > should fetch data from the given url
AssertionError: expected null to deeply equal { data: 'test' }
> tests/useFetch.test.ts:37:36
    35|          const [result, app] = withSetup(() => useFetch('your-test-url'));
    36|
    37|          expect(result?.data.value).toEqual({ data: 'test' });
      |                                      ^
    38|          expect(fetchSpy).toHaveBeenCalledWith('your-test-url');
    39|

  - Expected   - 3
  + Received   + 1

  - Object {
  -   "data": "test",
  - }"
  + "null"
```

Figure 11-7. Failing test for `useFetch`

To fix this issue, we need help from another package, Vue Test Utils (`@vue/test-utils`), the official testing utility library for Vue (*https://oreil.ly/dZILU*). This package offers a set of utility methods to help test Vue components. We will import and use `flushPromises` from this package to wait for the `fetch` API to resolve before asserting the `data` value:

```
import { flushPromises } from '@vue/test-utils'

it('should fetch data from the given url', async () => {
  //...

  await flushPromises();

  expect(result.data.value).toEqual({ data: 'test' });
});
```

The test should pass successfully (Figure 11-8).

```
 ✓ tests/useFetch.test.ts (1)

 Test Files  1 passed (1)
      Tests  1 passed (1)
   Start at  13:18:00
   Duration  602ms (transform 67ms,
```

Figure 11-8. Passing the test for `useFetch`

You can also assert the loading value by placing the assertion before the flush Promises call:

```
it('should change loading value', async () => {
  //...

  expect(result.loading.value).toBe(true);

  await flushPromises();

  expect(result.loading.value).toBe(false);
});
```

Another benefit of mocking the fetch API is that we can simulate the failure response by using the mockRejectedValueOnce method and test our composable's error-handling logic:

```
it('should change error value', async () => {
  fetchSpy.mockRejectedValueOnce(new Error('test error'));

  const [result, app] = withSetup(() => useFetch('your-test-url'));

  expect(result.error.value).toBe(null);

  await flushPromises();

  expect(result.error.value).toEqual(new Error('test error'));
});
```

That's it. You can apply the same mocking approach to external test APIs in your applications or mock any dependent functions that are already tested and reduce the complexity of your test suites. We have successfully tested our useFetch method with Vitest and Vue Test Utils.

Next, we will explore how to test a Vue component with Vitest and Vue Test Utils.

Testing Components Using Vue Test Utils

The Vue engine uses the configurations of the Vue components to create and manage component instance updates on the browser DOM. Testing components means we will test the components' rendering results to the DOM. We set our test.environment to jsdom in the vite.config.ts for simulating the browser environment, which doesn't exist in the Node.js environment where the tests are running. We also use the methods like mount, shallowMount, etc., from the @vue/test-utils package to help mount the component and assert the rendering results from a virtual Vue node to a DOM element.

Let's look at our PizzaCard.vue component, shown in Example 11-1.

Example 11-1. PizzaCard component

```
<template>
  <article class="pizza--details-wrapper">
    <img :src="pizza.image" :alt="pizza.title" height="200" width="300" />
    <p>{{ pizza.description }}</p>
    <div class="pizza--inventory">
      <div class="pizza--inventory-stock">Stock: {{ pizza.quantity || 0 }}</div>
      <div class="pizza--inventory-price">$ {{ pizza.price }}</div>
    </div>
  </article>
</template>
<script setup lang="ts">
import type { Pizza } from "@/types/Pizza";
import type { PropType } from "vue";

const props = defineProps({
  pizza: {
    type: Object as PropType<Pizza>,
    required: true,
  },
});
</script>
```

We will create a test file `tests/PizzaCard.test.ts` to test the component. We will
import the `shallowMount` method from `@vue/test-utils` to mount the element
within the file. The `shallowMount` function receives two main arguments: the Vue
component to mount, and an object containing additional data for mounting the
component, such as props' values, stubs, etc. The following code demonstrates how
the test file looks, with the initial value for the `pizza` prop:

```
/** tests/PizzaCard.test.ts */
import { shallowMount } from '@vue/test-utils';
import PizzaCard from '@/components/PizzaCard.vue';

describe('PizzaCard', () => {
  it('should render the pizza details', () => {
    const pizza = {
      id: 1,
      title: 'Test Pizza',
      description: 'Test Pizza Description',
      image: 'test-pizza.jpg',
      price: 10,
      quantity: 10,
    };

    const wrapper = shallowMount(PizzaCard, {
      props: {
        pizza,
      },
    });

    expect();
  });
});
```

Using shallowMount vs mount

The `shallowMount` method is a wrapper around the `mount` method with its `shallow` flag active. It is best to use `shallowMount` to render and test the component without caring about its children. If you want to try the children components, use the `mount` method instead.

The `shallowMount` method returns a Vue instance, `wrapper`, with some helper methods to allow us to mimic UI interactions with the component. Once we have the wrapper instance, we can write our assertions. For example, we can use the `find` method to find the DOM element with the class selector `pizza--details-wrapper` and assert its existence:

```
/** tests/PizzaCard.test.ts */
//...

expect(wrapper.find('.pizza--details-wrapper')).toBeTruthy();
```

Similarly, we can assert the text content of the `.pizza--inventory-stock` and `.pizza--inventory-price` elements with the `text()` method:

```
/** tests/PizzaCard.test.ts */
//...

expect(
  wrapper.find('.pizza--inventory-stock').text()
).toBe(`Stock: ${pizza.quantity}`);
expect(wrapper.find('.pizza--inventory-price').text()).toBe(`$ ${pizza.price}`);
```

The `shallowMount` method also provides the `html` property to assert the rendered HTML of the component. We can then use `toMatchSnapshot` to test the HTML snapshot of the element:

```
/** tests/PizzaCard.test.ts */

expect(wrapper.html()).toMatchSnapshot();
```

Upon running the test, the testing engine will create a snapshot file, `Pizza Card.test.ts.snap`, and store the HTML snapshot of the component. On the next test run, Vitest will validate the component's HTML rendering against the existing snapshot, ensuring the component's stability in complex app development.

Using Snapshots

If you change the component's template, the snapshot test will fail. To solve this issue, you must update the snapshot by running the test with the -u flag as `yarn test -u`.

Due to the limitations of snapshot testing, you should use it only for the components that are not likely to change. A more recommended approach is to test HTML rendering in E2E tests using PlaywrightJS.

The instance received from the `find()` method is a wrapper around the DOM element, with various methods to assert the element's attributes and properties. We will add another test case where we will assert the `src` and `alt` attributes of the `img` element using the `attributes()` method:

```
/** tests/PizzaCard.test.ts */

describe('PizzaCard', () => {
  it('should render the pizza image and alt text', () => {
    //...

    const wrapper = shallowMount(PizzaCard, {
      props: {
        pizza,
      },
    });

    const img = wrapper.find('img')

    expect(img.attributes().alt).toEqual(pizza.title);
    expect(img.attributes().src).toEqual(pizza.image);
  });
});
```

Let's make the test fail by changing the `pizza.title` to a text of `Pineapple pizza`. As Figure 11-9 shows, the test will fail and show this message.

```
───────────────────────────────────────── Failed Tests 1 ──────────

 FAIL  tests/PizzaCard.test.ts > PizzaCard > should render the pizza details
AssertionError: expected 'Test Pizza' to deeply equal 'Pineapple pizza'
❯ tests/PizzaCard.test.ts:27:34
    25|      const img = wrapper.find('img')
    26|
    27|      expect(img.attributes().alt).toEqual("Pineapple pizza")
      |                                    ^
    28|    });
    29|

  - Expected    "Pineapple pizza"
  + Received    "Test Pizza"
```

Figure 11-9. Assertion of image alt text failed

As this screenshot shows, the received value is `Test Pizza`, highlighted in red, and the expected value is green. We also know the reason for the failure: "expected `Test Pizza` to deeply equal `Pineapple pizza`," with a pointer to the line where the test fails. This information lets us quickly fix the test or check our implementation to ensure the expected behavior is correct.

Other practical methods for asserting the component's interaction and data communication are the `trigger()` method of the DOM wrapper instance and `emitted()` of the wrapper instance. We will modify the implementation of the `PizzaCard` component to add an "Add to cart" button and test the button's behavior.

Testing Interaction and Events of a Component

We will add the following code to the `PizzaCard` component for a new Add to cart button:

```
/** src/components/PizzaCard.vue */

<template>
  <section v-if="pizza" class="pizza--container">
    <!-- ... -->
    <button @click="addCart">Add to cart</button>
  </section>
</template>
<script lang="ts" setup>
//...
const emits = defineEmits(['add-to-cart'])

const addCart = () => {
  emits('add-to-cart', { id: props.pizza.id, quantity: 1 })
}
</script>
```

The button accepts a `click` event, which triggers the `addCart` method. The `addCart` method will emit a `add-to-cart` event with the `pizza.id` and the new quantity as the payload. We can then test the `addCart` method by asserting the emitted event and its payload. First, we will look for the button using the `find()` method, and then trigger the `click` event using the `trigger()` method:

```
/** tests/PizzaCard.test.ts */

describe('PizzaCard', () => {
  it('should emit add-to-cart event when add to cart button is clicked', () => {
    //...

    const wrapper = shallowMount(PizzaCard, {
      props: {
        pizza,
      },
    });
```

```
    const button = wrapper.find('button');
    button.trigger('click');
  });
});
```

We will execute the `wrapper.emitted()` function to receive a map of emitted events, with the key being the event name, and the value is an array of received payloads. Each payload is an array of arguments passed to the `emits()` function apart from the event name. For instance, when we emit the `add-to-cart` event with the payload `{ id: 1, quantity: 1 }`, the emitted event will be `{ add-to-cart: [[{ id: 1, quantity: 1 }]] }`.

We can now assert the emitted event and its payload with the following code:

```
/** tests/PizzaCard.test.ts */

describe('PizzaCard', () => {
  it('should emit add-to-cart event when add to cart button is clicked', () => {
    //...

    expect(wrapper.emitted()['add-to-cart']).toBeTruthy();
    expect(wrapper.emitted()['add-to-cart'][0]).toEqual([
      { id: pizza.id, quantity: 1 }
    ]);
  });
});
```

Testing a Component That Uses a Pinia Store

You can use `createTestingPinia()` from the `@pinia/testing` package to create a testing Pinia instance and plug it in the component as a global plugin during mounting. This will allow you to test the component without mocking the store or using the real store instance.

The test passes successfully, as expected. At this point, we have covered the basic testing of components and composables with Vitest and Vue Test Utils. The following section will look at using Vitest with a GUI.

Using Vitest with a GUI

In some scenarios, looking at the terminal (or command line) outputs can be complex, and having a Graphic User Interface (GUI) can be beneficial. For such cases, Vitest offers `@vitest/ui` as its extra dependency along the command parameter `--ui`. To start using the Vitest UI, you need to install **@vitest/ui** with the following command in the terminal:

```
yarn add -D @vitest/ui
```

When running the command `yarn test --ui`, Vite will start a local server for its UI app and launch it on the browser, as shown in Figure 11-10.

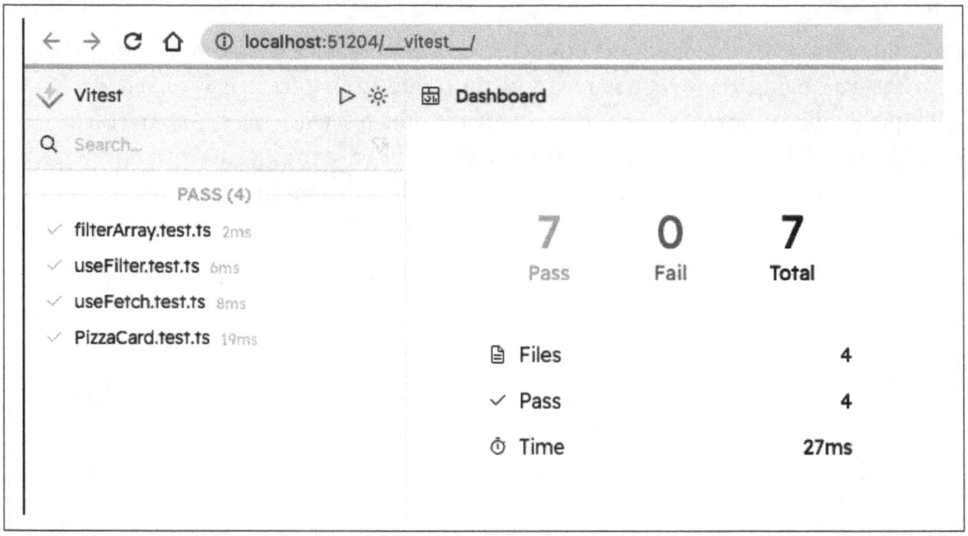

Figure 11-10. Vitest UI

On the left-side pane, we can see the list of test files with their status, indicated by relevant colors and icons. On the main dashboard is a quick summary of the test results, including the number of tests, the number of passed tests, and the number of failed tests. We can select a single test using the left-side pane and review each test case report, its module graph, and the implementation code for the tests. Figure 11-11 shows the test report for the `PizzaCard` component.

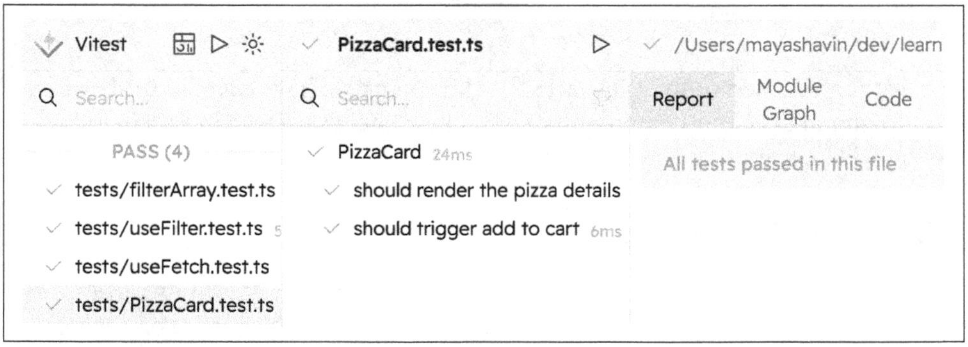

Figure 11-11. Vitest UI test report for `PizzaCard` component

You can also run the tests using the GUI by clicking the Run (or Rerun all) tests icon, as seen in Figure 11-12.

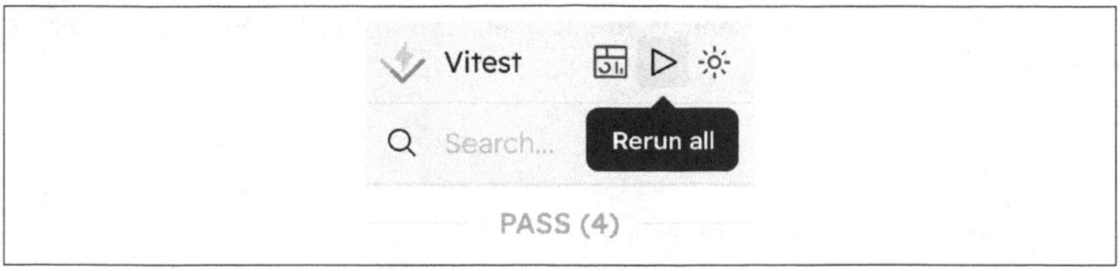

Figure 11-12. Run tests using the GUI

Using the GUI can be beneficial in some cases, but it can also be a distraction when you are working on a project and need to watch the tests during development. In this case, using the terminal may be a better option, and to review the test results, you can choose between the GUI, or the test coverage runner, which we will discuss next.

Using Vitest with a Coverage Runner

Writing tests is straightforward, but knowing if we write enough tests to cover all the scenarios of our test target is not. To create a sufficient testing system for our application, we use *code coverage* practice, which measures how much of our code we cover with our tests.

There are various tools for measuring code coverage and generating understandable reports. One of the most common tools is Istanbul, a JavaScript testing coverage tool. With Vitest, we can integrate Istanbul into our testing system using the `@vitest/coverage-istanbul` package. To install the package, run the following command in the terminal:

```
yarn add -D @vitest/coverage-istanbul
```

After installing the package, we can configure the `test.coverage` section in the `vite.config.ts` file with the provider as `istanbul`:

```
/** vite.config.ts */
export default defineConfig({
  //...
  test: {
    //...
    coverage: {
      provider: 'istanbul'
    }
  }
})
```

We also add a new script command in `package.json` to run the tests with coverage reports:

```
{
  //...
  "scripts": {
    //...
    "test:coverage": "vite test --coverage"
  }
}
```

When we run our tests using the command `yarn test:coverage`, we will see the coverage reports displayed in the terminal, as shown in Figure 11-13.

File	% Stmts	% Branch	% Funcs	% Lines	Uncovered Line #s
All files	83.87	20	88.88	83.87	
components	100	50	100	100	
PizzaCard.vue	100	50	100	100	6
composables	78.26	12.5	83.33	78.26	
useFetch.ts	84.61	50	100	84.61	13,18
useFilter.ts	70	0	75	70	14–17
utils	100	100	100	100	
filterArray.ts	100	100	100	100	

Figure 11-13. Coverage report in terminal

The Istanbul report tool will show you the percentage of your code in each file your tests cover during the testing execution process, dividing it into four categories: statements, branches, functions, and lines. It will also inform you of the line numbers of the uncovered code in the last column. For example, in Figure 11-13, for `composables/useFetch.ts`, we saw `13,18` in the *Uncovered Lines* column, indicating that our test for this file didn't cover the code in line 13 and line 18.

However, the terminal report is not always readable. For such a purpose, Istanbul will also generate a `coverage` folder in the `test.root` directory defined in `vite.config.ts`, or the root of the project. This folder contains the HTML reports for the coverage, denoted by `index.html`. You can open this file in the browser to see a prettier and more readable version of the coverage report, as shown in Figure 11-14.

All files

83.87% Statements 26/31 **20%** Branches 2/10 **88.88%** Functions 8/9 **83.87%** Lines 26/31

Press *n* or *j* to go to the next uncovered block, *b*, *p* or *k* for the previous block.

Filter: [   ]

File ▲		Statements		Branches		Functions		Lines	
components		100%	6/6	50%	1/2	100%	1/1	100%	6/6
composables		78.26%	18/23	12.5%	1/8	83.33%	5/6	78.26%	18/23
utils		100%	2/2	100%	0/0	100%	2/2	100%	2/2

Figure 11-14. Coverage report in HTML

If you set the `root` to point to the `src/tests` folder, you should change it to `src`. Otherwise, Istanbul can't locate and analyze the source files' coverage.

The HTML version displays test coverage by folders and files, with their names on the first column, *File*. The second column, with the progress bar, shows the coverage percentage for each file in colors (green means fully covered, yellow means partly covered, and red means not meeting the acceptance coverage level). The other columns show the coverage breakdown in statements, branches, functions, and lines.

We can click on each folder name to see the breakdown report per file within this folder, such as in */composables* in Figure 11-15.

All files composables

78.26% Statements 18/23 **12.5%** Branches 1/8 **83.33%** Functions 5/6 **78.26%** Lines 18/23

Press *n* or *j* to go to the next uncovered block, *b*, *p* or *k* for the previous block.

Filter: [   ]

File ▲		Statements		Branches		Functions		Lines	
useFetch.ts		84.61%	11/13	50%	1/2	100%	2/2	84.61%	11/13
useFilter.ts		70%	7/10	0%	0/6	75%	3/4	70%	7/10

Figure 11-15. Coverage report for composables

You can click on each file name to see the highlights of untested code lines in red and the number of times a line we covered (like 3x), as shown in Figure 11-16.

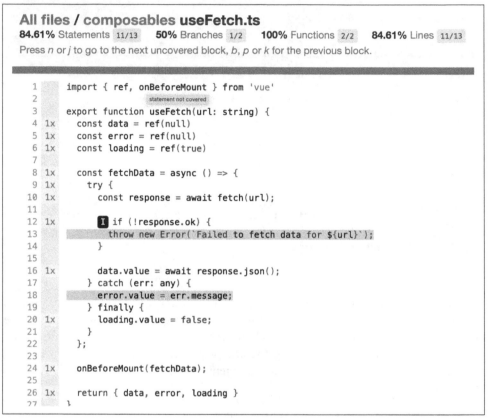

Figure 11-16. Coverage report for useFetch

The HTML report version is also interactive during watch mode, meaning that it will update the coverage report automatically when you change the code or the tests. This mechanism is handy during development, as you can see the coverage report changes in real time.

We can also set the coverage threshold for each category using the `test.coverage` section in `vite.config.ts`:

```
/** vite.config.ts */

export default defineConfig({
  //...
  test: {
    //...
    coverage: {
      provider: 'istanbul',
      statements: 80,
```

```
            branches: 80,
            functions: 80,
            lines: 80
        }
    }
})
```

In this code, we set the coverage threshold for each category to 80%. If the coverage percentage for any type is lower than the threshold, the test will fail with an error message, as seen in Figure 11-17.

```
Test Files  4 passed (4)
     Tests  7 passed (7)
  Start at  13:26:17
  Duration  839ms (transform 585ms, setup 0ms, collect 850ms, tests 34ms)

% Coverage report from istanbul
------------------|----------|----------|----------|----------|--------------------
File              | % Stmts  | % Branch | % Funcs  | % Lines  | Uncovered Line #s
------------------|----------|----------|----------|----------|--------------------
All files         |   83.87  |       20 |   88.88  |   83.87  |
 components        |     100  |       50 |     100  |     100  |
  PizzaCard.vue    |     100  |       50 |     100  |     100  | 6
 composables       |   78.26  |     12.5 |   83.33  |   78.26  |
  useFetch.ts      |   84.61  |       50 |     100  |   84.61  | 13,18
  useFilter.ts     |      70  |        0 |       75 |      70  | 14-17
 utils             |     100  |      100 |     100  |     100  |
  filterArray.ts   |     100  |      100 |     100  |     100  |
------------------|----------|----------|----------|----------|--------------------
ERROR: Coverage for branches (20%) does not meet global threshold (80%)
```

Figure 11-17. Error when a test doesn't meet the coverage threshold

Code coverage is essential for testing since it provides the benchmark to help you protect your code from bugs and ensure the quality of your application. However, it is just a tool to help you manage your tests, and you still need to write good tests to ensure your code quality and standards.

Setting the Threshold Number

Try to keep your coverage threshold number between 80% and 85%. It can be overkill if you set it to more than 85%. If less than 80%, it can be too low since you may miss some edge cases that cause bugs in your application.

We have explored unit testing using Vitest and other tools like Vue Test Utils for Vue-specific testing and Istanbul for code coverage. We will move to the next testing level, where we will learn how to write E2E tests for our application using PlaywrightJS.

End-to-End Testing with PlaywrightJS

PlaywrightJS (*https://oreil.ly/sIUKp*), or Playwright, is a fast, reliable cross-browser end-to-end testing framework. It supports programming languages besides Java-Script, such as Python, Java, and C#. It also supports multiple browser rendering engines like WebKit, Firefox, and Chromium, allowing us to perform testing in cross-browser environments on the same codebase.

To start using Playwright, run the following command:

```
yarn create Playwright
```

Yarn will run the creation script for Playwright, with the prompts asking for the test location (e2e), if we want to install GitHub Actions as the pipeline tool for CI/CD, and if it should install Playwright browsers. Figure 11-18 shows an example of a configuration for initializing Playwright in our application.

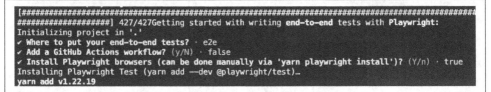

Figure 11-18. Initializing Playwright with prompts

After the initialization process, we will see a new e2e folder in the root of our project, with a single example.spec.ts file. Also, Playwright will generate a configuration file, playwright.config.ts, for our project, modifying the package.json with the relevant packages and another test-examples folder containing a working test example for a todo component using Playwright.

We can now add a new script command in our package.json to run our E2E tests using Playwright:

```
"scripts": {
  //...
  "test:e2e": "npx playwright test"
}
```

Similarly, we can add the following command to run the coverage reporter on our tests:

```
"scripts": {
  //...
  "test:e2e-report": "npx playwright show-report"
}
```

By default, Playwright comes with an HTML coverage reporter, and this reporter runs when any test fails during the test run. We can try to run the tests using these commands and see the example tests passed.

Let's look at the `playwright.config.ts` and see what it contains:

```
import { defineConfig, devices } from '@playwright/test';

/** playwright.config.ts */
export default defineConfig({
  testDir: './e2e',
  fullyParallel: true,
  forbidOnly: !!process.env.CI,
  retries: process.env.CI ? 2 : 0,
  workers: process.env.CI ? 1 : undefined,
  reporter: 'html',
  use: {
    trace: 'on-first-retry',
  },
  projects: [
    {
      name: 'chromium',
      use: { ...devices['Desktop Chrome'] },
    },
    {
      name: 'webkit',
      use: { ...devices['Desktop Safari'] },
    },
  ]
})
```

The configuration file exports an instance created by the `defineConfig()` method, based on a set of configuration options with the following main properties:

testDir

> The directory where we store the tests. We usually define it during the initialization process (**e2e** in our case).

projects

> The list of browser projects for running the tests. We can import `devices` from the same `@playwright/test` package and select the relevant setup to define the browser's configuration for Playwright to use, such as `devices[Desktop Chrome]` for the Chromium browser.

worker

> The number of parallel workers to run the tests on. This feature is helpful when we have many tests and need to run them in parallel to speed up the test process.

use

> The configuration object for the test runner, including an optional `baseURL` as the base URL and `trace` to enable the trace recording for failed tests on retry.

Other properties can customize our Playwright test runner as needed. See the complete list of configuration options at the Playwright documentation (*https://oreil.ly/nXapE*).

We will leave the file as is and write our first E2E test for our application. Let's head to the `vite.config.ts` and make sure we have the following configuration for the local server:

```
//...
export default defineConfig({
  //...
  server: {
    port: 3000
  }
})
```

By setting the port to 3000, we ensure our local URL will always be *http://localhost:3000*. Next, we will create a new E2E test file in the e2e folder with the name `Pizzas View.spec.ts`, dedicated to testing the *"/pizzas"* page. The *"/pizzas"* page uses the `PizzasView` view component to display a list of pizzas with the following template:

```
<template>
  <div class="pizzas-view--container">
    <h1>Pizzas</h1>
    <input v-model="search" placeholder="Search for a pizza" />
    <ul>
      <li v-for="pizza in searchResults" :key="pizza.id">
        <PizzaCard :pizza="pizza" />
      </li>
    </ul>
  </div>
</template>
<script lang="ts" setup>
import { usePizzas } from "@/composables/usePizzas";
import PizzaCard from "@/components/PizzaCard.vue";
import { useSearch } from "@/composables/useSearch";

const { pizzas } = usePizzas();
const { search, searchResults }: PizzaSearch = useSearch({
  items: pizzas,
  defaultSearch: '',
});
</script>
```

We want to write the tests for this page. Like Vitest, we start by wrapping the test file with a `test.describe()` block, where we import `test` from `@playwright/test` package. We then ensure the test runner will always navigate to our target page before testing the page content using the `test.beforeEach()` hook:

```
/** e2e/PizzasView.spec.ts */
import { expect, test } from '@playwright/test';

test.describe('Pizzas View', () => {
  test.beforeEach(async ({ page }) => {
```

```
    await page.goto('http://localhost:3000/pizzas');
  });
});
```

We also ensure the page is closed after finishing the tests using the `test.afterEach()` hook:

```
/** e2e/PizzasView.spec.ts */

test.describe('Pizzas View', () => {
  //...

  test.afterEach(async ({ page }) => {
    await page.close();
  });
});
```

We can start writing our first test for the page, such as checking the page title. We can use the `page.locator()` method to locate the page element. In this case, it is the `h1` element and asserts its content to be the text `Pizzas`:

```
/** e2e/PizzasView.spec.ts */

test.describe('Pizzas View', () => {
  //...

  test('should display the page title', async ({ page }) => {
    const title = await page.locator('h1');
    expect(await title.textContent()).toBe('Pizzas');
  });
});
```

We can run the test using the `yarn test:e2e` command and see the test passed (Figure 11-19).

Figure 11-19. Test report showing passing E2E tests with Playwright

Great! We can add more tests to the file, such as checking the search functionality. We can locate the search `input` element using its tag name or the `data-testid` attribute as a better approach. To use the `data-testid` attribute, we need to add it to the `input` in the `PizzasView` component template:

```
<input
  v-model="search"
  placeholder="Search for a pizza"
  data-testid="search-input"
/>
```

Then, we can locate the element using the `data-testid` attribute in our new test and `fill` it with the search term `Hawaiian`:

```
/** e2e/PizzasView.spec.ts */

test.describe('Pizzas View', () => {
  //...

  test('should search for a pizza', async ({ page }) => {
    const searchInput = await page.locator('[data-testid="search-input"]');

    await searchInput.fill('Hawaiian');
  });
});
```

To assert the result of the search, we will head to the `PizzaCard` implementation and add the `data-testid` attribute to the container element with the value of `pizza.title`:

```
<!-- src/components/PizzaCard.vue -->
<template>
  <article class="pizza--details-wrapper" :data-testid="pizza.title">
    <!--...-->
  </article>
</template>
```

Back to our `PizzasView.spec.ts` file, we can assert the visibility of pizza card with the `data-testid` attribute containing the search term on the page:

```
/** e2e/PizzasView.spec.ts */

test.describe('Pizzas View', () => {
  //...
  test('should search for a pizza', async ({ page }) => {
    const searchInput = await page.locator('[data-testid="search-input"]');

    await searchInput.fill('Hawaiian');

    expect(await page.isVisible('[data-testid*="Hawaiian"]')).toBeTruthy();
  });
});
```

We can rerun the test suite and see the tests passed (Figure 11-20).

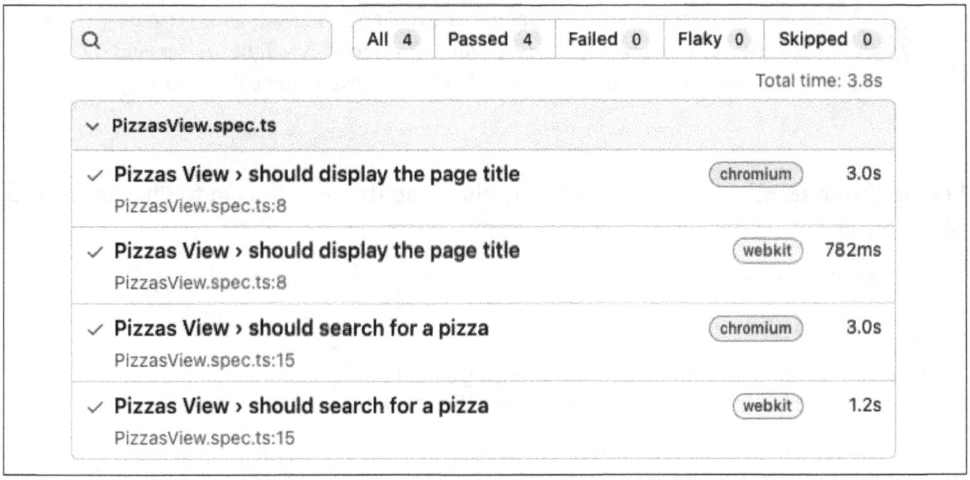

Figure 11-20. Test report showing the search tests passed

We can also click on each test displayed in the report to view the test details, including the test steps, their execution time, and any errors that occurred during the test execution in a target browser environment (Figure 11-21).

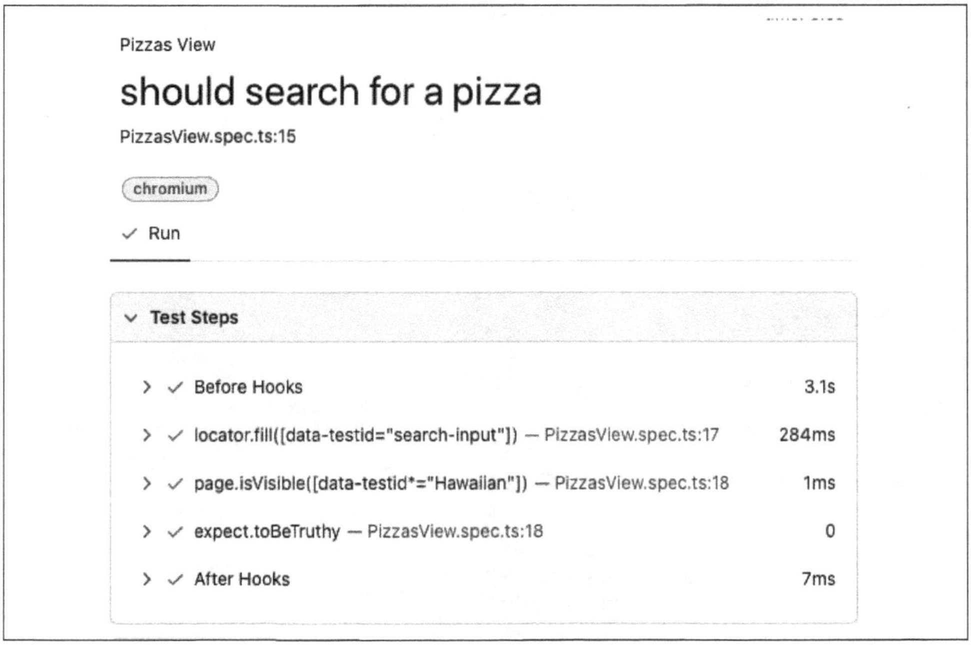

Figure 11-21. Details report for a single test run on Chromium

You must use `await` for `page.isVisible()` method, as it returns a Promise. Otherwise, the test will fail since Playwright will execute the assertion before the `isVisible()` process returns the result.

Let's edit our search test to make it fail by changing the search term to `Cheese` instead of `Hawaiian`:

```
/** e2e/PizzasView.spec.ts */

test.describe('Pizzas View', () => {
  //...
  test('should search for a pizza', async ({ page }) => {
    const searchInput = await page.locator('[data-testid="search-input"]');

    await searchInput.fill('Cheese');

    expect(await page.isVisible('[data-testid*="Hawaiian"]')).toBeTruthy();
  });
});
```

We can rerun the test suite and see if the test failed (Figure 11-22).

should search for a pizza

PizzasView.spec.ts:15

(chromium)

✕ Run
_____

> Errors

⌄ Test Steps

> ✓ Before Hooks	7.8s
> ✓ locator.fill([data-testid="search-input"]) — PizzasView.spec.ts:17	339ms
> ✓ page.isVisible([data-testid*="Hawaiian"]) — PizzasView.spec.ts:18	10ms
⌄ ✕ expect.toBeTruthy — PizzasView.spec.ts:18	2ms

```
17 |       await searchInput.fill('Cheese');
18 |       expect(await page.isVisible('[data-testid*="Hawaiian"]')).toBeTruthy();
   |
19 |     });
```

Figure 11-22. Test report showing the search test failed

The report shows which step the test failed. Let's debug it.

Debugging E2E Tests Using Playwright Test Extension for VSCode

We can install the Playwright Test for VSCode extension (*https://oreil.ly/9zlFB*) to debug a failed test. This extension will add another section on the Testing tab of VSCode, and auto-detect the relevant Playwright tests within the project, as shown in Figure 11-23.

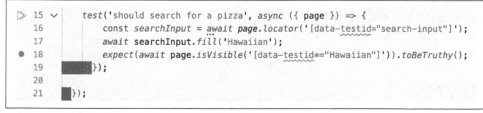

Figure 11-23. Testing tab displays the Playwright tests in the project

We can run the tests or a single test using the actions available on this view. We can also add breakpoints (denoted by the red dot) to debug a target test (Figure 11-24).

```
15 ∨    test('should search for a pizza', async ({ page }) => {
16           const searchInput = await page.locator('[data-testid="search-input"]');
17           await searchInput.fill('Hawaiian');
● 18           expect(await page.isVisible('[data-testid*="Hawaiian"]')).toBeTruthy();
19        });
20
21    });
```

Figure 11-24. Adding breakpoints to debug a test

To start debugging, navigate to the search test in the Test Explorer pane and click on the "Debug" icon (Figure 11-25). Hovering on the "Debug" icon will display the text "Debug Text."

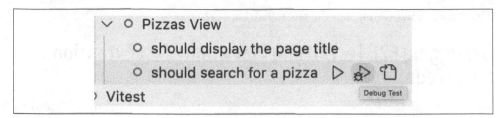

Figure 11-25. Run a test in debug mode

Upon running, Playwright will open a browser window (such as Chromium) and execute the test steps. Once the test runner reaches the breakpoint, it will stop and wait for us to continue the execution manually. Then we can hover over the variables to see their values or head to the testing browser to inspect the elements (Figure 11-26).

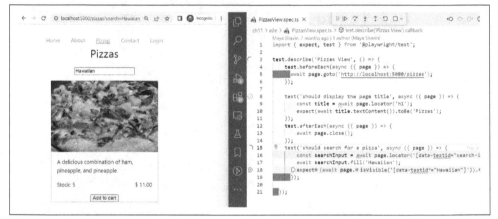

Figure 11-26. Debugging the search test

What's left is to fix the test and continue the debugging process until the test passes.

We have learned how to create basic E2E tests with Playwright and how to debug them with the help of external tools. Playwright provides many other features, such as generating the test based on the actual interaction with the application or performing accessibility testing with the `@axe-core/playwright` package. Check out other features and see how Playwright can help create better E2E tests for your application.

Summary

This chapter introduced the concept of testing and how to use Vitest as a unit testing tool for Vue applications. We learned how to write basic tests for components and composables with Vitest and Vue Test Utils and how to use external packages such as a coverage runner and Vitest UI for a better UI experience. We also explored creating E2E tests with PlaywrightJS, ensuring code confidence throughout our application.

CHAPTER 12

Continuous Integration/Continuous Deployment of Vue.Js Applications

The previous chapter showed us how to set up testing for our Vue application, from unit tests with Vite to E2E tests with Playwright. With our application covered with proper tests, we can move on to the next step: deployment.

This chapter will introduce you to the concept of CI/CD and how to set up a CI/CD pipeline using GitHub Actions for your Vue application. We will also learn how to use Netlify as our deployment and hosting platform for our application.

CI/CD in Software Development

Continuous integration (CI) and continuous delivery (CD) are combined software development practices aiming to speed up and stabilize the software development and delivery process. CI/CD includes monitoring the software lifecycle effectively through an automated integration, testing, and continuous software deployment to production process.

CI/CD offers many benefits to software development, including:

- Faster software delivery with automated deployment
- Stronger collaboration between different teams
- Better software quality with automated testing
- Faster response to bugs and software issues in a more agile approach

In short, CI/CD contains three main concepts: continuous integration, continuous delivery, and continuous deployment, and when combined, they form a robust software development process known as the CI/CD pipeline (Figure 12-1).

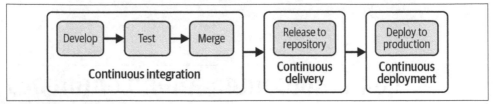

Figure 12-1. CI/CD pipeline

Continuous Integration

Continuous integration enables developers to integrate code into a shared repository frequently and simultaneously while working independently. With each code integration (or merge), we validate it using an automated build of the application and an automated system of different levels of testing. If there are conflicts between new and old code versions or any problems with the new code, we can detect and fix them quickly. Standard tools for continuous integration include Jenkins, CircleCI, and GitHub Actions, which we will discuss in "CI/CD Pipeline with GitHub Actions" on page 290.

Continuous Delivery

The next step after a successful continuous integration is continuous delivery. Continuous delivery automates the release of the validated application's code to the shared repository, making it ready for production deployment. Continuous delivery requires continuous integration since it assumes the code is always verified. It also includes another series of automated testing and release automation.

Continuous Deployment

Continuous deployment is the CI/CD pipeline's final step, automatically deploying the validated code to production. It relies significantly on a well-tested automation system for the codebase. Continuous deployment is the most advanced step of the CI/CD pipeline. It is only necessary for some projects, especially when manual approval is necessary before production deployment.

The three stages of the CI/CD pipeline form a more secure and flexible application development and deployment process. In the next section, we will learn how to set up a CI/CD pipeline for our Vue application using GitHub Actions.

CI/CD Pipeline with GitHub Actions

Provided by GitHub, GitHub Actions is a platform-agnostic, language-agnostic, and cloud-agnostic CI/CD platform. It is straightforward to use and free for projects hosted on the GitHub platform. Each CI/CD pipeline in GitHub Actions contains single or multiple workflows, denoted by a YAML file. Each workflow includes a series of jobs and executes in parallel or sequentially. Each job has a series of steps containing many sequential actions. And each action is a standalone command or a script that gets executed in the designated runner environment (Example 12-1).

Example 12-1. Example GitHub workflow file

```
name: Example workflow
on: [push, pull_request]
jobs:
    first-job:
        steps:
        - name: First step
            run: echo "Hello world"
        - name: Second step
            run: echo "Second step"
    second-job:
        steps:
        - name: First step
            run: echo "Do something in second job."
```

> The workflow file follows YAML syntax. You can learn how to use YAML syntax at the workflow syntax for GitHub Actions documentation (*https://oreil.ly/uIIkh*).

To start using GitHub Actions, within our Vue project directory, we will create a new directory named .github/workflows with a workflow file, ci.yml. This file will contain the configuration for our CI/CD pipeline. For example, the following is a simple workflow file that runs our unit tests:

```
name: CI for Unit tests
on:
    push:
        branches: [ main ] ❶
    pull_request:
        branches: [ main ] ❷
jobs:
    unit-tests:
      timeout-minutes: 60
      runs-on: ubuntu-latest
      steps:
      - uses: actions/checkout@v3      ❸
      - uses: actions/setup-node@v3    ❹
        with:
          node-version: 18
      - name: Install dependencies ❺
        run: npm i
      - name: Execute unit tests
        run: npm run test:coverage ❻
      - name: Uploading artifacts ❼
```

```
uses: actions/upload-artifact@v3
with:
  name: test-results
  path: test-results/
  retention-days: 30
```

❶ The workflow will be triggered when there is a push to the `main` branch or

❷ When there is a pull request to merge to `main`

❸ Checkout the testing branch to a runner environment using built-in GitHub Actions, `actions/checkout`

❹ Set up the node environment with Node.js version 18.x using built-in GitHub Actions, `actions/setup-node`

❺ Install dependencies

❻ Run unit tests with reporting coverage

❼ Upload the test report to GitHub Actions as artifacts

Each job is a standalone process and does not share the same environment. Therefore, in its steps, we need to install dependencies for each job separately.

On GitHub, we can navigate to the Actions tab to see the status of our workflow (Figure 12-2).

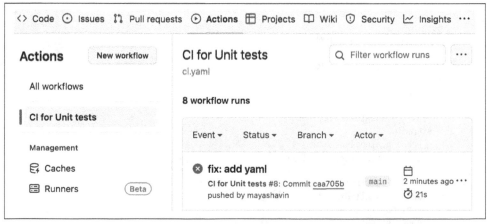

Figure 12-2. GitHub Actions page with workflow running

GitHub displays the workflows according to the commits, with their status and the target branch (main). We can then view the status of each job within a workflow by clicking on the job name, such as how we can see the status of the *unit-tests* job in Figure 12-3.

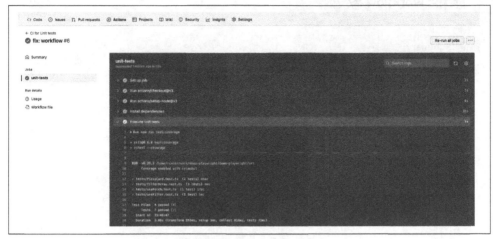

Figure 12-3. Unit-tests of the job's running status in steps

Once the workflow finishes running, we can see the test report uploaded to the Artifacts section (Figure 12-4).

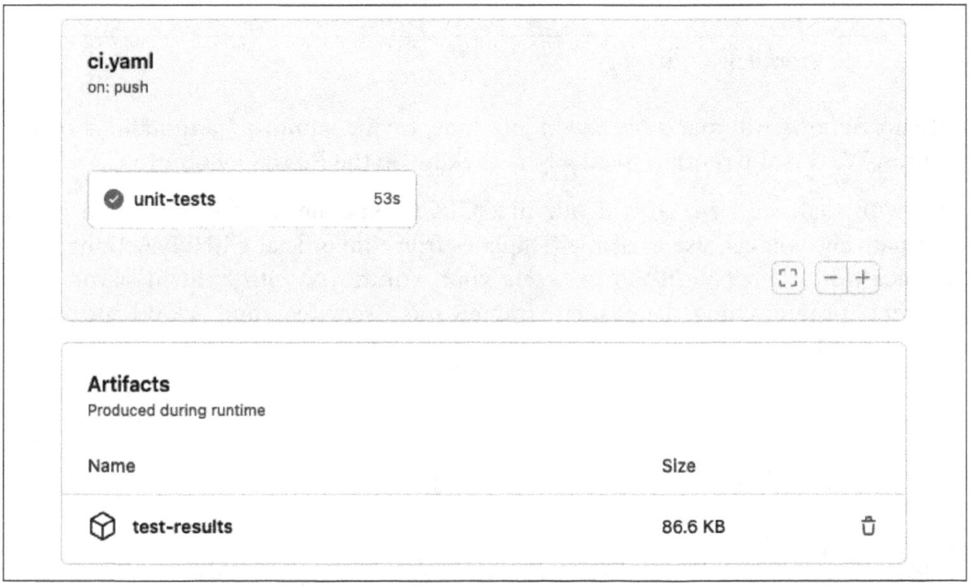

```
ci.yaml
on: push


    ✓   unit-tests                    53s


                                           [ ] ( - | + )


Artifacts
Produced during runtime

Name                                   Size

📦  test-results                        86.6 KB                🗑
```

Figure 12-4. Artifacts section with test report

We also can check the status result of a workflow, broken down by jobs, by clicking on the workflow name (Figure 12-5).

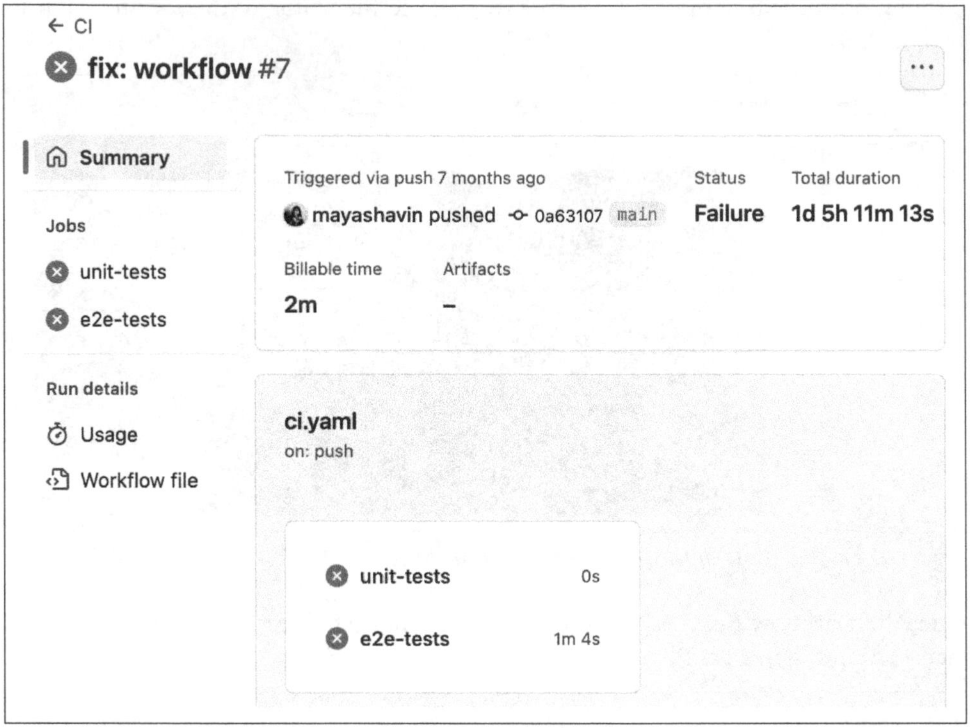

```
← CI
❌ fix: workflow #7                                              ...

🏠 Summary        Triggered via push 7 months ago          Status      Total duration
                  👤 mayashavin pushed  -o- 0a63107  main   Failure     1d 5h 11m 13s
Jobs
❌ unit-tests     Billable time      Artifacts
❌ e2e-tests      2m                 –

Run details
⏱ Usage          ci.yaml
📄 Workflow file  on: push

                         ❌ unit-tests              0s

                         ❌ e2e-tests               1m 4s
```

Figure 12-5. Workflow status page

GitHub Actions will mark any failed job and provide summary annotations of the failures. We can also rerun a failed job by clicking on the *Re-run jobs* button.

And with that, we have created our first CI/CD pipeline for our Vue application. Alternatively, you can use available templates from the official GitHub Actions marketplace (*https://oreil.ly/ch9V2*) to create your workflows, with built-in support for different programming languages, frameworks, services, and cloud providers (Figure 12-6).

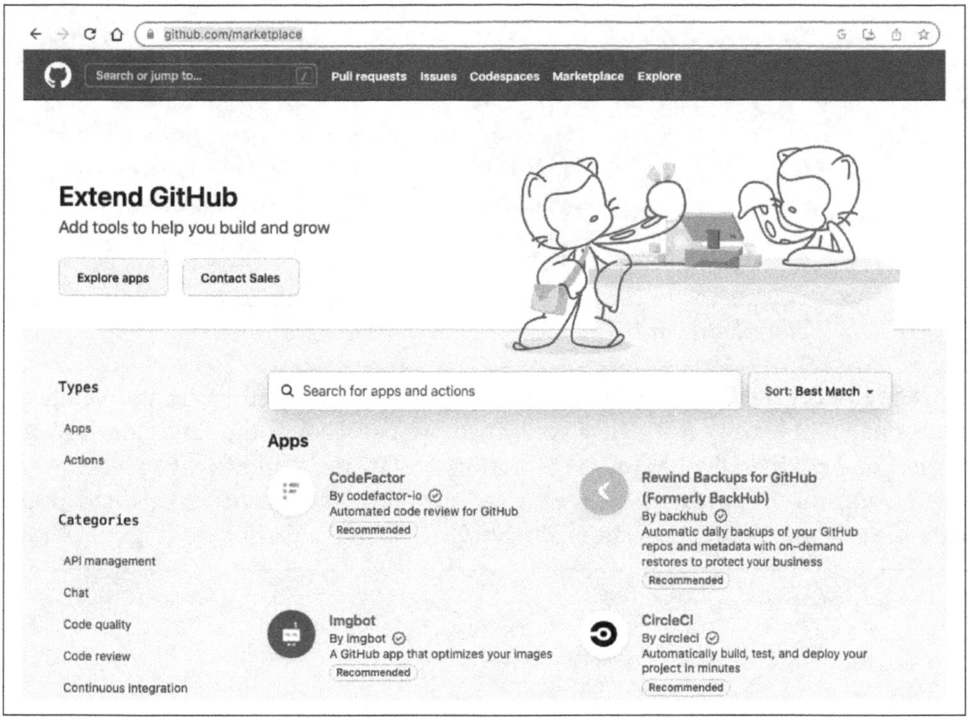

Figure 12-6. GitHub Actions marketplace

Based on our workflow example, you can create more workflows for your application if required or extend the current workflow to include more steps, such as deployment. In the next section, we will learn how to set up continuous deployment for our application using Netlify.

Continuous Deployment with Netlify

Netlify is a cloud platform that offers a wide range of services for hosting modern web applications, including hosting, serverless functions APIs, and CI/CD integration. It is free for personal projects while offering a generous free tier for commercial ones.[1]

To deploy our Vue project on Netlify, we need to create a Netlify account (*https:// oreil.ly/uLHpQ*) and log in. Once logged in to the dashboard, we can head to the *Sites* tab and click on the *Add new site* button to import our project from the GitHub provider for automatic deployment, or deploy manually (Figure 12-7).

---

1 Other alternatives are Azure Static Web Apps and Vercel.

Figure 12-7. Netlify dashboard

Next, we select the Git provider for our project (GitHub) and authorize Netlify to access our GitHub account. Once confirmed, we can choose the repository for our project and click on the `Deploy site` button to start the deployment process. After completing the deployment, we can view our site deployment's status and other details, such as a PR preview on the *Site overview* tab of the dashboard (Figure 12-8).

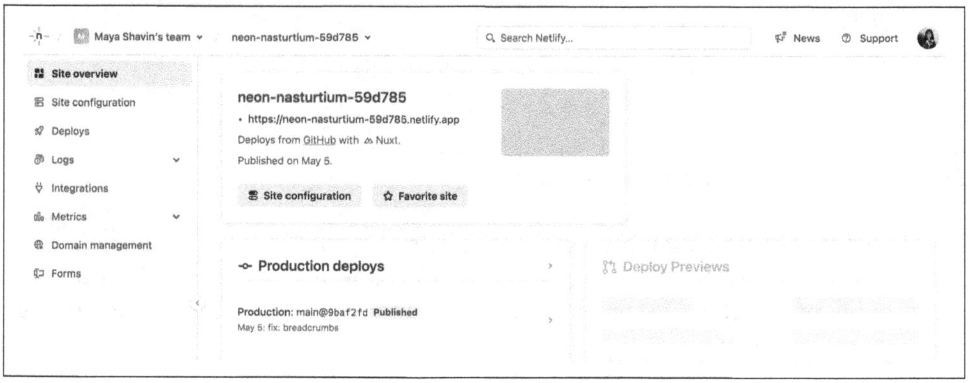

Figure 12-8. Netlify site overview

Once deployed successfully, Netlify will provide a temporary URL to access the application. In fact, you can configure your site's custom domain by navigating to the *Domain Management* section (Figure 12-9).

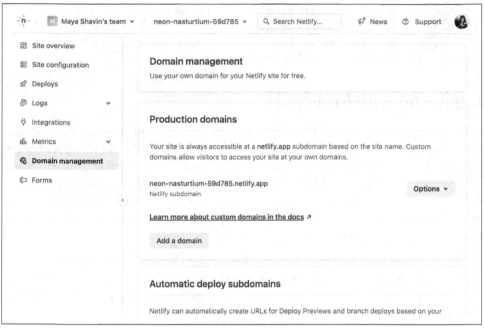

Figure 12-9. Netlify domain settings

By default, once integrated, Netlify will automatically deploy your application whenever a new commit is merged to the main branch. Additionally, it will generate a preview build for each pull request. Within this view, you can also configure additional settings such as build command, deployment context for continuous deployment, and environment variables for your application. Netlify also offers build hooks as a unique URL for triggering build and deployment with a third-party service like Github Actions workflow via HTTP requests (Figure 12-10).

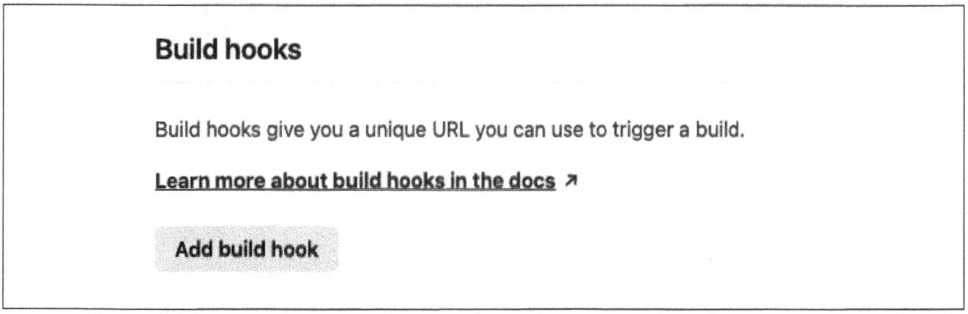

Build hooks

Build hooks give you a unique URL you can use to trigger a build.

Learn more about build hooks in the docs ↗

Add build hook

Figure 12-10. Build a hook section in Site settings

You can manually build your application using the `yarn build` command locally, then drag and drop the `dist` folder to the Netlify app (*https://oreil.ly/LInwT*) to deploy your application to a temporary URL provided by Netlify.

Deploying with Netlify CLI

Alternatively, we can install the Netlify CLI as a global tool in our local machine, using the command `npm install -g netlify-cli`. With this CLI installed, we can initialize our project for Netlify using the command `netlify init`. This command will prompt us to log in to the relevant account (GitHub) and prepare our project for deployment. Once initialized and ready, we can run the command `netlify deploy` to deploy our project to a temporary URL for previewing or `netlify deploy --prod` to deploy to production directly.

We have successfully deployed our first Vue application to Netlify. Other advanced features Netlify offers include serverless functions, form handling, and split testing. You can explore these features per the project's requirements using the Netlify official documentation (*https://oreil.ly/6X9F6*).

Summary

In this chapter, we have learned about the concept of CI/CD and how to set up a simple CI/CD process for our Vue application using GitHub Actions. We also learned about Netlify and how to automatically deploy our application to Netlify hosting. In the next chapter, we will explore the final aspects of the Vue ecosystem, server-side rendering (SSR) and static site generation (SSG) using Nuxt.js.

CHAPTER 13

Server-Side Rendering with Vue

In the previous chapter, we learned how to set up our Vue application's complete CI/CD pipeline. We also learned how to deploy our application using Netlify for production. Our application is now ready for users to access via the web. With that, we have almost finished our journey with learning Vue. This chapter will explore the other aspect of using Vue, the server-side rendering and static site generation with Nuxt.js.

Client-Side Rendering in Vue

By default, Vue applications are for client-side rendering, with a placeholder `index.html` file, JavaScript file (usually compiled in chunks by Vite for performance optimization), and other files like CSS, icons, images, etc., for a complete UI experience. In the initial load, the browser sends a request to the server for the `index.html` file. In return, the server will deliver the original placeholder file (often with a single element with a unique id selector `app` for the Vue engine to mount the app instance, and a `script` tag pointing to the required JavaScript file containing the main code. Once the browser receives the HTML file, it will start parsing and request additional resources, such as the desired `main.js` file, then execute it to render the rest of the content accordingly (Figure 13-1).

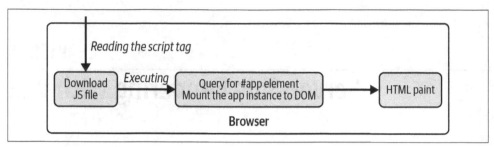

Figure 13-1. Flow of rendering a client-side Vue application

From this point on, the application finishes initialization, and the user can start interacting with it. Vue will dynamically handle the view-changing requests by users with the built-in routing system. However, if you right-click the page and select *View page source*, you will see only the code of the original root index.html file but not the current UI view. This behavior can be problematic, especially when building a website or an app that requires good Search Engine Optimization[1] (SEO).

In addition, the process of loading and executing JavaScript code before displaying any content to the user can cause a long waiting time for the user due to factors such as heavyweight JavaScript files to download, slow networks, the amount of time the browser takes to paint the content (First Paint), etc. As a result, the whole process can lead to a slow Time To Interactive[2] (TTI) and a slow First Contentful Paint[3] (FCP). All of these factors affect the overall app performance and user experience and often are challenging to fix.

In such scenarios, there may be better choices than client-side rendering applications, such as server-side rendering, which we will explore next.

Server-Side Rendering (SSR)

As its name indicates, server-side rendering (SSR) is an approach to compile everything on the server side into a fully working HTML page and then deliver to the client side (browser) on demand, instead of performing on the browser.

To develop a local SSR Vue application, we will need a local server to communicate with the browser and handle all the data requests. We can do this by installing Express.js[4] as our project's dependency with the following command:

---

1 SEO is the process of making your app better for search engines to index in the search results.

2 The time when the user can interact with the page.

3 The first time when content is visible to the user.

4 Express.js is a Node.js web application framework.

```
yarn add express
```

Once this is installed, we can create a server.js file in our project's root directly with the code in Example 13-1 to set up our local server.

Example 13-1. The server.js file for the local server

```
import express from 'express'

const server = express()
```

```
server.get('/', (req, res) => {
    res.send(`
        <!DOCTYPE html>
        <html>
        <head>
            <title>Vue SSR Example</title>
        </head>
        <body>
            <main id="app">Vue SSR Demo</main>
        </body>
        </html>
    `)
})

server.listen(3000, () => { console.log('We are ready to go') })
```

❶ Create a server instance

❷ Define the handler for any request for the entry URL "/"

❸ The handler will return a string acting as an HTML page that displays *Vue SSR Demo* on the browser.

❹ We set up the local server to run and listen at port 3000.

Within the project's root directory, we can start our local server using the node server.js command. Once our server is ready, we must create our application on the server with the method createSSRApp from the vue package. For example, let's compose a Vue application that displays a digital clock with the current date and time in a dedicated file, app.js, with the code in Example 13-2.

Example 13-2. The app.js file for the Digital Clock application

```
import { createSSRApp, ref } from 'vue'

const App = {
    template: `
        <h1>Digital Clock</h1>
        <p class="date">{{ date }}</p>
```

```
          <p class="time">{{ time }}</p>
    `,
  setup() {
      const date = ref('');
      const time = ref('');

      setInterval(() => {
          const WEEKDAYS = ['SUN', 'MON', 'TUE', 'WED', 'THU', 'FRI', 'SAT'];
          const MONTHS = [
              'Jan', 'Feb', 'Mar',
              'Apr', 'May', 'Jun',
              'Jul', 'Aug', 'Sep',
              'Oct', 'Nov', 'Dev'
          ];

          const currDate = new Date();
          const minutes = currDate.getMinutes();
          const seconds = currDate.getSeconds();
          const day = WEEKDAYS[currDate.getDay()];
          const month = MONTHS[currDate.getMonth()].toUpperCase();

          const formatTime = (time) => {
              return time < 10 ? `0${time}` : time;
          }

          date.value =
            `${day}, ${currDate.getDate()} ${month} ${currDate.getFullYear()}`
          time.value =
            `${currDate.getHours()}:${formatTime(minutes)}:${formatTime(seconds)}`
      }, 1000)

      return {
          date,
          time
      }
    }
}

export function createApp() {
  return createSSRApp(App) ❷
}
```

❶ We define the options for our main application's component, App.

❷ We use `createSSRApp()` to build the application on the server side with `App` options.

This file exposes a single method, `createApp()`, to use in both server and client, returning a Vue instance ready for mounting.

In our `server.js` file, we will use this `createApp()` from `app.js` to create the server-side app instance and render it into an HTML formatted string with the `renderToString()` method from the `vue/server-renderer` package. Once `renderToString()` resolves with a content string, we will replace the content in the returned response with it, as shown in Example 13-3.

Example 13-3. Update `server.js` to render the app instance into an HTML string

```
import { createApp } from './app.js'
import express from 'express'
import { renderToString } from 'vue/server-renderer';

const server = express()

server.get('/', (req, res) => {
  const app = createApp(); ❶

  renderToString(app).then((html) => {
    res.send(`
    <!DOCTYPE html>
    <html>
      <head>
        <title>Vue SSR Demo - Digital Clock</title>
      </head>
      <body>
        <div id="app">${html}</div> ❷
      </body>
    </html>
    `);
  });
});

server.listen(3000, () => { console.log('We are ready to go') })
```

❶ App instance creation with `createApp()`

❷ Place the generated HTML string from `renderToString()` within a `div` of `#app` as its id.

When we head to *http://locahost:3000/*, we will see the browser displays only the title, *Digital Clock* (Figure 13-2), with the fields `date` and `time` empty.

Figure 13-2. Empty Digital Clock

This behavior happens because we only generate the HTML static code to return to the client side, but no Vue is available in the browser. The same goes for any interactive behavior, such as the onClick event handler. To solve this interactive problem, we need to mount our app in hydration mode, allowing Vue to take over the static HTML and make it interactive and dynamic once the HTML is available on the browser side. We can do this by defining an entry-client.js, which will use the createApp() from app.js to get the app instance. The browser will execute this file and mount the Vue instance to the correct element in the DOM (Example 13-4).

Example 13-4. The entry-client.js file for mounting the app instance in hydration mode

```
import { createApp } from './app.js';

createApp().mount('#app');
```

We will also update the server.js file to load the entry-client.js file in the browser using the <script> tag, and enable serving client files in the browser (Example 13-5).

Example 13-5. Update server.js to load entry-client.js in the browser

```
//...

server.get('/', (req, res) => {
  const app = createApp();
```

```
renderToString(app).then((html) => {
  res.send(`
  <!DOCTYPE html>
  <html>
    <head>
      <title>Vue SSR Demo - Digital Clock</title>
      <script type="importmap"> ❶
        {
          "imports": {
            "vue": "https://unpkg.com/vue@3/dist/vue.esm-browser.js"
          }
        }
      </script>
      <script type="module" src="/entry-client.js"></script> ❷
    </head>
    <body>
      <div id="app">${html}</div>
    </body>
  </html>
  `);
  });
});

server.use(express.static('.')); ❸
```

❶   Load the source for the vue package using importmap

❷   Load the entry-client.js file in the browser using a <script> tag

❸   Enable serving client files in the browser

When we restart the server and refresh the browser, we will see the clock displayed with the updated date and time.

Digital Clock

MON, 24 APR 2023

19:58:41

Figure 13-3. Digital Clock

Using DOM API and Node API in SSR

You can't use DOM APIs and web APIs in SSR, since those are browser-only APIs. You also can't use Node API for client-side components only, such as fs for file reader.

We have learned how to create a simple SSR Vue application. Nevertheless, when we need to handle a more complex application, such as using Vue SFC, code splitting, Vue Router, which may require window API, and so on, we may need to build an engine to handle application code bundling, rendering with the right bundled code, wrapping Vue Router to work, etc., which can be a tedious task.

Instead, we can use a framework that already provides this engine, such as Nuxt.js, discussed in the next section.

Server-Side Rendering with Nuxt.Js

Nuxt.js (Nuxt) is an open source modular-based SSR framework built on Vue. It offers many features out of the box, such as file-based routing systems, performance optimization, different build mode, etc., while focusing on the developer's experience (Figure 13-4).

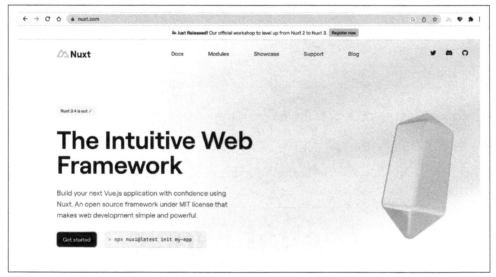

Figure 13-4. Nuxt.js official website

As a modular-based framework, the Nuxt package acts as the core, where we can plug other Nuxt-supported modules into the app to extend an application's core functionality. You can find the list of available Nuxt modules at Nuxt modules official documentation (*https://oreil.ly/hkdnj*), including modules for SEO, PWA, i18n, etc.

> Visit Nuxt's official documentation (*https://oreil.ly/1B2vg*) to learn more about its API documentation, installation, and primary use cases for reference. At the time of writing, Nuxt 3.4.2 is the latest version.

In this section, we will create our Pizza House application featured in Chapter 8 using Nuxt. We will start with the following command to create a new Nuxt application:

```
npx nuxi init pizza-house
```

`pizza-house` is our project name, and `nuxi` is the Nuxt CLI that will scaffold a Nuxt application with the following main files:

`app.vue`
The root component for the application.

`nuxt.config.ts`
The configuration file for Nuxt, including setting up the plugins, CSS path, application metadata, etc.

 Nuxt will create the application with TypeScript support by default.

Nuxt will also create script commands for building and running the application locally in `package.json`, as seen in Example 13-6.

Example 13-6. The `package.json` file for Nuxt application

```
"scripts": {
    "build": "nuxt build",
    "dev": "nuxt dev",
    "generate": "nuxt generate",
    "preview": "nuxt preview",
    "postinstall": "nuxt prepare"
},
```

After running the `yarn` command to install the dependencies, we can run the `yarn dev` command to start the application locally and visit *http://localhost:3000* to see the default Nuxt landing page.

Since Nuxt supports file-based routing using the `pages` folder, we will now define our routing systems under this folder:

index.vue
The home page for the application. Nuxt will automatically map this page to the root path (/).

pizzas/index.vue
The page displaying the list of pizzas, with the path */pizzas*.

pizzas/[id].vue

This is a dynamic nested page, where [`id`] is the placeholder for the pizza's id for displaying the pizza details. Nuxt will automatically map this page to the path */pizzas/:id*, such as */pizza/1*, */pizza/2*, etc.

Next, we need to replace the content of app.vue with the code in Example 13-7 to have the routing system working.

Example 13-7. Update app.vue to use Nuxt's layout and page components

```
<template>
  <div>
    <NuxtLayout>
      <NuxtPage/>
    </NuxtLayout>
  </div>
</template>
```

NuxtLayout is the layout component for the application, and NuxtPage is the page component for the application. Nuxt will replace these components with the defined pages and layout components automatically.

Let's add the code from Example 13-8 to pages/index.vue to display the home page.

Example 13-8. Home page for the Pizza House application

```
<template>
    <h1>This is the home view of the Pizza stores</h1>
</template>
```

And the code from Example 13-9 to pages/pizzas/index.vue to display the list of pizzas.

Example 13-9. Pizzas page for the Pizza House application

```
<template>
  <div class="pizzas-view--container">
    <h1>Pizzas</h1>
    <ul>
      <li v-for="pizza in pizzas" :key="pizza.id">
        <PizzaCard :pizza="pizza" />
      </li>
    </ul>
  </div>
</template>
<script lang="ts" setup>
import { usePizzas } from "@/composables/usePizzas";
import PizzaCard from "@/components/PizzaCard.vue";
```

```
const { pizzas } = usePizzas();
</script>
```

This page uses the `PizzaCard` component from Example 11-1 and the `usePizzas` composable from `composables/usePizzas.ts` to get a list of pizzas for displaying, with the code from Example 13-10.

Example 13-10. Composable for the Pizza House application

```
import type { Pizza } from "@/types/Pizza";
import { ref, type Ref } from "vue";

export function usePizzas(): { pizzas: Ref<Pizza[]> } {
  return {
    pizzas: ref([
      {
        id: "1",
        title: "Pina Colada Pizza",
        price: "10.00",
        description:
          "A delicious combination of pineapple, coconut, and coconut milk.",
        image:
      "https://res.cloudinary.com/mayashavin/image/upload/Demo/pina_colada_pizza.jpg",
        quantity: 1,
      },
      {
        id: "2",
        title: "Pepperoni Pizza",
        price: "12.00",
        description:
          "A delicious combination of pepperoni, cheese, and pineapple.",
        image:
      "https://res.cloudinary.com/mayashavin/image/upload/Demo/pepperoni_pizza.jpg",
        quantity: 2,
      },
      {
        id: "3",
        title: "Veggie Pizza",
        price: "9.00",
        description:
          "A delicious combination of mushrooms, onions, and peppers.",
        image:
      "https://res.cloudinary.com/mayashavin/image/upload/Demo/veggie_pizza.jpg",
        quantity: 1,
      },
    ]),
  };
}
```

When we run the application using `yarn dev`, we will see the home page (Figure 13-5) and the pizzas page (Figure 13-6), respectively, displayed in the browser.

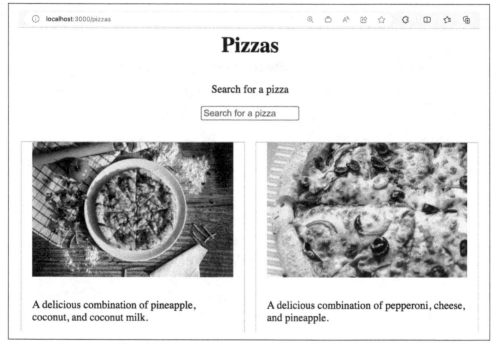

Figure 13-5. Home page for the Pizza House application

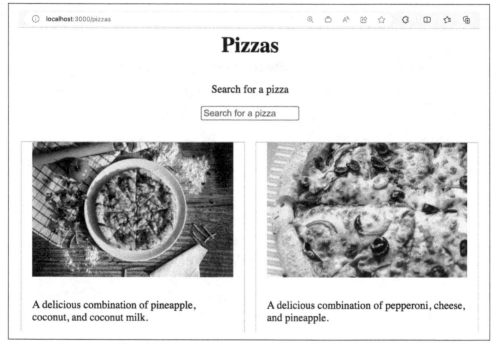

Figure 13-6. Pizzas page for the Pizza House application

Now we will implement the pizza details page by adding the code from Example 13-11 to `pages/pizzas/[id].vue`.

Example 13-11. Pizza details component

```
<template>
  <section v-if="pizza" class="pizza--container">
    <img :src="pizza.image" :alt="pizza.title" width="500" />
```

```
  <div class="pizza--details">
    <h1>{{ pizza.title }}</h1>
    <div>
      <p>{{ pizza.description }}</p>
      <div class="pizza-stock--section">
        <span>Stock: {{ pizza.quantity || 0 }}</span>
        <span>Price: ${{ pizza.price }}</span>
      </div>
    </div>
  </div>
</section>
<p v-else>No pizza found</p>
</template>
<script setup lang="ts">
import { usePizzas } from "@/composables/usePizzas";

const route = useRoute(); ❶

const { pizzas } = usePizzas();

const pizza = pizzas.value.find(
    (pizza) => pizza.id === route.params.id ❷
);
</script>
```

❶ Use useRoute, the global composable from Vue Router, to get the current route's information.

❷ route.params.id is the id of the pizza in the URL.

When we go to *pizzas/1*, we will see the pizza details page displayed in the browser (Figure 13-7).

Figure 13-7. The details page of pizza with id 1

Unlike a regular Vue application, we can't map the routing params id to the id props of the PizzaDetails component. Instead, we need to use the useRoute composable to get the current route's information, including its parameters.

Next, we will implement a default layout for our application with a navigation bar. We will create a new file, layouts/default.vue, with the code from Example 13-12.

Example 13-12. Default layout for the Pizza House application

```
<template>
    <nav>
        <NuxtLink to="/">Home</NuxtLink> ❶
        <NuxtLink to="/pizzas">Pizzas</NuxtLink>
    </nav>
    <main>
        <slot /> ❷
    </main>
</template>
<style scoped>
nav {
    display: flex;
    gap: 20px;
    justify-content: center;
}
</style>
```

❶ NuxtLink is the Nuxt component for rendering link elements, similar to Router Link in Vue Router.

❷ <slot /> is the slot element to render the page's content.

Nuxt will replace NuxtLayout with the default layout, and we will see the navigation bar displayed in the browser (Figure 13-8).

Figure 13-8. Default layout for the Pizza House application

We can also create different layout files in `layouts` and pass the desired layout file name to the props `name` of `NuxtLayout`. Nuxt will pick up the suitable layout component to render based on its value. For example, we can create a new layout file, `layouts/pizzas.vue`, with the code from Example 13-13.

Example 13-13. Pizzas layout for the Pizza House application

```
<template>
    <h1>Pizzas Layout</h1>
    <main>
        <slot />
    </main>
</template>
```

In `app.vue`, we will pass the layout name to the `name` props of `NuxtLayout` conditionally (Example 13-14).

Example 13-14. Using pizzas layout for PizzaDetails component

```
<template>
    <NuxtLayout :name="customLayout">
        <NuxtPage />
    </NuxtLayout>
</template>
<script setup lang="ts">
import { computed } from "vue";

const customLayout = computed(
    () => {
      const isPizzaLayout = useRoute().path.startsWith("/pizzas/");
      return isPizzaLayout ? 'pizzas' : 'default';
    }
);
</script>
```

When we head to */pizzas/1*, we will see the pizza details page rendered with the `layouts/pizzas` layout (Figure 13-9).

> Apart from the `pages` structure, the rest of the application structure is the same as a regular Vue application. Hence, converting a Vue application to a Nuxt application is straightforward.

With SSR, we can achieve a quicker initial page load and better SEO since the browser receives our app's fully populated HTML file. However, a disadvantage of

SSR is that with every browser refresh, the app requires complete reloading, compared to the client-side rendering with single-page application approach.[5]

Pizzas Layout

Pina Colada Pizza

A delicious combination of pineapple, coconut, and coconut milk.

Stock: 1   Price: $10.00

Figure 13-9. Pizza details page rendered with custom layout

In addition, since SSR requires populating the page content dynamically on the server before returning the page content file to the browser, it can lead to a delay in rendering the page, and any interaction that requires page content changes can cause multiple server requests, affecting the app's performance overall. We can use the static side generator (SSG) approach to address this issue.

Static Side Generator (SSG)

The static side generator (SSG) is a type of server-side rendering. Unlike regular server-side rendering, SSG will generate and index all the pages in the application at build time, and serve those pages to the browser on demand. By doing so, it ensures the initial load and the performance on the client side.

> This approach is suitable for applications that don't require dynamic content, such as blogs, documentation, etc. However, if your application contains dynamic content such as user-generated content (authentication, etc.), consider using SSR or a hybrid approach (*https://oreil.ly/zqTn1*) instead.

---

5 Single-page application is an approach to dynamically replace the current view with new data without the need to reload the entire page.

Using SSG in Nuxt is straightforward. We can use the `yarn generate` command, in the same codebase. This command will generate the static files for the application in the `dist` directory, ready for deployment.

The `generate` command will generate the static files for the application in the `.out put/public` directory, ready for deployment (Figure 13-10).

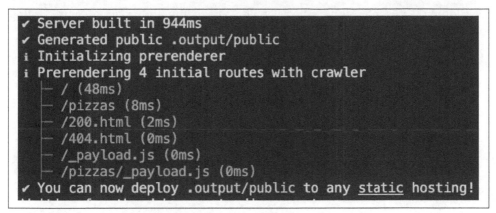

```
✔ Server built in 944ms
✔ Generated public .output/public
ℹ Initializing prerenderer
ℹ Prerendering 4 initial routes with crawler
  ├─ / (48ms)
  ├─ /pizzas (8ms)
  ├─ /200.html (2ms)
  ├─ /404.html (0ms)
  ├─ /_payload.js (0ms)
  ├─ /pizzas/_payload.js (0ms)
✔ You can now deploy .output/public to any static hosting!
```

Figure 13-10. The `.output` directory after running `yarn generate`

That's all it takes. The last step is to deploy the `dist` directory to a static hosting service, such as Netlify, Vercel, etc. These hosting platforms will deliver the static files to the browser on demand using a Content Delivery Network (CDN) with caches.

Last Words

In this chapter, we learned how to build SSR and SSG applications with Nuxt. With that, we end our journey together in this book.

We have covered all the basics of Vue, including the core concepts, the Options API, the lifecycle of a Vue component, and how to use the Composition API effectively to create a robust and reusable component system in a Vue application. We also learned how to integrate Vue Router and Pinia to create a fully working Vue application with routings and data state management. We explored different aspects of developing a flow for a Vue application, from unit testing with Vitest and E2E testing with Playwright to creating a deployment pipeline with GitHub workflows and hosting using Netlify.

You are now ready to explore more advanced Vue topics, and you have the necessary skills to build your own Vue projects. So, where should you go from here? A variety of possibilities await you. Start building your Vue applications and explore the Vue ecosystem further. If you want to develop content-based sites, consider digging deeper into Nuxt. If you are into making a UI library for Vue, check out Vite and design systems concepts like atomic design.

Regardless of your choice, the skills you have learned in Vue will always be handy on your journey to becoming a great frontend engineer and Vue developer. Hopefully this book will be your companion as a reference and foundation along the way.

Developing web applications, especially with Vue, is fun and exciting. Start creating and share what you achieve!

Index

Symbols

(pound sign) for v-slot, 88
: (colon), for v-bind, 31
? (question mark) syntax for query field in passing data between routes, 199
@ (at symbol) for v-on, 41
` (backtick) for multi-level HTML code, 21
{} (curly braces)
    binding data with JSX, 177
    {{}} (mustache syntax), 22

A

AboutView sample component, 189
actions, stores, 221, 225, 229-233, 237
activeClass, 198
after-enter transition event, 249
after-leave transition event, 249
afterEach hook
    E2E testing with Playwright, 282
    navigation guard, 204
alias route configuration property, 191
.alt key modifier, 46
anchor, in URLs, 188
animation property, 239
animations, 239
    (see also transitions)
    controlling with transition events, 249
    defining, 239
    third-party libraries, 248-250
any type, avoiding, 169
app root component, mounting, 19
appear prop, 245
applications
    client-side rendering, 299

configuration options, 9
connecting to databases, 170
creating, 9-11, 18
creating with NPM, 5
directories and file structure, 9
loading, 12
server-side rendering, 300-306
arrays
    iterating over with v-for, 35-39
    style arrays, 34
    two-way binding with v-model, 29
asynchronous calls
    E2E testing with Playwright, 286
    loading data with Axios, 161, 165-170
    reusable fetch component with Axios, 167-171
    testing composables, 267
at symbol (@) for v-on, 41
attributes
    binding style attributes, 33-35
    transition attributes, 244, 245
attrs, functional components and, 178
Axios
    advantages, 159
    external data incorporation with, 159-171
    fetch and, 159, 167-171
    installing, 160

B

back(), 214
::backdrop selector, 133
backtick (`) for multi-level HTML code, 21
base URLs, 194, 281
before-enter transition event, 249

317

createRouter(), 193
createSSRApp(), 301
createTestingPinia(), 273
createWebHistory, 194
creating phase, components' life cycle, 62
Cross-Site Request Forgery, 159
CSS, 97
  (see also animations; style; transitions)
  accessing data values with v-bind, 102
  CSS Modules, 103-105
  display rule, 49
  order of style tags, 97
  scoped styling components, 97-105
  Single File Component structure and, 57-59
CSS Modules, 103-105
css prop, disabling default transition classes, 249
.ctrl key modifier, 46
curly braces ({})
  binding data with JSX, 177
  mustache syntax {{}}, 22

D
data
  binding with JSX and render(), 177
  binding with lazy modifier, 30
  binding with v-model, 26-31
  binding, one-way, 24, 31
  binding, two-way, 26-31
  composables and, 154-158
  connecting application to external database, 170
  creating reactive data from other reactive date with computed(), 152-153
  data flow and nested components, 107-117
  data flow and state management, 217-218
  data flow diagram, 107
  emitting data between components, 107, 117-123
  external data incorporation with Axios, 159-171
  handling with reactive(), 138, 142-145
  handling with ref(), 138-143, 145
  iterating with v-for, 35-39
  loading with Axios, 160-164
  loading with Axios, asynchronous challenges, 165-170
  passing between routes, 199-203

passing dynamic data with provide/inject pattern, 123-125
  reusable fetch component with Axios, 167-171
  state handling and Options API, 19-24
data property
  creating local state with data(), 20, 22-24
  editing, 24
  reactivity of, 24
data(), creating local data state with, 19, 22-24
data-testing attribute, E2E testing with Playwright, 283
data-v and scoped styling components, 99
debugging
  CI/CD and, 289
  E2E testing with Playwright Test for VSCode, 287-288
:deep() and scoped styles, 101
deep, watcher field, 79-82, 148
default in props syntax, 111
defineComponent(), 60, 119
defineConfig(), E2E testing with Playwright, 281
defineEmits(), 121
defineProperty(), 25
defineProps(), 64, 116
defineStore(), 221
.delete key modifier, 46
deployment, 194
  (see also Continuous Integration/Continuous Deployment (CI/CD))
  base URL and, 194
  server-side rendering with static-side generators, 315
describe()
  E2E testing with Playwright, 282
  grouping tests in Vitest, 260
Description component, 20
destroyed hook, 68
Devtools (see Vue Devtools)
dialog element modals with Teleport component, 127-135
directories, projects, 9
disabled prop and Teleport, 126, 135
display property and conditional display of elements with v-show, 49, 241
dist directory, 315
DOM (Document Object Model), 18

(see also Virtual Document Object Model
   (DOM))
accessing with Composition API hooks, 147
accessing with refs attribute, 91-92, 147
conditional rendering with v-if, v-else, and
   v-else-if, 46-49
data structure, 13
event phases and, 42
reactivity and, 24-26
render() and, 173-177
server-side rendering and, 305
template command syntax, 21
understanding, 13-18
domains with Netlify, custom, 296
dynamic class names, 33

E

E2E (end-to-end) testing, 252
   debugging, 287-288
   with PlaywrightJS, 280-288
   setup, 280-282
   testing HTML rendering with PlaywrightJS,
      271
   writing tests, 282-284
e2e folder, 280
Edge, V8 engine and, 3
effect-move class, 247
.$el property, 63, 67
Electron, Vue Devtools and, 6
elem as alias for elements, 36
elements
   conditional display of with v-show, 49
   elem alias, 36
   element binding and key attribute, 39
emits
   custom events with defineEmits(), 121
   functional components and, 178
   modals, 129
   passing data between components, 107,
      117-123
emits(), testing emitted events, 272
emitted(), testing event components, 273
emitters, event
   custom event emitters and functions, 108
   functional components and, 178
   modals, 129
   passing data between components, 107,
      117-123

testing, 272
end-to-end testing (see E2E (end-to-end) testing)
.enter key modifier, 45
enter state, transitions, 241
enter transition event, 249
enter-active-class transition attribute, 244
enter-cancelled transition event, 249
enter-class transition attribute, 244
enter-to-class transition attribute, 244
entry-client.js, 304
env. prefix, 194
environment files and base URL, 194
environment parameter, Vitest, 254
errors
   error messages and unknown routes,
      215-216
   loading data with Axios, 161, 164
   unit testing, 268
.esc key modifier, 46
ESLint, 10, 40
event listeners
   binding with v-on, 40-46
   custom props, 197
   event modifiers, 42-44
   event modifiers, chaining, 44
events
   binding event listeners with v-on, 40-46
   controlling animations with transition
      events, 249
   custom event emitters and functions, 108
   custom events with defineEmits(), 121
   emitting, 107, 117-123
   event modifiers, 42-44
   event modifiers, chaining, 44
   keyboard events and key code modifiers, 45
   modals, 129
   phases of, 42
   testing interactions, 272
.exact key modifier, 46
exactActiveClass, 198
expect(), unit testing with Vitest, 256-261
Express.js, 300

F

fadein-enter-active transition attribute, 246
fadein-enter-to transition attribute, 246
fadein-leave-active transition attribute, 246

installing
  Axios, 160
  Istanbul, 275
  Netlify CLI, 298
  Node, 3
  NPM, 3-5
  packages with NPM, 5
  packages with Yarn, 6
  Pinia, 220
  Pinia plugin, 181
  plugins, 179-182
  Vitest, 253
  Vitest UI, 273
  Vue Router, 181, 189
  Yarn, 3, 5
integration (see Continuous Integration/
  Continuous Deployment (CI/CD))
integration testing, 252
interface, declaring custom types, 115
is prop, dynamic rendering with component
  tag, 182
Istanbul, 275-279
isVisible()
  dynamic class names and, 33
  E2E testing with Playwright, 286
  v-if and, 46
it(), unit testing with Vitest, 256-261
iterating
  object properties, 38-40
  with v-for, 35-39, 91

J

JavaScript
  client-side rendering and, 299
  JSX and render(), 176
  transitions and animations, 240, 248-250
Jenkins, 290
JSDOM, 254
JSON and Axios, 159
JSX
  configuration option for new projects, 10
  registering JSX components, 177
  render() and, 176
  syntax, 177

K

keep-alive component, 183
key attribute

binding with, 39
group transitions, 246-247
iteration with v-for and, 37-40
provide/inject pattern and, 124
syntax, 40
uniqueness of, 37
valid values for, 40
key code modifiers, 45
keyboard events and key code modifiers, 45
@keyframes, animations and transitions, 239,
  244

L

lang="ts" attribute, 59
layouts file, server-side rendering with Nuxt,
  313
lazy two-way binding, 30
leave state, transitions, 241
leave transition event, 249
leave-active-class transition attribute, 244
leave-cancelled transition event, 249
leave-class transition attribute, 244
leave-to-class transition attribute, 244
libraries, third-party
  animations and transitions, 245, 248-250
  file repository structure, 11
lifecycle hooks, 63
  (see also setup hook)
  accessing this with, 23
  Composition API and, 146-148
  diagram, 69
  loading data with Axios, 160-167
  Options API and, 19
  order of, 69-72, 95
  Server-Side Rendering (SSR) and, 67
  table of, 146
  testing composables with, 264-268
  understanding, 61-72
  using, 63-72, 146-148
  when to use, 72
state, 217
limit and plugins, 180
linkActiveClass, RouterOption property, 193
linkExactActiveClass, RouterOption property,
  193
links
  custom class names for, 198
  RouterOption configuration, 193

installing Yarn, 6
resources on, 5
version, 5
npm command, 3
numbers, two-way binding with v-model, 31
nuxt.config.ts file, 307
Nuxt.js, 306-315
NuxtLayout, 308, 312
NuxtLink, 312
NuxtPage, 308

O

object dereferencing syntax and scoped slots, 86
object properties, iterating with v-for, 38-40
oldValue, watcher option field argument, 148
$onAction, 237
onBeforeMount() hook, 146, 265-268
onBeforeMounted() hook, 146, 165
onBeforeRouteLeave(), 207
onBeforeRouteUpdate(), 207
onBeforeUpdate() hook, 146
.once event modifier, 44
one-way binding, 24
onMounted() hook, 146, 165
onTrack, watcher field, 148
onTrigger, watcher field, 148
onUnMounted() hook, 146
onUpdated() hook, 146, 165
open attribute, modals, 129
Options API, 18
    (see also setup hook)
    data(), 22-24
    directive basics, 26-54
    disadvantages, 137
    navigation guards, 208
    properties, 19
    registering components globally, 54
    routing and, 203
    state handling, 19-24
    storing state, 22-24
    template property, 19-22, 173
    understanding, 18-21
    watchers, 77-83
options, in watch() syntax, 148
order
    CSS styles, 97
    lifecycle hooks, 69-72
    lifecycle hooks and mixins, 95

mounting components, 63
navigation guards, 208
rendering and Teleport component, 135
side effects, 238
unit tests, 260

P

package-lock.json file, 5
package.json file
    installing packages with NPM, 5
    server-side rendering with Nuxt, 307
packages
    managing with NPM, 4
    managing with Yarn, 4, 5
    versions, 5
pages folder, server-side rendering with Nuxt, 307
.passive event modifier, 44
path route configuration property, 191
path section in URLs, 187
pathMatch parameter, 215
:pathMatch(), 215
paths
    dynamic routes, 211
    nested, 210
    regular expressions patterns, 215
    route configuration property, 191
performance
    client-side rendering, 300
    computed properties, 76
    layout update problem, 14
    object reactivity, 25
    optimizing rendering with v-once and v-memo, 51-54
    reactive(), 145
    ref(), 142
    server-side rendering, 314
    side effects, 238
    static-side generator (SSG), 314
    Virtual DOM and, 16-18
    Vue size and, 2
    watchEffect(), 151
    watchers, 76, 81
Pinia
    configuration option for new projects, 10
    creating instances, 220
    installing, 181, 220
    resources on, 219

state
  composables and, 154-158
  creating local state with data(), 20, 22-24
  data flow and state management, 217-218
  keep-alive component, 183
  loading property and, 166
  management with Pinia, 217-238
  Options API role in handling, 19
  reusable fetch component with Axios,
    167-171
  skeleton placeholder for, 167
state management systems
  connecting applications to databases and,
    170
  Pinia, 217-238
  tools for, 219
state, store property, 221
static-side generator (SSG), 314
.stop event modifier, 44
stores
  activating, 235
  adding items to cart, 226-229
  creating, 220-226, 235
  displaying cart items with actions, 229-233
  file repository structure, 11
  names, 221
  with Pinia, 224-238
  properties of, 220
  removing items from, 233-235
  resetting state, 234
  setup stores, 222
  side effects, 236
  state management role, 219
  testing, 235, 273
  using in cart component, 226
stores folder, file repository structure, 11
storeToRefs(), 224
strict route configuration property, 191
string property key, unit testing with Vitest, 256
strings
  declaring props with, 111
  injecting plain HTML code for dynamic dis-
    play with v-html, 50
style
  accessing data values with v-bind, 102
  binding attributes, 33-35
  conditional display of elements with v-
    show, 49
  CSS modules, 103-105

modals, 133
navigation bar, 198
nested routes, 211
order of style tags, 97
rendering pages with RouterView, 196
scoped styling components, 90, 97-105
style arrays, 34
Vue SFCs, 57-59
style attribute, binding to, 33-35
$style property, scoped styles, 104
style section, Vue SFCs, 58
style tag, 97-99
$subscribe, 237
.system key modifier, 46

T

.tab key modifier, 46
target
  dynamic rendering with component tag,
    182
  modals with Teleport component, 126,
    134-135
  phase and events, 42
TDD (see test-driven development (TDD))
Teleport component
  disabling, 126
  modals and, 127-135
  rendering issues, 134
  using, 126-135
template property, 19-22, 173
template section, Vue SFCs, 57
template tag, named slots, 88-91
templates
  CI/CD with GitHub Actions, 294
  Options API role in, 19-22
test field, configuring Vitest runner, 255
test(), 261
test-driven development (TDD), 252, 256, 259,
    261
test.root directory, 276
testDir, 281
testing, 251
  (see also E2E (end-to-end) testing; unit test-
    ing; Vue Test Utils)
  CI/CD and, 254, 289, 292
  components, 268-273
  composables, 158, 261-268
  configuration options for new projects, 10

About the Author

Maya Shavin is a Senior Software Engineer at Microsoft, marked by a distinguished educational background that includes an MBA, BSc in Computer Science, and a BA in Economics. Specializing in the web and frontend development, her proficiency spans TypeScript, React, and Vue.

As a core maintainer of StorefrontUI, an open source ecommerce framework, she prioritizes delivering performant and accessible components while emphasizing the importance of solid vanilla JavaScript knowledge.

Beyond coding, she shines as an internationally recognized speaker and published author, advocating passionately for web development, UX/UI, accessibility, and robust coding standards. She enjoys sharing her knowledge on her blog (*https://maya shavin.com*) and on X (Twitter) @mayashavin, speaking at conferences, and delivering hands-on workshops on web development, and Vue in particular.

Colophon

The animal on the cover of *Learning Vue* is a Eurasian golden oriole (*Oriolus oriolus*). These birds can be found as far west as Western Europe and Scandinavia and east toward China. They are migratory birds that tend to spend winters in southern Africa.

Male Eurasian golden orioles are predominantly a bright golden yellow. They have a black tail and wings with yellow-tipped covert feathers. Their eyes are a deep maroon and their beaks are a dark pink. Females are more green than yellow compared to males. Their underbellies are a yellowy-white with dark streaks, and their wings are a greenish brown. Despite their bright colors, Eurasian golden orioles can be difficult to spot in the leafy tree canopies where they nest.

Because of their expansive range, Eurasian golden orioles can be found in a variety of habitats. They can be found in deciduous forests (mainly oak, poplar, and ash trees), riverine forests, orchards, large gardens, and mixed coniferous forests. In winter, they live in semi-arid to humid woodlands and forest-savanna mosaic.

For food, Eurasian golden orioles use their beaks to peck insects out of crevices on the ground and in trees. They are mostly insectivores and frugivores, but they have occasionally been seen eating small vertebrates, seeds, nectar, and pollen.

The biggest threats to these birds are severe weather, habitat loss, and deforestation. However, Eurasian golden orioles are still an abundant species that is considered to be of least concern on endangered species lists. Many of the animals on O'Reilly covers are endangered; all of them are important to the world.

The cover illustration is by Karen Montgomery, based on an antique line engraving from *British Birds*. The series design is by Edie Freedman, Ellie Volckhausen, and Karen Montgomery. The cover fonts are Gilroy Semibold and Guardian Sans. The text font is Adobe Minion Pro; the heading font is Adobe Myriad Condensed; and the code font is Dalton Maag's Ubuntu Mono.

O'REILLY®

Learn from experts.
Become one yourself.

Books | Live online courses
Instant answers | Virtual events
Videos | Interactive learning

Get started at oreilly.com.